Small States in the Modern World

Small States in the Modern World

Vulnerabilities and Opportunities

Edited by

Harald Baldersheim

Professor, University of Oslo, Norway

Michael Keating

Professor, University of Aberdeen, UK

Edward Elgar
PUBLISHING

Cheltenham, UK • Northampton, MA, USA

Published by
Edward Elgar Publishing Limited
The Lypiatts
15 Lansdown Road
Cheltenham
Glos GL50 2JA
UK

Edward Elgar Publishing, Inc.
William Pratt House
9 Dewey Court
Northampton
Massachusetts 01060
USA

A catalogue record for this book
is available from the British Library

Library of Congress Control Number: 2015943178

This book is available electronically in the **Elgar**online
Social and Political Science subject collection
DOI 10.4337/9781784711443

ISBN 978 1 78471 143 6 (cased)
ISBN 978 1 78471 144 3 (eBook)

Typeset by Servis Filmsetting Ltd, Stockport, Cheshire
Printed and bound in Great Britain by TJ International Ltd, Padstow

Contents

Figures

Tables

Contributors

Alyson J.K. Bailes is Adjunct Professor of Political Science at the University of Iceland.

Harald Baldersheim is Professor of Political Science at the University of Oslo, Norway.

Jozef Bátora is Associate Professor of Political Science at Comenius University, Bratislava, Slovakia.

Nik Brandal is a historian and project manager and researcher for the public committee on the treatment of Norwegian travellers at the Centre for Human Rights, University of Oslo, Norway.

Øivind Bratberg is Senior Lecturer in the Department of Political Science, University of Oslo, Norway.

Licia Cianetti is a Ph.D. candidate in the School of Slavonic and East European Studies, University College London, England.

Malcolm Harvey is Research Fellow at the Centre on Constitutional Change at the University of Aberdeen, Scotland.

Michael Keating is Professor of Politics at the University of Aberdeen, Scotland.

Jeffrey McNeill is Senior Lecturer in Planning at Massey University, New Zealand.

Diana Panke is Professor of Governance in Multilevel Systems at the Albert-Ludwigs-Universität Freiburg, Germany.

Stéphane Paquin is Professor of International Political Economy and Public Policy at École nationale d'administration publique, Montréal, Canada.

Allan Sikk is Senior Lecturer in Comparative Politics at the School of Slavonic and East European Studies, University College London, England.

Anton Steen is Professor of Political Science at the University of Oslo, Norway.

Baldur Thorhallsson is Professor of Political Science at the University of Iceland.

Preface: outline of the issues

Michael Keating

SMALL STATES IN THE GLOBAL ERA

Some 30 years ago Peter Katzenstein's (1985) *Small States in World Markets* showed how, rather than disappearing under the effects of modernization and global change, some small states were not only surviving but thriving. This was a major challenge to received wisdom at the time, although Katzenstein's sample was limited to a small number of European democracies practising corporatist modes of making public policy. During the 2000s there was a further wave of writing about small states, drawing on a wider set of cases. The collapse of the Soviet and Yugoslav unions had spawned new states, most of which were small. Singapore fascinated some; the New Zealand experience interested others. Some of these studies relied on quantitative analyses of the relationship between size and economic success (Skilling 2012a). Alesina and Spoloare (2003) claimed to have found an inverse relationship between size and global free trade, with the size of states somehow adapting to global market imperatives.

We are sceptical of such general explanations. We argue that small states do have some issues in common, which they need to resolve, but that there are different forms of adaptation, which are contextual and path-dependent. Some are more successful than others. Our aim has therefore been to trace different modes of adaptation and their success in different contexts.

It would seem incumbent on us to define exactly what we mean by 'small' and indeed 'size'. Most obviously, size could refer to population, area or wealth but is usually a combination of these; essentially we refer to population, but this is not something that is fixed but is itself subject to public policy. More importantly, size is not merely an arithmetical concept but a functional one. We are interested in the problems and opportunities created by being large or small in relation to particular tasks, which themselves change over time and in relation to particular modes of production, market conditions and security regimes. Size is also relative in a world or regional context. In this sense distance is also important, since being both small and remote poses particular challenges. We do not therefore stipulate any fixed threshold for size but do exclude the large established states and also city-states and micro-states.

Because we are defining size as much functionally as numerically, we restrict our cases to developed industrial countries with welfare states, facing similar challenges in sustaining economic competitiveness and social cohesion. We do not claim to have a universe of cases or even a scientific sample but rather have taken cases to illustrate our main themes. There is an admitted bias to the northern European countries, but this is because they illustrate so many of the themes. We also include two 'state-less nations' where there are strong movements for independence, inspired to a great extent by the model of small states in world markets. The kinds of challenges and opportunities facing small countries may not be a function of formal independence; indeed in an interdependent world the very concept of independence has lost much of its meaning. Rather, sustaining an economic and social project may be about very specific powers, relationships with broader systems, and institutional performance. An extra-European case is New Zealand, which is both small and remote, and has attracted a lot of outside interest and become the 'poster-child' for a particular form of adaptation to world markets.

VULNERABILITY AND OPPORTUNITY

A key concept is that of vulnerability, the way in which size increases this and how states respond. Small states are vulnerable in regard to international security, unable to provide for their own defence. They are economically vulnerable, lacking large domestic markets and subject to global trading rules. They may have difficulty defending their own social model in the face of competitive pressures. Their culture and languages may similarly be exposed to dangers from without.

In order to cope with this vulnerability, states need two things. One is external shelter, which may take various forms. Remoteness may in itself provide security shelter. Neutrality, if it is respected, may provide another form. Otherwise, security shelter is provided by alliances, whether bilateral or multilateral, or global and regional security systems. We have examples of all of these. Economic shelter these days rarely takes the form of protectionist trade policies, which are unaffordable, as the New Zealand case shows. Rather, small states tend to be export-oriented in order to compensate for the small internal markets. Shelter may be provided by global or regional free-trade regimes of bilateral links. These may provide protection but at the same time are constraining, and there is a question of how much influence small states can have in international regimes, including the European Union (EU). We note different answers to the question of whether small states are better inside or outside the EU.

The second requirement is an internal buffer, or mode of responding to external shocks. While Katzenstein focused on the importance of corporatism, that is structured negotiation among the state, capital and labour, we now see a variety of responses, from going with the market to formalized social concertation. This raises the important question of institutions, taken in the broad sense to include structures of government, social relations, modes of policy-making and shared understandings of the national interest and how matters should be handled. Many of these factors are not peculiar to small states, but our interest is in how small states use them to overcome vulnerabilities, whether successfully or unsuccessfully. Institutions, as we know, are path-dependent and often evolve over a long time, shaped by critical experiences, but they are not unchangeable, so states can enter on to distinct trajectories under various circumstances.

Some of the literature on small states has attempted to show that they are naturally better at achieving some goals, usually economic growth. This is problematic, if only because the goals of states may differ. There may be trade-offs to be made among economic growth and social cohesion and, if there are, states may make different choices. We would argue, in any case, that what matters is not size in the numerical sense but the vulnerabilities and the opportunities that arise from relative size in particular contexts. For this purpose, we need case studies that explore the complexities of temporal and geographical context, and the decisions made by policy-makers. Small states can do well or badly by whatever criteria are used.

THE CHAPTERS

Michael Keating starts by considering the size of states historically and how they have adapted to different global conditions. He then explores modes of adaptation of economic and social policy, deploying two ideal types. The market liberal approach accepts global constraints and emphasizes low costs and deregulation. The social investment approach combines high spending and taxes, with a focus on the conditions for growth. Each is supported by a particular institutional configuration. Nik Brandal and Øivind Bratberg pursue this theme, distinguishing the social investment state from its social democratic variant. The Nordic model combines these, and most of the Nordic states proved relatively successful during the global financial crisis after 2008, by constantly adapting and changing. Baldur Thorhallsson shows how Iceland was an exception, failing to secure either external shelter or internal buffer mechanisms and so proving extremely vulnerable to the crash. Jeffrey McNeill's chapter on New Zealand traces a very different mode of adaptation, based on exposing the country to international market forces, combined with deregulation and New Public Management at home. Anton Steen looks at the Nordic states together with the Baltic countries. While the former are usually seen as predominantly social democratic and the latter neo-liberal, Steen shows that this is a simplification. Bureaucratic and business elites across both zones show varying attitudes to how to adapt to market challenges, with Nordic businesses hankering for less state control while elites in the Baltics appreciate the need for a strong state framework. Harald Baldersheim looks at a different form of vulnerability, that of a wealthy small state dependent on natural resource revenues. The case is Norway, which has built up a massive sovereign wealth fund based on oil but must maintain strict fiscal discipline in order to safeguard the capital and remain within the economy's capacity to absorb the revenues.

Alyson J.K. Bailes examines the security dilemmas of small states, with particular emphasis on the Nordic cases. Again there is variation around a common theme, as each country has adopted a distinct combination of European, NATO and neutralist stances during the Cold War and after.

Three chapters deal with the European Union and small states. Diana Panke identifies the main factors explaining the influence of small states, again noting the importance of institutions and relationships. Jozef Bátora looks at diplomatic representation and the way in which small states can use European channels to compensate for their own small-scale operations. Allan Sikk and Licia Cianetti focus in detail on how the Baltic states use the European Parliament.

Stéphane Paquin and Malcolm Harvey examine two cases of autonomous but not independent polities, Quebec and Scotland respectively. In both cases, there are independence movements with a broad reach but inspired by the Nordic small-state model, with a significant social democratic element. Paquin and Harvey ask whether they are also equipped with the institutions and social practices that would enable them to emulate the Nordic countries were they to become independent or even in the absence of independence.

Finally, Harald Baldersheim returns to the key themes to summarize the findings and look ahead.

Michael Keating and Malcolm Harvey acknowledge the support of the Economic and Social Research Council, which funded a Senior Fellowship under the Future of the UK and Scotland programme in 2012–2013 and further work in the Centre on Constitutional Change in 2013–2015. Harald Baldersheim acknowledges the support of the Democracy Programme at the University of Oslo, which funded our two workshops in Oslo and Berlin at which draft papers were discussed.

PART I

Introduction

1. The political economy of small states in Europe

Michael Keating

STATES IN HISTORY

History has known many different types of polity, to use the neutral term that Ferguson and Mansbach (1996) employ to avoid the loaded connotations of 'state'. These have evolved and changed according to changing international and domestic circumstances. Over much of European space and history the dominant mode of rule has been the empire, from the Roman and Byzantine, through the Holy Roman, to the Habsburg, Ottoman, Romanov and Hohenzollern empires, the last three enduring until the First World War. Empires are characterized by a concentration of military power at the centre but diverse means for ruling the periphery, including direct control and the use of intermediaries. There is no need for a homogeneous culture, national identity or unified institutions.

In the western part of the continent, the end of the Roman Empire saw a fragmentation of political authority, followed by the rise of states (Rokkan 1999). During the fifteenth century, large polities consolidated, while several smaller projects failed (Burgundy, Catalonia, the Lordship of the Isles). Other polities survived at the interface between the powers. Scotland played England against France for centuries and survived despite the weakness of its monarchy. The Netherlands emerged in the context of war between England and Spain. Stein Rokkan (1999) drew attention to the 'shatter-belt' of territories that maintained their identities. The Netherlands, born from a religious revolt in a group of varied provinces in the sixteenth century, developed into a strong and unitary state. Belgium split away in 1830, only itself to experience territorial tensions in the late twentieth century. Finland emerged from successive Swedish and Russian overlordship, while the Baltic states emerged twice during the twentieth century.

During the eighteenth century, there was some consolidation of the state system, continued into the nineteenth century with the 'unification' of Germany and Italy and the integration of France. Nationalism served the cause of larger units in Germany, Italy and France. In central and eastern Europe, on the other hand, it was a factor in disintegration of empire and the creation of smaller units.

The nation-state was not inevitable, and it faced many competitors (Spruyt 1994). Nor did a single model of nation-state emerge in Europe. Different sizes of states do, however, face distinct challenges at particular historical moments. There are varied explanations for these trends. Some studies emphasize force and the strategies of leaders seeking to control the maximum territory (Tilly 1975). Changing military technologies featured, as the need for large standing armies and weaponry from the nineteenth century privileged large states. Previously, small polities could mobilize their own military power (as with the Venetian navy and arsenal), but otherwise troops could be purchased. Some explanations are more sociological, emphasizing communication, cultural integration and the rise of nationalism (Deutsch 1966). Dynastic marriages, the strategies of state-building elites and opportunism played a role.

This chapter focuses on economic factors and the way they condition the size of states. It is important here to avoid any functional determinism or teleology, since there is no automatic process that aligns the size of states with economic optimality. Tilly (1990) has noted the combination of economic and military factors (capital and coercion) as interacting in the construction and consolidation of states. So we might say that prevailing economic circumstances and trading orders condition the choices of state leaders, providing constraints and opportunities, but that the size of states themselves is the product of a combination of the factors outlined above.

In the early modern period, small polities such as Venice, Genoa, Rijeka and the Hanseatic cities, along with the provinces and cities of Flanders, were located on trade routes (Tilly 1994). Other polities survived at the periphery of the state system, as in Scandinavia, or turned towards global empire, as did Portugal. During the nineteenth century, economic development and industrialization pointed to the need for larger internal markets, although this was rarely simple. German unification was preceded by a free trade area and itself deepened economic integration. The creation of a single market in Italy, however, was less of a success, bringing together units whose role in the international trading order was very different, often defying economic logic. The aftermath of the First World War saw the triumph of the nation-state model in Europe, but this was not the product of economic logic. On the contrary, it broke up integrated markets in parts of Europe such as the Danube basin and was followed by a retreat to national protectionism in the 1930s.

THE ADVANTAGES OF BEING BIG

During the twentieth century, it was often assumed that large states represented the future because they were functionally more efficient. At a time of expanding industry, it helped to have a large internal market and a wide range of productive activities. Having a large and diversified internal market can help a country to weather 'asymmetrical shocks'. Larger states were also credited with economies of scale, in overseas representation, domestic administration and defence and in expensive items like research and development. Small states were vulnerable to external economic shocks and to predatory behaviour, including beggar-my-neighbour economic protectionism.

When the world trading system collapsed between the two world wars, small states were particularly badly hit, forced back on their own restricted domestic markets. The advantages of scale seemed to increase after the Second World War, when governments accepted responsibility for economic management including full employment, economic growth, price stability and regional balance. Keynesian macroeconomic management was best managed at a large scale, with central governments mobilizing resources; the danger, in a small country, is that the benefit will leak abroad on imports. Gradually, Keynesian macroeconomic policy was complemented with an active government role in sponsoring 'national champions' in key economic sectors, and engaging in various forms of indicative planning in conjunction with the private sector.

The welfare state in the twentieth century also favoured big states. Welfare rights were rooted in a common political community, which was assumed, without a great deal of analysis, to correspond to the nation-state, which in turn was both an administrative unit and a community of belonging. It seemed logical that large states would be better at welfare, as they could mobilize larger resources across large geographical spaces. There were explicit mechanisms for transferring resources to local governments on the principle that rich and poor regions should be able to provide the same level of services irrespective of fiscal capacity. If national solidarity was strong enough, such transfers could even be permanent rather than sporadic, the price paid for national unity. Decentralization of taxes and welfare, on the other hand, might lead to a 'race to the bottom' as poorer polities cut taxes and services to attract business investment. Welfare states were thus a centralizing influence and both drew on and in turn strengthened a sense of common destiny and solidarity.

Finally, in an uncertain and dangerous world, size seemed to offer a degree of protection against aggression. Only large states could afford large armies, navies and the modern military technology of the late-nineteenth- and early-twentieth-century arms races. Small states might rely on international guarantees, but these were often swept aside, as happened to Belgium in 1914. The fate of Czechoslovakia in 1938 showed that even their supposed protector could connive in their destruction. Since the Congress of Vienna in 1815 it had been the big powers that disposed of the affairs of the continent, including recognition of states, installation of monarchs and any moving of boundaries. Intellectual cover was given to great power pretensions by the geo-politics school of geographers, who believed that nations had destinies determined by their geographical location and strategic interests. Influence stemmed from size, resources and command of land or the seas, while the great powers struggled for supremacy.

GLOBALIZATION AND THE END OF THE STATE?

During the 1990s, the debate about 'globalization' posed the question of whether the nation-state itself had been superseded. International trade flows made the idea of national economies meaningless. Free movement of capital could overwhelm efforts by governments to manage their currencies. Transnational corporations could shift investment and production at will, so forcing national governments to meet their demands on taxation and regulation. Keynesianism was no longer viable in an open economy where any stimulus would leak away. A cultural version of globalization refers to the rise of global culture based on mass consumerism. The information revolution was another contributing factor, with trade in goods giving way to information and instant communications breaking down national borders.

In retrospect, all this talk of globalization and the end of nations and states proved overblown. It is true, however, that the freedom of action of nation-states has been circumscribed by economic forces over which they have ever less control. States with their own currencies are vulnerable to speculative attacks. States with high taxes on companies and wealthy individuals may risk losing investment and a tax base. As capital and production could so easily be moved around it became ever more difficult to tax corporations at all. The result was a gradual reduction in corporate taxation and a blind eye to corporate tax avoidance.

National welfare states can be undermined by the unbalancing of social relationships under globalization. They were built on social compromises between capital and labour in a situation in which neither had an 'exit' option and were obliged to accommodate each other. If capital and highly skilled workers can now move around while the rest of the labour force is immobile, there is less incentive to come to these agreements. Multinational firms, in particular, are often known for their anti-trade union attitudes and unwillingness to engage in broader bargaining. So the decline of trade unions has been linked to the internationalization of the economy and a division between workers in more or less globalized sectors. This in turn has unbalanced the domestic political compromises between capital and labour that underpinned the post-war welfare state.

If all states were impotent in the face of globalization and competitive imperatives then *a fortiori* small states should be even more disempowered and vulnerable. They are even less able to master global forces, to balance their economies or to resist external pressure. Lacking large internal markets, they must export and accept the disciplines of the global economy. Yet, from the late twentieth century, a literature emerged arguing that small states might actually possess some advantages in a global era. Quantitative comparative analyses suggested that they did no worse, and often did better, than large states on most economic and social indicators (Katzenstein 1985; Armstrong and Read 1995, 1998; Easterly and Kraay 2000; Skilling 2012a). Attention also turned to the new states that were emerging following the collapse of the Soviet Union and Yugoslavia. Globally, states have proliferated, and the United Nations currently has 193 members, against 154 in 1980.

THE RETURN OF SMALL STATES

Global and European free trade reduces the capacity of states to manage their economies in the old way, but for small states it can be liberating. They no longer need large domestic markets, since the home market is now the whole of Europe or even the world. International rules protect them by outlawing protectionism and trade barriers and preventing large states bullying them or unilaterally changing the rules.

The same argument can be made about defence and national security. Collectivization of security under NATO and other transnational bodies reduces threats from neighbours as well as more remote powers. It eliminates the need for autonomous national defence or costly armaments across the whole spectrum. Small states have adapted to this in various ways (see Chapter 2). Some, such as Denmark and Norway, joined NATO, while Austria was neutral by international agreement. Finland was neutral but with a care not to provoke the Soviet Union, while Sweden practised armed neutrality. Ireland was formally neutral, for historical reasons, but not politically impartial between East and West and was able effectively to free-ride on Western security, since the Western powers would not allow it to fall into the hands of their enemies. All these countries effectively sheltered under the umbrella of NATO, which prevented wars within the Western sphere. Strategic security, in turn, allowed small states to seek their own place in the global division of labour.

Alesina and Spoloare (2003) argue that global or continental free trade actually produces small states. That is a piece of functional determinism and does not correspond to the historical facts. In fact, most small states are the result of decolonization or, in Europe, the fall of empires, including the Habsburg, Ottoman and Russian empires after the First World War and the Soviet Union in the late twentieth century, and had nothing to do with free trade. Economic considerations hardly featured in early-twentieth-century debates about independence, which were driven by nation-building and identity politics, and nationalists tended to be economic protectionists (Bohle and Greskovits 2012).

It is more accurate to say that free-trading conditions may provide new opportunities for small states, as well as vulnerabilities. Deprived of many of the classic mechanisms of macroeconomic management and unable to control international markets, small states must adapt. They are, in many ways, policy-takers rather than policy-makers (Skilling 2012a). The key issue here has become that of national competitiveness. This is a difficult and contested idea. Since the demise of mercantilism, the dominant theory about the international division of labour has been that of Ricardian comparative advantage. This suggests that global welfare, as well as that of individual states, will be maximized when each specializes in what it does best. Authors like Porter (1990), in *The Competitive Advantage of Nations*, argue that comparative advantage (under which every state has its own niche) has now given way to absolute or competitive advantage. As Porter (1990, p. 8) puts it, 'exposure to international competition creates for each industry an absolute productivity standard necessary to meet foreign rivals, not a relative productivity standard compared to other industries within its national economy'. Ohmae (1995) and Alesina and Spoloare (2003) go further, to argue that the size of the state itself is determined by the exigencies of competition and that this explains the re-emergence of small states in the contemporary era.

This is another instance of functional determinism. Moreover, many economists also argue that national competitiveness is meaningless, since only firms compete (confusingly, Porter 1990 also argues this at one point, p. 33). The idea must therefore be seen as much as a political construction as a fact and one that has a strong ideological component. Whatever its merits, however, it has been embraced by states and international organizations. The European Commission has preached a relentless message about competitiveness not only among states but among regions as well.

Of course, since competitiveness is always measured in relation to one's competitors, it is impossible for all states to become more competitive at the same time, as opposed to becoming more productive.

Porter, Ohmae and Alesina and Spoloare are at one in arguing that adaptation to global markets requires neo-liberal policy responses, which they present as both necessary and desirable. An earlier literature, however, had drawn rather different conclusions. Small states tended to be open economically, seeking global markets to compensate for their small domestic ones, and supporting trade liberalization (Katzenstein 1985). On the other hand, they tended to have rather large public sectors and high taxes. Rodrik (1998) attributed this to the needs of economic stabilization. While large states could mobilize resources over a larger space and recover from downturns more easily, small states were more vulnerable to economic fluctuations, which a larger public sector could help to cushion. Many of them focused on specialized types of production in which economies of scale are less important than in the basic industries of the old industrial era. In defiance of the 'race to the bottom' hypothesis, large states were not better at welfare and distribution than smaller ones. On the contrary, the most generous welfare provision and the highest levels of public services are found in some of the smaller states. So there is not one small-state model of adaptation to global change but several. Here we summarize them under two ideal types, the market liberal and the social investment models, to show that small states do have policy choices, even if these are constrained.

THE MARKET LIBERAL MODEL

The market liberal mode of adaptation accepts the logic of global competition and the corollary that states are policy-takers. This implies keeping production costs low and catering to mobile investment capital, skilled workers and professionals. Measures include reductions in business regulations, low taxes on business and high earners, and flexible labour markets and wages. The public sector generally is seen as a charge on the productive economy and so should be small. The ideal type also includes free movement of labour so that in bad times workers can migrate while in good times they come back. The market liberal strategy of going with the economic flow entails accepting economic cycles and the 'creative destruction' they can bring and concomitant rises and falls in income. It is marked by sharp inequalities in income and wealth, as those in internationally competitive jobs and sectors can command a premium.

New Zealand embarked on a market liberal experiment in the 1980s after it had lost a large part of its export market when the United Kingdom joined the (then) European Economic Community and its protectionist industrial strategy became unaffordable (see Chapter 10). The strategy has been applied in the Baltic states, where it is presented as a logical part of the transition to the market economy. Trade unions there are weak, and workers and the general public more tolerant of sharp changes in their material conditions, given their recent experiences (Bohle and Greskovits 2012). Enlargement of the European Union has provided opportunities for out-migration when jobs are scarce and to return when times are better.

It is difficult to reproduce these policies in mature European welfare states, where public services are seen as a permanent social gain and cannot easily be dismantled. Trade unions are still part of the national life, however weakened in recent decades. Voters will not easily tolerate sharp fluctuations in living standards without social and political instability. Taxes on businesses in Europe have been driven down by international competition, with new EU member states having some of the lowest levels, but small countries do not appear to be especially vulnerable to this (Elschner and Vanborren 2009).

The market liberal strategy is open to objections that it is ineffective even on its own terms. Studies have questioned the effectiveness of low corporation taxes in attracting industrial investment (Jensen 2012). The cases of Ireland and central and eastern Europe may be distinct, since they adopted low corporate taxes at a time when there was little private domestic industry and little existing revenue to lose. Marginal differences in taxation appear to be rather low down the list of criteria for choosing investment locations, compared with skilled labour, infrastructure and other locational characteristics. Tax cutting encourages 'brass-plate' relocations and transfer pricing, whereby profits are declared in the low-tax jurisdiction but production is done elsewhere. Tax cutting can also set off a tax competition in which small states may ultimately lose out.

There is now a lot of evidence that inequality, far from stimulating economic growth, may be a drag on performance (Wilkinson and Pickett 2010; Stiglitz 2012; Ostry et al. 2014). Public services are not just a burden on the productive economy but may provide the physical and human capital on which private production depends, especially in advanced economies. Small states may be even more in need of these public goods, as they lack the large private corporations which might invest heavily in research and development. As a consequence, publicly funded and university research is vital.

While small states often have high foreign direct investment (FDI), this can also create vulnerabilities to external changes and decisions taken elsewhere. There may be a loss of diversity, and the FDI sector can become detached from the domestic economy, trading in global markets and generating profits but without spreading the benefits back. Small local firms may find difficulty in competing with multinational enterprises able to offer higher wages for the most skilled workers and mobilizing huge resources for investment. This can create an economic dualism between a foreign-owned sector effectively able to set its own rules and a weaker and vulnerable domestic sector, as in Ireland.

THE SOCIAL INVESTMENT STATE

An alternative conception is that of the social investment state (Crouch 2013; Hemerijck 2013), in which public expenditure is seen not as a drain on the productive economy but as part of it. So education represents investment in human capital, while health spending can enhance productivity. Research is a contribution to innovation and economic renewal. Publicly financed childcare allows mothers to remain in the labour market, so expanding the workforce and retaining skills. Investment in the early years of childhood contributes to economic prosperity, improving skills while reducing the later burden of social marginalization.

Social investment implies not just sustaining public expenditure but redefining it and shifting the priorities towards efficiency-enhancing measures. There is now a broad consensus that the most effective way of tackling deprivation and other social problems is to get people into work, but sharp differences on how it might be achieved. While neo-liberals favour punitive approaches to unemployment, by reducing welfare benefits and imposing strict requirements, the social democratic approach privileges preparation. So active labour market policy, seeking to align training, benefits and economic development, has become central to policy debates. This is consistent with modern ideas about supply-side measures as the key to economic success, given the limitations of states, and especially small states, to engage in traditional Keynesian economic management or, within currency unions like the Euro, to use monetary policy to regulate demand.

It is also consistent with the move within welfare policy, away from the male breadwinner and the family facing predictable lifetime challenges, towards a more complex society in which gender and age, as much as class, structure the labour market. There are 'new social risks' which include precarious and low-paid employment and marginalization of under-prepared workers. The old model was based on insurance against the contingencies of life, which would balance out in due course. Unemployment was seen as cyclical so that national insurance funds could accumulate in boom times and be drawn down in recessions. Old age pensions were built up in the working years and consumed after retirement at a fixed age. Whether in the form of investment funds or as obligations on the part of the state, they represented claims on future production, which was generally assumed to be ever-increasing. In the new way of thinking, there are multiple types of household and routes into employment. There is also a need for continually upgrading skills to meet new technologies and modes of production.

Social investment thus stated appears to reconcile otherwise competing priorities between economic competitiveness and social welfare. Indeed, it can look like a magic formula to escape from one of the central dilemmas of public policy. Education both improves the economy and aids social mobility by giving people from poorer backgrounds the opportunity to prosper. Health spending has both economic and social benefits. Active labour market policies help individuals out of poverty and increase the productive labour force at the same time. Reskilling and training can ease the transition into high-productivity activities and so raise wages. If more equal societies are indeed more productive, then again the social and economic imperatives can be reconciled. The formula might have particular appeal to small states, for which the dilemma between national competitiveness and social cohesion is especially acute, given their market vulnerability. It is not surprising that social investment has had particular appeal to social democrats as they seek to adapt their policies to the modern age. Trade unions have welcomed the emphasis on human capital enhancement.

In practice, matters are more complex. The phrase 'social investment' may amount to little more than a way of legitimizing public services at a time of financial constraint and neo-liberal hegemony. It often seems to subordinate the claims of social justice and equality to those of the economy. By focusing on productive labour, it might favour the better-off or those who could most easily be brought into the workforce (Rhodes 2013). The stress on new social risks might be exaggerated, since the old social risks have not gone away. Preparation and job training are not going to get people into work if there are not enough jobs available.

A social democratic version of the strategy is marked by an emphasis on social equality for its own sake. As social inequalities rise as a result of the new international division of labour, it is difficult to tackle them through taxes and benefits alone, hence the interest in enhancing human capital. Spreading the benefits, however, still requires the right kinds of domestic institutions, including labour markets and collective bargaining. Social investment is a long-term strategy, and citizens must defer consumption and immediate gratification in favour of the long term, while the present generation needs to think of future ones. It implies higher taxes. Given the volatility of taxes on high earners and their propensity to migrate, taxes need to be broad and weigh also on the middle classes. Politically, this is sustainable only when all citizens feel that they benefit from the public services financed. This explains the tendency in the Nordic countries to universal rather than selectively available public services, so binding in the whole population to the social contract. Social justice is assured by providing the same level for rich and poor rather than by explicitly redistributive tax policies.

Some states have a better starting point than others. Some legacies go back to the nineteenth century, while others date to historical crises and social compromises in the twentieth. The Nordic states had crucial experiences in the inter-war period, which shaped institutions and expectations in the longer run. Even among the transition states of eastern and central Europe, emerging from Communism, some were better placed than others because of historic legacies or because they had started to adapt even before the Berlin Wall came down (Bohle and Greskovits 2012).

In the next two sections we consider the institutional and cultural conditions for building different forms of response to these external vulnerabilities.

CORPORATISM AND CONCERTED ACTION

In the 1980s, Katzenstein (1985) identified the secret of adaptation of small states to global markets as corporatism, a mode of policy-making in which government, business and trade unions get together to thrash out agreements on long-term goals and commitments (Schmitter 1974). Coordination can thus overcome problems of collective action and benefit both sides. Unions accept nominal wage restraint and thus contain inflation and business costs, in return for full employment and increases in real wages. They may accept lower individual wages in return for enhancement of the 'social wage' in the form of public services such as health and education. Business commits to investment in the knowledge that markets will expand, wages will be under control and infrastructure will be provided. Government agrees to fund public services and expand infrastructure, relying on other partners to deliver and thus sustain the tax base. Corporatism may be used in good times to control booms, and in crisis to recover production levels without massive unemployment. While corporatism was not confined to small states it may be that their vulnerabilities make it more attractive, while their size makes it feasible. In its classic form, however, it depended on certain preconditions.

One is the existence of domestically owned businesses with a stake in the prosperity of the country and unable to relocate easily. Locked in by national boundaries, they had an incentive to cooperate with the other social partners to produce public goods. While neo-liberal economists regard all firms as following a single capitalist logic, sociologists have often drawn attention to different models of capitalism (Hall and Soskice 2001). In liberal market economies, firms compete with each other according to individualistic market principles. They typically aim to maximize profits in the short term and, nowadays, the value of their shares. In coordinated market economies, on the other hand, business is organized in associations, which regulate their own affairs and cooperate (as well as competing) to produce public goods from which they can all benefit, such as skilled labour. Firms look to the long term and often aim at increasing market share and expanding production, rather than maximizing profit in the short term. Such firms are more likely to be amenable to corporatist bargaining and collective action.

A second condition is strong and centralized associations representing business and labour. These can control their own members and come to agreements, knowing that they can deliver. Finally, corporatism needs a strong government, able to tax and spend effectively and to deliver on its commitments. Corporatist arrangements are often combined with proportional representation, which ensures that a wide spectrum of political opinion is incorporated in decisions.

The central feature of corporatist bargaining has often been national wage negotiations, conducted by employers and unions, sometimes with a role for the state. This secures a basic agreement on the distribution of the social product, with universal trade unionism ensuring that wage differentials are not excessive. On top of this are built a variety of other elements, including the 'social wage', commitments to public investment and measures to meet the needs of particular groups within the community.

By the 1980s corporatism appeared to have declined as a result of globalization and the opening of markets (E. Jones 2008). The idea of national capitalism made little sense in a world dominated by global corporations and mobile investment. Trade unions were in retreat, especially in the private sector and in multinational corporations. Rising welfare costs meant that governments could not continually increase the social wage but rather sought containment and retrenchment. Economic problems in coordinated market or corporatist states were attributed to the sclerosis brought on by having to negotiate change and allowing declining sectors a veto on innovation. From being the secret of success, corporatism became the scapegoat for failure.

Corporatism was never confined to small states but was particularly important to them, given their need to adjust to global markets without provoking excessive social divisions or unsustainable levels of unemployment. It has proved most enduring in Norway, in Belgium and in Austria. In

Sweden it has largely been abandoned in favour of market adjustment, although the strength of trade unions means that the ideas of compromise have not totally vanished. The Netherlands moved from corporatism to a looser form of coordination labelled the 'polder model'. Ireland moved towards concerted action in the 1980s but abandoned it in the economic crisis of the late 2000s. The experience of the transition states of eastern and central Europe has been highly diverse. The Baltic states embarked on a market liberal strategy from the outset, especially in Estonia. Slovenia, in contrast, practised neo-corporatism with a significant role for trade unions (Bohle and Greskovits 2012). In the Visegrad countries (Poland, Hungary, the Czech Republic and Slovakia), social concertation was tried but never quite worked out and was eventually abandoned.

In the 1990s, however, a number of European states came back to negotiation among the social partners in an effort to regain competitiveness and to qualify for the single European currency through what Martin Rhodes (2001) called 'competitive corporatism'. This was not the full corporatism of old, with binding agreements among peak groups, but described as 'lean corporatism' (Traxler 2004), 'social concertation' (Compston 2002), 'social pacts' (Avdagic et al. 2011), 'social dialogue' or 'social partnership'. The European Commission has promoted the idea, emphasizing social investment and economic theories that incorporate human capital, research and entrepreneurship.

Wage negotiation, to sustain international competitiveness, often remains at the core of these social bargains. They can provide business with knowledge of future costs, thus encouraging investment. Training and active labour market policy are linked to competitiveness and sometimes go beyond individual wages to the social wage, public services and welfare. There is some tendency to escape the old corporatist insider deals by extending partnership to other groups, including social interests, the voluntary sector and environmentalists. Business interests however have the biggest influence, while unions occupy a less central position, and social and environmental interests come still further behind.

Large business and multinational firms tend to stand aside from social partnerships, but they still benefit from wage stability, public services and trained human resources. In some countries, vocational training is entrusted to partnerships of employers and unions and financed from business levies, which provides a disincentive to free riding and a motive for participation. Small businesses are often not organized in effective associations – sometimes they have to work within bodies dominated by the big firms, and are unable to make their voices heard. It is medium-sized enterprises that often have the most to gain from social concertation, tied as they are into the national system and needing support that big firms can provide for themselves. Accordingly it works most effectively where there is such a tier of firms.

Social concertation is more flexible than classic corporatism. There is scope to change plans if external circumstances change. Rather than a single set of peak negotiations, there may be multiple venues for concertation and negotiation, reducing veto points and blockages, while providing incentives for cooperation; an issue blocked in one negotiating forum can be taken elsewhere. Sometimes it is very lightly institutionalized, but, even where formal partnership bodies have been disbanded, the idea of negotiation and compromise persists. Where a crisis hits, there may still be a tendency to organize a summit or social partnership. In this way, the shadow of corporatism survives its formal demise, and the search for consensus continues.

Small states can respond more or less effectively to vulnerabilities by institutional adaptations, but this still raises the question of why and how this is done. It may be that small size in itself fosters positive forms of adaptation, but this might be argued either way. Alternatively, the secret may lie in culture or in historically ingrained patterns of behaviour.

DOES SIZE MATTER?

Small states may have advantages in adaptation in that their leaders, whether in government, business or civil society, know each other personally, and there are short lines of communication. The relevant people can gather in one room to sort out deals. There may be less social distance between groups and a sense of shared destiny. External challenge may foster a habit of working together and a sense of social cohesion and encourage trust.

On the other hand, small states, where everyone knows everyone else, could be risk-averse and prone to group-think. The need for consensus could stifle innovation and creativity. Vested interests could be stronger, and domestic producers could be in a strong position to demand protection and support of various sorts, and so inhibit economic change and dynamism. The very closeness of actors may encourage rent-seeking, in which groups each try to enlarge their own share of the social product rather than expanding the total. Outdated and uncompetitive sectors may exercise undue influence.

There is also a danger of clientelism, a mode of government based on doing favours for individuals and small groups and distributing resources in small packages. This avoids large issues, prevents resources being applied where they can produce the largest social benefit and discourages long-term planning. Clientelism may thrive in small societies where people know each other and reputations are important. In larger states, the population is so large that politicians are unable to bribe them all. It follows, therefore, that the patterns of behaviour themselves matter.

CULTURE

Since the 1980s there has been a debate about social capital as a third factor of production alongside physical and human capital (Coleman 1988; Portes 2001). It refers to the ability of societies to sustain virtuous patterns of behaviour, including non-simultaneous reciprocity, that is contributing to the common good in the knowledge that the individual will gain in the longer term. This contrasts with market exchange, in which there is a simultaneous exchange, and with patrimonial systems, in which there is a non-market exchange of favours. A central element in social capital is trust, especially trust in people whom we do not know personally. Studies have regularly shown high levels of such trust in the Nordic states (Marien 2011). The concept of social capital was popularized by Robert Putnam (1993) in a study of Italy purporting to show very different levels of social and economic performance in different regions. Putnam's work has been subjected to some devastating criticism on both methodological and empirical grounds (see the special issue of *Politics and Society*, **24** (1), 1996) but remains influential, since it appears to offer policy-makers the holy grail of a combination of economic prosperity and social cohesion. The main problem with the way the concept has been used is in its operationalization and measurement. Typically, there are surveys of individuals asking them about attitudes and levels of trust, drawing on the 'civic culture' tradition (Almond and Verba, 1965, 1980). Social capital, however, is essentially about relationships, which are mediated by institutions and circumstances. Putnam attributes the differences among Italian regions to history going back to the Middle Ages,[1] but historians have shown that societies regularly undergo changes in their self-understanding and that they can sometimes shift radically in short periods of time (Plumb 1967).

Alesina and Spoloare (2003) also tend to a reductionist view of culture and attitudes. They start from public goods theory, to argue that smaller states will better serve their citizens by giving them policies that they like. Small states are more desirable because, with a smaller population, their citizens are more likely to have the same preferences for public policies. In fact, this does not follow, since there is no reason to think that a population of 5 million people is more likely to agree among themselves than one of 50 million. Some of the smallest polities are deeply divided. Alesina and

Spoloare (2003), however, back up their argument by assuming that small regions and countries will be more ethnically homogeneous. As they put it, 'in today's world of free trade, relatively small ethnic regions can "afford" to stay small and homogeneous' (2003, p.14). Ethnicity is a highly problematic concept, and sociologists these days are practically unanimous that it is socially constructed. Individuals have multiple identities, which they use for different purposes (class, gender, nationality or age, for example), and share these differently with different other people. In so far as ethnicity can be measured, it is as a compound of other characteristics including language, religion, subjective feelings and intersubjective meanings, which are always contested and always changing. Race, a term that Alesina and Spoloare also use rather freely, is even more problematic. Biologists are agreed that it is not a scientific category. It is rather a sociological category, in which an arbitrary characteristic like skin colour is used to unite people who are otherwise highly varied and to differentiate them from others. Nations are socially stratified societies, with rich and poor, employers and workers and a host of other divisions. Social concertation and negotiation happen not because everyone has the same preferences and interests but precisely because they do not and must therefore arrive at positive-sum compromises.

Culture in itself does not, therefore, explain very much and ethnicity even less. In fact, the cultural stereotypes that are invoked to explain success and failure of social projects are usually merely rationalizations of the outcome rather than real causes. Often the same qualities are invoked to account for success at one time and place and for failure at another (Keating et al. 2003; Keating 2008). So individualism can be presented as an entrepreneurial virtue, to explain success, or as a lack of social capital and cooperation, to explain failure. Collectivism and a sense of community can be presented as social capital or as a lack of entrepreneurial spirit. A strong sense of tradition can be spun as evidence of being trapped in the past or as the basis for community and social capital. Cultural homogeneity can be invoked to explain common purpose, but cultural diversity can equally be used to explain innovation. It is not, therefore, embedded cultural characteristics of society that explain the capacity for adaptation but the way that cultural images and traditions are pressed into service to underpin a project.

A different and more sociologically informed idea of trust rejects both essentialist arguments based on shared ethnicity and purely individualist accounts. Instead, it looks at relationships, examining what Sabel (1993) calls 'studied trust', the emergence of effective common purposes and trust as a result of experience. It is not necessary for everyone to share the same beliefs and values as long as they share the same political space and engage in compromises and cooperation. In this way, individual short-term interest can be linked to the pursuit of mutual shared interests.

The past matters, since it leaves a legacy of policies and institutions, which cannot always be changed overnight. History, however, is no more determinate than other social and economic circumstances, and small states can adapt to changed conditions. What the path dependency theorists often neglect, moreover, is that history is as often the product of the present as its cause, continually revised and reinterpreted to make sense of the present, whether in a positive or a negative sense. The national imaginary is thus a compound of what happened and how it is interpreted. Small nations faced with big neighbours may be particularly attached to their national myths and, while these are not objective reality, they are important elements in the construction and reproduction of the polity.

PATHS TO ADAPTATION

Small states are vulnerable to external economic shocks in the modern interdependent world. On the other hand, they may have offsetting advantages that allow them to adapt to external change and provide themselves with some room for manoeuvre. This is not because of any determinist relationship between global trading conditions and state size, nor because of embedded and immutable cultural traits. Nor is it true to say that small states can always adapt better, still less that the demands of the modern interdependent world have actually brought small states into being. It is rather that small states have experienced different ways of managing the interactions of global markets with local institutions and politics. There is no one model for success but rather multiple modes of adaptation. This does not mean small states can adopt any policy mix they choose, since there is a complementarity among policies in different fields that can ensure that they are mutually sustaining. The experience of Ireland illustrates the problems that arise when seeking to combine different modes of adaptation (Dellepiane and Hardiman 2012). Once set on a particular path, however, it is often difficult for states, locked into particular modes of policy-making, to change. Doing so may leave them particularly vulnerable to external shocks and pressures, as the experience of the transition countries of eastern Europe shows.

NOTE

1. History, to put it charitably, is not his strong point.

PART II

The modern world – a less dangerous place for small states?

2. Small states and security: does size still matter?

Alyson J.K. Bailes

INTRODUCTION

Security is the field where the drawbacks of being a small state in the international system are most glaringly obvious. As one author puts it, being small 'has been viewed as a handicap to state action, and even state survival' (Browning 2006, p. 669). Whether smallness is defined by statistical parameters such as size of population, or by a state's relative capacity vis-à-vis its neighbours,[1] its gravest effect is to leave the state in question with little chance of preventing a hostile physical takeover – which in turn heightens the risk of political and economic blackmail. Being on the wrong side of an asymmetrical power balance further constricts a state's space for manoeuvre, minimizing its chances of acting as leader or rule-setter at any international level (Wivel et al. 2014). The consequences of existing in a system built by and for players of other sizes were summed up in the fifth century BC by Thucydides as 'the weak accept what they have to accept' (Thucydides 1972, p. 302).

The modern tradition of small-state studies, after the Second World War, began by stressing small actors' basic problems of survival. Annette Baker Fox in 1959 voiced the prevailing view that 'Not only could such a state have no security under modern conditions of war; it could have no future in the peace that presumably one day would follow' (Fox [1959] 2006, p. 39). 'Security' in this context meant the military defence of territory, a sphere in which small states' plight was exacerbated by the growing quantity and quality of large-state arsenals. Their most obvious survival strategy was to find one or more stronger states capable of 'sheltering' them, and to join them in a formal or informal alliance (Walt 1987). Such a relationship could also be described as 'bandwagoning': requiring the protégé to align its behaviour with the sponsor's, and perhaps to pay more concretely, for example by accepting bases on its territory. A further small-state option was 'balancing', seeking leverage by working with a wider range of partners, and perhaps even reinsuring with other large powers.

Balancing made sense against a hostile neighbour, but could also offset the risks of over-dependence on a single friend (Walt 1987; Scheuerman 2009).

The only clear alternative to such commitments was to declare neutrality, non-alignment or non-allied status, thus in principle opting out of local and global power-play. The Non-Aligned Movement (NAM) founded at Belgrade in 1961 currently shows a high, though by no means dominant, proportion of small states as members.[2] For small states in all but the most peaceful regions, however, building an independent defence capacity to deter violations of neutrality is no easy task; and avoiding political encroachments – such as Germany's demands on Sweden during the Second World War – may be even harder (Karsh 1989).

This stark analysis, chiming with realist theories of international relations (Scheuerman 2009), still works for much of the world today. Numerous small states, for instance in the Gulf and South-east Asia, still face unstable local power systems with potentially aggressive neighbours. Others are threatened by internal risings and coups, which may involve exploitative as well as altruistic international interventions. Even within the greater Europe, the Russian war of 2008 with Georgia exploited the smaller side's vulnerability in classic fashion, and the latest Russian actions in Ukraine have re-ignited a sense of military threat for the three small Baltic states.

Few analysts today, however, would find this account of small-state security complete. The context has been changed, above all, by new multidimensional definitions of security in which military action is just one extreme of a spectrum of deliberate threats and human-made or natural risks. The capacity of a state to act effectively in the international system, or in some cases even to survive, depends also on its economic, energy and environmental security, on aspects of social robustness such as internal order, solidarity and health, and on how well it handles major accidents and natural disasters (Buzan 2007). As further argued below, these nonmilitary dimensions of security are ones in which state size and strength no longer correlate directly with success, for several reasons.

Already under the former realist vision, individual small states could find better, or worse, security solutions according to their skills; and this applies even more strongly today. Worldwide, small states include some that top the global list of GDP per capita and the annual Global Peace Index,[3] as well as some of the world's most wretched cases of conflict, injustice and want. The reasons for such variation are best illustrated by exploring concrete examples, and later in this chapter the five Nordic states (Denmark, Finland, Iceland, Norway and Sweden) are taken as a case study. Rich, peaceful and respected for their global contributions, they have made remarkably varied national choices in internal and external security. Investigating these may illuminate, among other things, the linkages that potentially exist in all states from domestic politics to international behaviour.

TWENTY-FIRST-CENTURY SECURITY: A SHIFTING SMALL-STATE ENVIRONMENT

The Wider Concept of Security

The trend towards multi-dimensional understandings of security, seen both at the intellectual and the executive level since the late twentieth century, has had several drivers. The end of the Cold War made military threats less dominant for Europe and some other regions, while threat or risk perceptions were coloured by events such as the terrorist atrocities of 2001, the SARS and bird flu epidemics and the Indian Ocean tsunami. NATO, the European Union and the Organization for Security and Co-operation in Europe (OSCE) all published security strategies in the early 2000s that highlighted the hazards of internal conflict, 'new' threats such as global terrorism and crime, and 'softer' issues such as the environment (see for example OSCE 2003). In the North–South context, the UN Human Development Report of 1994 produced one of the first multiple security constructs: 'human security', with its seven dimensions of economic, health, food, environmental, political, community and personal security (UNDP 1994). A similar concept for advanced societies was the 'societal security' adopted as a framework for handling non-military challenges by the Nordic states (Buzan 2007; Bailes 2014).

In modern circumstances, non-state actors like insurgent groups, terrorists and arms smugglers are important even in armed conflict. In the functions vital for non-military security – such as energy, food and water supplies, infrastructure maintenance or drug production – the private business sector stands squarely in the front line (Bailes 2008). A sizeable literature on the so-called 'privatization of security' has drawn attention to how this weakens the nation-state's supposed monopoly of power over life and death (e.g. Matláry and Østerud 2007, which includes Nordic case studies). Less often noticed is the way that such developments complicate the relation between size and security. A small state can be a base for large and powerful non-state actors – offshore banks, shipping lines, Radio Luxembourg – which bring it new options as well as risks and temptations (Baldacchino 2014). If it must seek non-state expertise and supplies abroad, its dependence on (for example) a large multinational company or on foreign scientists will have a different cost/benefit balance from that of

Table 2.1　Some key aspects of multi-dimensional security for small states

'Hard' security	Non-state violence	Economy-related	Accidental/natural
Military attack	Terrorism	Poverty and under-development	Major accidents
Caught in crossfire	International crime	Lack of resources	Infrastructure breakdown
Sabotage	Non-state cyber-attack	Import dependence	Pandemics
External coup	Large-scale smuggling	Supply issues: food, energy, etc.	Natural disasters
State cyber-attack	Illegal migration	Social weaknesses and divisions	Environment degradation
Internal conflict		Corruption risks	Climate change
Major civil disorder			

Source:　Adapted and updated from Bailes et al. (2014).

being a military satellite. Importantly for overall strategy, the power providing the best 'hard' military security is unlikely to be able to offer a quick fix for all non-military challenges too. A small state today must 'balance' not only among traditional sponsors but also among multiple state and non-state providers required for different aspects of security provision and civil emergency management.

How do the practical implications of smallness differ from one type of security challenge to another? Table 2.1 divides a typical comprehensive security spectrum into four issue-sets, running from the most traditional, state-bound dimensions to the 'softest' ones. Generally speaking, the classic vision of small-state weakness holds good for other human-made threats besides 'hard' security. The smallest governments might fall to a mere handful of terrorists or coup-makers. Even moderately sized nations find it hard to develop autonomous expertise in cyber-defence or to manage the smuggling of goods and people without significant outside help. Further, small polities risk being 'captured' by criminal and other corrupt interests, as has happened in the past with Caribbean islands and the drugs trade. That region has been a laboratory for attempts to check non-state threats reaching across national borders by equally more-than-national action (Shaw 2014).

The picture on economic security is more complex. First, security in this connection is not the same as wealth or growth, but refers rather to stability and resilience in face of the shifts and shocks of an open, globalized system (Buzan 2007). Very poor small states are intrinsically insecure, as they cannot meet even their citizens' basic needs without outside aid. Above this level, however, traditional ideas of state power are challenged by the dynamics of a global free trade system that even the largest state cannot 'control' as it might manage a military relationship. The recent Euro-crisis showed that larger countries (Spain, Italy, Greece) can suffer from upheavals as much as smaller ones (Ireland, Iceland, Portugal), and perhaps face a tougher recovery.

Irreducible aspects of small states' economic vulnerability include their limited resources and small internal markets, leading to typically high import dependence even for such basics as food (Commonwealth Advisory Group 1997). The hazards facing a small currency were illustrated when the Icelandic krona lost nearly half its value in the 2008 crash. Sources of earnings not tied to size and resources such as tourism, gambling, ship-flagging and offshore banking have been profitable for many small players, but bring increased exposure to external trends and to the temptations of illegality and corruption.

Many attempts have been made to quantify and combine such factors in indexes of economic risk (e.g. Cordina and Farrugia 2005), but the best small-state economic solutions are more debatable. Katzenstein (2003) sees flexibility and speed of adjustment as helping small polities both to find profitable niches and to cope with adversity. Griffiths (2014) discusses ways of cushioning external fluctuations, such as a stabilization fund, but also stresses the importance of good governance. One current hypothesis is that a corporatist[4] approach in the domestic economy, as practised in most Nordic states, can palliate the risks of neo-liberal market policies combined with high external exposure (Thorhallsson and Kattel 2013). Whatever the reason, small states have been shown to survive vicissitudes better than similarly sized provinces of neighbouring large states, confirming that *prima facie* state power is no yardstick of security in this field (Griffiths 2014).

In coping with the fourth, accidental and natural, set of security challenges, small states combine vulnerability with certain advantages. Reliant on imports for so many vital supplies, they suffer equally through their neighbours' and suppliers' emergencies. One large accident or natural disaster can leave even relatively rich countries needing external rescue, while some oceanic islands fear total immersion from sea-level rises following climate change. This last point, however, can be turned around to highlight the 'canary in a coal-mine' value of small polities. Greater exposure helps them see emergent threats and risks faster, and often pushes them into greater international activism ('punching above their weight') as they seek to sensitize the global community (Ingólfsdóttir 2014). The Alliance of Small Island States (http://aosis.org/), created to publicize climate-related risks, illustrates the point. Besides, small populations can make governments' task simpler in handling some hazards, for example maintaining emergency stocks, or vaccinating against a pandemic. Internal homogeneity, though not always a given (two-thirds of Liechtenstein's workforce are foreigners), should both ease policy-making in the 'softer' fields of security and promote social solidarity when things go wrong. It makes it harder for terrorism and criminal infiltration, or internal radicalization, to fester undetected.

The New Range of 'Shelters' and Security Providers

If a single protector state is unlikely to supply answers for all crucial dimensions of security, who can? The answer lies in the multiplication and development of multilateral organizations since the mid-twentieth century, at global, regional and sub-regional (neighbourhood) level. As a minimum, in any security dimension where it has competence, a multilateral community should be able to apply collective resources and mobilize mutual help. Unlike a protector state, moreover, it can also develop transnational models and regulations that harmonize members' practices, offering smaller states a 'level playing field'. Thirdly, institutional mechanisms give smaller members a seat at the table and – EU weighted voting aside – ostensibly equal representation, thus softening (if never wholly overcoming) the realist logic of power relations. Globally active institutions like NATO and the EU give small members openings for activism in fields where the classic small-state analysis would deny them any standing.

The UN and its agencies provide the main comprehensive security cover for many non-European small states, but other institutional options vary from region to region. In Europe itself and other areas such as Central and South America, South-east Asia and much of Africa, small states may use both large regional groups and smaller sub-regional ones for different security needs. Large groups like NATO or the EU provide the strongest cover but also impose the strongest burdens. Small states must join in policies addressing the larger members' usually broader and graver concerns, and are expected to tap their small military resources for collective operations abroad (Bailes and Thorhallsson 2013). Sub-regional organizations like the Nordic grouping (www.norden.org) or Central European Initiative (www.cei.int) more often consist only or mainly of medium and small states and, with their 'light' central mechanisms and non-binding decisions, cost little in terms of cash or sovereignty. They can however help in 'softer' functions like border management, health and environmental security, and in easing neighbourhood tensions, besides offering even the smallest members a taste of leadership when holding the presidency (Cottey 2009).

Normative Expectations

Security prospects and options for small states also reflect prevailing ideas and norms in a self-aware international community. Several trends in the last century have improved their hopes of survival: from the UN's Trusteeship Council sheltering small ex-colonies (see http://www.un.org/en/mainbodies/trusteeship/), through the expansion of international aid programmes and disaster relief,[5] to the latest experiments in temporary international administration of territories gaining statehood through conflict (East Timor, Kosovo). In the West at least, willingness has grown not only to recognize new states on moral grounds rather than assessing their viability (Bolton and Visoka 2010), but to do what it takes to make and keep them viable.

In more active mode, small-state representatives are often preferred for fact-finding and mediation initiatives given their non-threatening and supposedly impartial nature. Oscar Arias Sanchez (Costa Rica) and Martti Ahtisaari (Finland) are successful examples from states of around 5 million. Small states can increasingly hope to be heard if they offer good ideas for international governance, not least in the security sphere where they can also protect their own interests by peace-making, arms-limiting, humanitarian and pro-environment proposals. This phenomenon has been christened 'norm entrepreneurship' (Ingebritsen 2002; Thorhallsson 2012), and Sweden and Norway are among the best-known examples.

As already noted, the shift in patterns of conflict since 1945 and the proliferation of military and civilian peace operations have allowed, but also pressured, small states with armies to use them in new ways. The smallest members of NATO, for instance, might not be expected to do much more in their own defence than to wait for reinforcements; but the image factors mentioned above make them popular as contributors and even commanders for external missions. Preparing even minuscule inputs of this sort, however, makes military-technical demands that divert attention from home needs, leaving the state even less ready to face its local enemies (Rickli 2008). Combined with other institutional demands and forms of activism where it is hard to avoid 'taking sides', this is arguably placing some neutral, non-aligned or non-allied small states in an increasingly ambivalent position.

Finally, small states' perceived responsibilities are affected by a general growth of concern for good governance in defence and security (Bailes et al. 2014). Peace-building doctrine now typically aims not just to restore central power but to make sure it is exercised in a constitutional and legal framework that protects democracy and human rights. The notion of Security Sector Reform (SSR),[6] espoused by the UN, NATO and the EU for these purposes and also applied during non-violent political transitions, is as relevant and necessary for many small polities as for large ones. Further, efforts to curb the transnational phenomena of terrorism, crime, arms and WMD smuggling, and cyber-violence nowadays demand cooperation from all states, including small ones which are commonly short of the experience as well as specialized assets required. Small states may resent the ensuing burdens of compliance and reform; but in the 'softer' areas of security, including disaster resilience, it is in their own interest to develop law-based, transparent and cooperative policies so as to draw best value from the strengths of their business actors, volunteer bodies and ordinary citizens (Bailes et al. 2014).

These last points underline how globalizing forces, and the heightened potential of non-state actors, are subverting the traditional logic of states and power. While explored elsewhere in the volume, this also has consequences for the security sector. The US found it difficult enough to complete a traditional military conquest in Iraq, but it is even more plainly dependent on international cooperation – including from small partners – in the fields of economic, environmental, health and cyber-security, not to mention anti-terrorism and anti-proliferation efforts. What Russia did to its smaller neighbours in Georgia and Ukraine has been revenged partly by the verdict of international financial markets. Arguably, large powers are suffering more from globalization's increasing inroads into traditional sovereignty than the small players that could never fully exercise it.

THE NORDIC REGION AS A CASE STUDY

Introduction to the Region

Five Nordic countries with their autonomous territories[7] belong to the Nordic Council, a parliamentary cooperation body supplemented since 1971 by the Nordic Council of Ministers (NCM). As shown in Table 2.2, all have populations smaller than 10 million, and all have similar political (democratic), social (welfare-oriented, egalitarian) and cultural (secular, open and liberal) systems. They occupy a region once characterized by violent rivalry between Sweden and Denmark and by major incursions into wider European conflicts, such as Sweden's role in the Thirty Years War and its (unsuccessful) attempt in the early eighteenth century to nip Russian power in the bud.

Table 2.2 Comparison of the Nordic states and Danish autonomous territories

	Territory (sq. km.)	Population (thousands)	GDP (US$, constant prices, in billions)	GDP per capita (PPP, in current US$)	Military spending (% of GDP)	Institutional membership (all belong to UN, OSCE, Council of Europe)
Denmark	43 094	5590	314 242	38 521	1.4%	NATO, EU
Finland	338 145	5414	250 024	37 012	1.5%	EU (and PfP*)
Iceland	103 000	320	13 657	40 401	(0.1%)**	NATO, EEA***
Norway	323 802	5019	499 667	56 663	1.4%	NATO, EEA
Sweden	450 295	9517	525 742	42 037	1.2%	EU (and PfP*)
Faroe Islands	1 393	50	2 198	–	–	(NATO)
Greenland	2 166 086	57	1 268	–	–	(NATO)

Notes:
All facts correct for 2013.
* PfP = NATO's Partnership for Peace.
** Iceland has no armed forces; the figure relates to civil security spending, e.g. on the Coastguard.
*** EEA = European Economic Area.

Since Sweden declared neutrality in the early nineteenth century, however, the Nordics have built a new image as a non-aggressive, high-minded family of states whose troops go abroad only for peace missions. This restraint is not only normatively based but reflects sober strategic calculations as Russia's strength has grown, reaching an apogee in Cold War times when Soviet forces were massed in the Kola Peninsula, and the Baltic Sea and Russia's Arctic coasts were key break-out areas. Unable to deter or defeat Russian threats with their own small forces, the Nordics after the Second World War had to balance the logic of seeking big-power protection against that of avoiding provocation and distancing themselves from the military actuality of East–West confrontation. After a fluid period when an inclusive Nordic pact was mooted (Salmond and Insall 2012), the five states jumped different ways in 1949: Iceland, Norway and Denmark becoming founding members of NATO, and Sweden and Finland settling for neutral status, with the latter more obviously under the Soviet shadow.

Nordic relations with the EU have been equally diverse, and often idiosyncratic. Denmark entered together with the UK and Ireland in 1973; Sweden and Finland entered only in 1995, at which time Norway also negotiated terms for entry but its people voted 'No'. Iceland applied for membership in 2009 following its traumatic economic crash, but froze the application in 2013 under a new government. In 1994 Iceland and Norway joined the European Economic Area (EEA), which makes them part of the Single Market; they also belong to the Schengen system of border control and cooperate with the agencies Europol and Eurojust. The three Nordic members of the Union each have a distinct status, with only Finland participating fully in all EU policies including Economic and Monetary Union (EMU). Denmark gained four opt-outs in 1993 at the time of ratifying the Maastricht Treaty: from EMU, EU defence, European citizenship, and justice and home affairs. In 2003 Sweden's people voted against participating in the Eurozone. Denmark's autonomous possessions, the Faroe Islands and Greenland, have opted not to share its EU membership and have *sui generis* relationships with Brussels.

Together with the countries' varying NATO statuses, this picture clearly distinguishes the Nordics from the default model of other small states on Europe's edges, whose strategy is – put simply – to join everything in sight.[8] Sweden's and Finland's choice of neutrality in the 1940s arguably served a higher security logic, by avoiding direct superpower confrontation in the region and allowing relatively relaxed local relations with Russia: with results often described as 'Nordic balance' or 'the Nordic peace' (Arter 1999, pp. 286ff.). It is hard, however, to find a corresponding strategic imperative for Norway and Iceland to avoid EU membership, and here domestic attitudes and structural factors seem more decisive (see for example Thorhallsson 2014 on Iceland). Nor can the Nordics' chequered attitude to Europe-wide integration be explained by their having found an equally effective local equivalent. Nordic Cooperation – as discussed further below – is a loose and non-binding system, strongest in social and cultural dimensions, that has never achieved or even aimed at a full defence pact or local-grown common market (Ojanen 2014).

Two hypotheses may help explain this curious Nordic arrangement and – thus far – its apparent success. First, each country's conscious-ness of smallness is offset by a strong and unrepentant sense of national identity, connected with Sweden's and Denmark's position as born-again aggressors and the other three states' fairly recent dates of independence,[9] which in turn brings a strong attachment to sovereignty and national par-ticularities. Secondly, other players have their own motives for protecting the Nordic zone without demanding absolute conformity, or the cruder manifestations of small-state gratitude, from local nations in return. The bargain works partly because the benign international activism that the Nordics can consequently pursue and their own local cooperation are seen as 'goods' by the international community including their largest sponsors. One may well query, however, whether this model holds good for any other small states and, indeed, whether it can work indefinitely for the Nordics themselves.

Nordic Solutions for 'Hard' Defence

It is both the curse and the blessing of the Nordics to exist in an area that is central to the US–Russian strategic confrontation – most superpower nuclear weapons have Arctic flight-paths – and crucial for maritime and air operations in the event of war. As a result, the US and NATO would wish to deter Soviet or Russian incursions in the area almost regardless of who lived there. During the Cold War, NATO's deterrent posture lowered conflict risks in the region and maintained stable, even relaxed, neighbour-hood relations in a way that actually benefited the two non-allied Nordics just as much as the others.[10]

With the end of the Cold War, the strategic salience of all parts of Europe for US planners began to wane; but, as Russian forces evacu-ated former Warsaw Pact territories and NATO expanded, the remaining concentration of Russia's strength along its northern coastlines actually increased the relative importance of Nordic stability. Since 2008–2009, strategic interest has been attracted back to the area by speculations on the opening up of the Arctic (Le Mière and Mazo 2013), as well as the evi-dence of Russian aggression in Georgia (2008) and Ukraine (2014). Under its new Strategic Concept of 2010 (NATO 2010), the Alliance has offered

Nordic and Baltic member states enhanced contingency planning for possible attacks, and in 2014 – in reaction to Ukrainian events – both Sweden
and Finland signed up for closer territorial defence cooperation with the
Alliance (Klus 2014).[11]

For strategically exposed small players to seek superpower and/or
alliance protection fits the most basic paradigm of small-state security.
The Nordic case, however, is more complicated than this. Unlike proté-
gés such as Israel and Taiwan that seek constant demonstrations of US
support, Norway, Denmark and Iceland have insisted that no foreign
forces or nuclear objects (American or other) be based on their territories
in peace-time. Norway has a still-valid agreement with NATO to avoid
force exercises too close to the Russian border, and its most northerly
possession – Svalbard – is de-militarized under an international treaty
of 1920 (Chillaud 2006). Iceland has no armed forces at all: the US provided a troop presence under the bilateral defence agreement of 1951, but
withdrew unilaterally in 2006.

In terms of small-state theory these choices might be interpreted as
balancing: designed to permit calm and mutually profitable relations
with Russia, which the Nordics have developed both bilaterally and
through sub-regional structures (see below). The Nordics can also be seen,
however, as practising what Ole Wæver and his 'Copenhagen School' call
de-securitization[12] (Joenniemi 1999): deliberately not voicing a *prima facie*
security threat, but side-lining it in order to seek common ground with
the possible aggressor. The benefits of successful de-securitization for the
smaller parties in an asymmetrical relationship are clear *if* they can count
on their protectors to hold the umbrella steady over them without constant
nagging.[13] In the Nordic case, Western protectors – and arguably Russia
too – have welcomed a degree of regional relaxation that reduces their own
costs and risks. For the Nordics themselves, it is a situation that suits their
largely de-militarized societies and pro-peace cultural norms, though their
everyday 'strategic culture' varies widely from the unmilitary Icelanders to
the highly defence-minded Finns (Howlett and Glenn 2005).

These Nordic national singularities surface in many contexts: attitude,
strategy, and defence or security structures.[14] While many factors are at
work, the most appealing rationalization of the pattern is a geo-strategic
one. Iceland and Denmark have the most 'Atlantic' attitudes, including the
episodes of greatest closeness to the US as a protector. From 1951 to 2006
the dominant Icelandic political and economic forces aligned themselves
with Washington in a classic model of bandwagoning (Ingimundarson
2011). Denmark moved from an earlier NATO-sceptic position to become
one of the US's closest followers in the post-Cold War era of enlargement
and military intervention – showing how a small protégé may vary its

'payment' according to a sponsor's demands (Archer 2014). This reliance on US cover made it practical for Iceland to do without armed forces and for Denmark to provide only symbolic protection for the Faroes and Greenland. For its own defence, Denmark in 2004 adopted a strategy that defined main force tasks as peacekeeping and support for civil security (Lunde Saxi 2006), implicitly leaving territorial cover to someone else – a strategy more plausible after Polish and Baltic NATO membership dramatically deepened the country's glacis towards the East.

For the two most easterly, non-allied Nordics, the indirect and informal nature of Western strategic cover after 1949 left a gap to be filled first and foremost by independent national defence, but also more scope to play bridging roles between East and West (e.g. Finland's hosting of the Conference on Security and Co-operation in Europe[15]). After joining the EU in 1995 Finland and Sweden also played an influential role in the development of the Union's military arm, now the Common Security and Defence Policy (CSDP) (Strömvik 2006). While keen that it should not compete with NATO or risk provoking Russia, they had reason to value whatever 'soft' protection might come from equal involvement in a militarily active European family. Both welcomed new language in the EU's Treaty of Lisbon (entering into force 1 December 2009) that commits EU members – albeit with strictly limited practical effect – to help each other in case of military attack, regardless of alliance status.[16]

Despite such parallels in their balancing and reinsurance policies, however, the defence cultures and systems of Sweden and Finland are as different as they could be. As seen in Table 2.3, Sweden has remarkably few armed force personnel – now all professionals – while Finland, roughly half its size, retains conscription and has by far the biggest Nordic army. This contrast extends to their reserve and civil defence systems and to public attitudes, where trust in the military is low in Sweden (limiting their domestic role) and highest in Finland (Cronberg 2006), while Sweden's attachment to neutrality appears the deeper and more norm-driven of the two. The Finns have a simple explanation – 'Sweden has a better neighbour to the East than we have' – but other factors such as wartime experiences, longer-term history, and the size of the Swedish arms industry[17] surely play a role.

Norway stands in the middle of the spectrum, not only geographically. It has strong practical reasons to cooperate with Russia and minimize tension in the Barents and White Seas; its values are often offended by US positions, so that it was – for instance – more dubious than Denmark about the Iraq campaign (Lunde Saxi 2006). The resulting urge for balancing is seen for instance in Norway's Arctic strategy, which highlights cooperation with Russia on oil, gas, fisheries and border management (Government of

Table 2.3   Comparison of Nordic armed forces

State (population)	Active forces	Of which, Army	Central staffs	Deployed abroad	Arms trade*
Denmark (5.5 million)	17 200 (home guard 50.6k)	7 950	3100	372 + 1 vessel	30th
Finland (5.3 million)	22 250 (reserves 354k)	16 000	(2800 paramilitary)	374	19th
Norway (4.8 million)	25 800 (reserves 46k)	9 350	7500 + 1 vessel	141	22nd
Sweden (9.3 million)	15 300 (volunteer auxiliaries 22k)	5 500	3450	372	11th

Note: * Position on list of top arms exporters worldwide, 2013.

Source: Arms trade position from www.armstrade.sipri.org/armstrade/html/export_toplist. php; other information from IISS (2014).

Norway 2006). Ultimately, however, Norway can only maintain such room for manoeuvre while its Western strategic shelter is strong, securing its rear and preventing Russian political or economic blackmail. The toughest issue dividing Norwegian defence thinkers for nearly two decades has been how far Norway should 'pay' for this protection by joining in new-style peace missions, and how much of its small resources it should conserve for territorial defence (Lunde Saxi 2006).[18]

This background helps explain the limits of Nordic 'hard' defence cooperation. It cannot include guaranteed mutual defence[19] because of different institutional statuses, but also for reasons less often voiced: Sweden's 200-year-long defaulting from its natural leadership position, the others' varied attitudes to the Swedes, and the fact that even the tightest Nordic defence league could still not make much impression on Russia. If Nordics must sacrifice their precious sovereignty and free choice in defence, they will do so for partners who really can protect them, not for each other. Accordingly, when in April 2011 Nordic foreign ministers issued a mutual 'solidarity' declaration (Nordic Ministers 2011), they promised to assist each other in all major security emergencies *other than* warlike attack.

For many years, also, overt intra-Nordic defence cooperation was limited to the external sphere of peacekeeping (see NORDCAPS).[20] Only since the end of the Cold War has cooperation in equipment schemes – though normally with just two to three states per project – and in operational areas such as training, exercising and air patrolling been gradually developed, within a framework now called NORDEFCO[21] (Forsberg

2013; Ojanen 2014). Reactions to the Russia–Ukraine crisis have spurred new talk of, notably, a Finnish–Swedish axis; but a Swedish independent policy review in 2014 (the Bertelman Report) warned that no degree of cooperation, with anyone, can release Sweden from the quandary caused by its own defence cuts (Government of Sweden 2014).

Nordic Solutions for Non-military Security

The Nordic states have been rather little exposed in some parts of the security spectrum, such as internal conflict and disorder, terrorism, violent crime, and nuclear proliferation (as distinct from nuclear pollution). In these fields, their role is to share the burden of international counter-measures – more for their partners' sake than themselves – and to campaign for global reductions in violence. In other areas, however, and notably in environmental security, the Nordics have been prominent in drawing international attention to 'softer' brands of risk (Ingólfsdóttir 2014). They have highlighted women's and children's security needs, playing a strong role in adopting and implementing UN Security Council Resolution 1325.[22] At home, all five states now apply multi-dimensional concepts of security, for which Norway and Sweden (and increasingly Iceland) use the 'societal' label, while Finland has a particularly well-thought-out 'security in society' doctrine (Government of Finland n.d.). There are, however, practical differences in the threat/risk constellation for each state, with Iceland and Finland – for instance – having very different environmental agendas, Sweden and Finland less directly exposed to Arctic risks, Denmark the only state yet seriously affected by Islamic extremism, and so forth. In energy security, Norway and Iceland are self-sheltered by their natural resources; Finland is the most import-dependent, still drawing 100 per cent of its gas and 64 per cent of its oil from Russia, which helps us understand why its population widely support the expansion of nuclear energy for greater self-sufficiency.

Nordic economic security solutions vary as much as the countries' 'hard' defence choices. Their starting-points are similar in terms of high economic and welfare standards combined with relatively large state sectors, requiring the private sector to produce high added value. Norway and Iceland, however, profit mostly from natural resources (fish, oil, gas, other power sources and tourism) and this, as well as political culture and geography, may help explain why they have not seen strong enough protective benefits in the EU to be willing to cede on sovereignty. For Sweden and Denmark, with their more continental orientation and greater agricultural and industrial exports, the appeal of the EU market has been stronger. Finland's motives for EU entry and its commitment to EMU are the most clearly security-related: the EU helped compensate for the collapse of former Soviet trade, and sealed the Western character of the Finnish land and people (*Economist* 1997). Just as with defence, moreover, some of these national solutions appear more easily sustainable than others. While Norway hardly wavered with the economic crash of 2008, Iceland suffered abject failure in the attempt to diversify its narrow economic base by building up banking services – a classic small-state ploy – and has yet to find a convincing path to revival. There are persistent murmurs of Euro-scepticism in Sweden, and Finland has recently bridled at paying a share of bail-outs for Southern Europeans.

All Nordic states have cooperated in one endeavour, the building of overlapping sub-regional structures designed to engage Russia in practical cooperation and thus reinforce regional understanding and stability. The Barents Euro-Arctic Council (BEAC; www.beac.st) and the Council of the Baltic Sea States (CBSS; www.cbss.org) were Norwegian and Danish brain-children respectively, while Finland pioneered the Northern Dimension (ND), an EU framework incorporating Iceland, Norway and Russia (http://eeas.europa.eu/north_dim/index_en.htm). All of these concern themselves to some degree with environmental security, migration controls, anti-crime, infrastructure improvement, health and other specialized security issues such as nuclear safety (Oldberg 2014). Their strategic functionality can be seen in terms of balancing, plus providing an extra layer of multilateral or institutional shielding for the Nordics – the EU is represented, and large European states are members or observers, in all of them. As noted above, they give even the smallest members a shot at influence when holding the chairmanship (Cottey 2009).

Last and not least, the Nordic states have cooperated among themselves in 'soft' security since the 1950s, notably through networks of police and rescue organizations. In 2009 a programme to boost mutual learning and collaboration when dealing with civil emergencies was launched as the 'Haga process'. A Swedish initiative, the Haga system has by now reviewed many specific issues and operational areas, albeit with sparse visible results (Bailes and Sandö 2014). Its latest studies, notably on host nation support for cross-border civil operations, have highlighted the considerable variations in national structures and laws regarding non-military security. Cultural differences over central and local burden-sharing, over how far to trust the military, and over public–private relations further complicate the picture. Haga's limitations are, however, to some extent compensated by other advances being made, for example in Nordic cyber-security cooperation and cooperative research into societal security (Bailes and Sandö 2014).

LESSONS AND CONCLUSIONS

Answering this chapter's title question, size still matters a lot in 'hard' defence, and in face of other deliberate human threats. Small states in still-violent regions may, however, now find other routes to survival besides bandwagoning with a single large helper: notably, a UN rescue or shelter within regional institutions. Within the 'softer' security dimensions, the nature of small states' vulnerability and the options for protection both shift significantly, often providing a wider range of palatable options *if* the small state gets its policies (and internal arrangements) right. The growing roles of non-state actors, the effects of globalization, and ongoing institutionalization all tend to blur old power calculations, while smallness makes certain economic, accidental or natural risks more manageable. Further, the expanding agenda and changes in normative views of smallness – at least in some parts of the international community – have unlocked the traditional constraints on small actors' ability to play active parts in shaping and running the world system. They can be and are listened to on security topics, both in their own right and when representing the institutions they belong to.

The Nordic states are often seen as a prime example of this last phenomenon, and of 'escaping from smallness'. The case study above suggests that (a) their success depends on successful correction by larger actors of the inherent asymmetry in their region, and (b) when looked at closely there is no single Nordic security model. The countries remain diverse not just because a Nordic 'balance' still has some residual stabilizing effect, but because they attach normative value to difference, have inadequate motive to harmonize with each other, and (except Finland) place little trust in security via supranational integration. One might well ask whether their example is therefore too 'advanced' for other small states to follow, or not advanced enough (notably in its understanding of the sovereignty/security trade-off) to be commendable. What is clear is that each of the five has drawn significantly different conclusions from the common facts of Russian challenge and US protection, and that some of their solutions are starting to look less comfortable and sustainable than others.[23] The shock of Russian actions in 2014 has led all four larger Nordics to contemplate a sharp hike in defence spending, and the new leader of Sweden's conservatives to call for urgently investigating NATO membership (*Local, The* 2015). As the Bertelman Report puts it, 'The tension between the requirements of effectiveness, solidarity and sovereignty is increasing' (Government of Sweden 2014, pp. 65–66).

In the last analysis, small states around the world vary too much to allow any single security prescript. Some *methods* are more advisable than others, but they hardly differ from what constitutes good security governance in any state.[24] A realistic assessment of threats and risks is the starting-point, followed by a review of potential outside providers for solutions beyond the state's own capacity. In modern conditions, the old wisdom of balancing is reinforced by the need to look in different directions for military and various non-military inputs. Hopes of escaping crude one-sided dependence are further improved when states can join effective regional organizations. To enjoy the most congenial solutions, however (and even more to 'escape smallness' in terms of international influence), small states need good home politics as well as sharp brains. Conflict suppression, solidarity, transparency, policy consultation and (in some experts' view) economic corporatism: these do not come automatically even in the tiniest society, but any state not attempting them is merely doubling its disadvantages.

NOTES

1. The author does not offer any new viewpoint on the vexed question of defining 'smallness', as discussed by Wivel et al. (2014). For security purposes, the simple statistical approach, the 'relational' approach to smallness, and an approach that explores 'feeling small' all have explanatory merit. All test-cases and other examples used here come from states with populations under 10 million.
2. Finland, Ireland and Sweden never joined the NAM, and Malta and Cyprus have withdrawn.
3. Luxembourg, Liechtenstein, Qatar and Singapore are regularly in the world's top ten for GDP per capita, and Iceland frequently tops the Global Peace Index; see http://www.visionofhumanity.org/sites/default/files/2014%20Global%20Peace%20Index%20 REPORT.pdf.
4. Corporatism implies organized cooperation between the government and 'social partners' (business and workers) in managing economic policy.
5. On the importance of this for small West Indian states see Kirton (2013).
6. An excellent source of information and analysis on SSR is the Centre for the Democratic Control of Armed Forces in Geneva (see www.dcaf.ch).
7. Besides Greenland and the Faroes, Finland has sovereignty over the Åland Islands and Norway over Svalbard, also called Spitsbergen. These last two territories have distinct international statuses as well as tiny populations and are not included in Table 2.2.
8. Malta and Cyprus do remain outside NATO, but for more political reasons. The Nordics are the largest single group of European neighbours to show such diversity.
9. Norway and Finland gained full sovereignty in 1905 and 1917 respectively. Iceland was accorded it in 1917 but conducted its foreign and defence affairs through Denmark until 1944.
10. '[T]he success of the old policy of non-alignment leading to neutrality in the event of war, was all along dependent on a cohesive and strong NATO' (Margaretha af Ugglas, Swedish Defence Minister, *NATO Review*, April 1994, available at http://www.nato.int/ docu/review/1994/9402-3.htm).
11. The new agreements focus on host nation support cooperation to facilitate the *ad hoc* entry of NATO forces into Finnish and Swedish territory.
12. In brief, to securitize something is to declare that it is a security issue, and therefore deserving of tough handling (possibly beyond the limits of ordinary politics): to desecuritize is to do the reverse. See Buzan et al. (1998).

13. Small states without an urgent external threat may, of course, also securitize internal concerns like ethnic minorities.
14. For more on Nordic comparisons see Bailes (2009) and Archer (2014).
15. The CSCE was created with the 'Helsinki Final Act' signed in 1975 after three years of negotiation.
16. The relevant clause, Article 42.7 (text at European Union 2007), specifies that the EU commitment does not change the non-alliance policy of countries like Sweden and will be implemented with the help of NATO structures. Denmark has been particularly sceptical about this article.
17. A native arms industry supports a high level of mechanization in Swedish forces but also draws away expenditure from personnel. Recently, the Swedish government has decided to start buying off the peg abroad in hopes of halting further erosion of capability (Government of Sweden 2014).
18. Another effect of the US, NATO and EU demand for support in peace missions has been to draw down on Nordic contributions to UN peacekeeping: in 2014 their rankings on the list of largest UN military and police contributors were Finland 45th, Sweden 56th, Norway 75th and Denmark 84th (www.un.org/en/peacekeeping/contributors/2014/dec14_2.pdf).
19. True, Sweden's parliament adopted in 2009 a unilateral 'solidarity' pledge promising aid in a military emergency to all its neighbours. But the language was a less specific echo of Sweden's existing EU obligations under the Treaty of Lisbon (see above), and the other Nordics have not reciprocated (Government of Sweden 2014, pp. 65–73).
20. This cooperation of the four Nordic military states began in 1997 and later drew in UK support; see https://www.regjeringen.no/en/dokumenter/NORDCAPS---MOU-between-Denmark-Finland-Norway-and-Sweden/id419404/.
21. See www.nordefco.org. NORDEFCO is a lightly institutionalized structure, not legally based.
22. Text at http://www.un.org/womenwatch/osagi/wps/.
23. This is argued at more length in Bailes (2009).
24. See note 6.

3. Do small states need shelter? The economic and political turmoil in Iceland

Baldur Thorhallsson

INTRODUCTION

Iceland was badly hit by the latest international economic crisis. No other European country experienced a currency crisis and the fall of practically all of its financial institutions at the same time. The depreciation of the króna substantially increased the debt burden borne by those households and firms that had borrowed in foreign currency – and many bond (account) holders lost their savings. Inflation rose to double figures, and unemployment reached levels similar to those of the Great Depression. This led to a societal and political crisis: violent protests on the streets of Reykjavik for the first time in over 50 years, the fall of the government, a general election and a dramatic drop in confidence (to record low levels) in politicians, the Althingi (the national parliament) and other public institutions. The question that arises is: Why was Iceland impacted so severely, economically and politically, by the crisis? Did the fact that Iceland is one of the smallest European states play a part in the sudden downturn?

The aim of this chapter is to examine the position of Iceland in the new era of globalization and whether its smallness had something to do with how badly it was hit by the financial crisis. The chapter will place the case of Iceland within the small-state literature, examining it as an example of how small states seek to compensate for their weakness by making specific domestic and external arrangements. The chapter argues that the Icelandic government has failed to guarantee its citizens sufficient domestic buffer and external shelter. These are of fundamental importance, according to the literature, in order for small states to minimize the risk associated with their fluctuating economies (see Handel 1981; Katzenstein 1984, 1985) and obtain foreign assistance in times of need (see Rothstein 1968; Keohane 1969), as laid out in Chapter 1.

This chapter will place economic and political developments in Iceland in a historical context. Iceland is closely associated with the other Nordic states and has adopted many of their domestic characteristics (buffers), with important exceptions. These are related to the dominance of the primary sectors and their closeness to the main ruling political parties and the neo-liberal economic policies that swept the country from the early 1990s.

Also, Iceland's smallness and its location on the geographical map – one could also say the geopolitical map – have had a profound influence on its domestic and foreign affairs. The traditional historical narrative tells a story of a remote, isolated nation that has developed a unique culture. Its people fled oppression in Norway in the ninth and tenth centuries and created their own commonwealth. Unfortunately, the nation lost its freedom to foreign rulers (first the Norwegian kingdom in the latter half of the thirteenth century and later Denmark) and did not prosper again until it was in full control of its affairs in the early twentieth century (Iceland received home rule in 1904, became a sovereign state in 1918 within the Danish kingdom and became a republic in 1944). Accordingly, the sacred duty of politicians is to protect the nation's independence: the country's sovereignty must be protected from foreign influence and dominance. Hence, Icelandic politicians have found it difficult to associate themselves closely with regional and international institutions – especially those which require transfer of power to supranational bodies. Thus, they are reluctant to advocate participation in the European project and only reluctantly accepted membership of the European Economic Area (EEA) and Schengen in the 1990s. The political backing needed in the Althingi for making a European Union membership application only came into existence after the 2008 crash (Thorhallsson 2013).

Historically, Iceland came under American influence – despite heavy domestic opposition to the American military presence in the country – and politicians were repeatedly unwilling to involve the country deeply in the functions of NATO and the UN. American direct economic and political protection came to an end with the closure of the US/NATO military base in Keflavík in 2006. Accordingly, two years later, Iceland found itself without allies when the international financial crisis hit it with full force. It was stranded in the mid-Atlantic without buffers built into its domestic order or external political, economic and societal shelter.

DOMESTIC AND EXTERNAL PROTECTIVE ARRANGEMENTS IN SMALL STATES

The small-state literature primarily focuses on structural weaknesses associated with states' smallness. Small states are seen as facing a challenging task owing to the structural weaknesses associated with their small population, their size in terms of economy and territory and their limited military and administrative capacities compared with their larger neighbours (Archer and Nugent 2002). The viability of the small state – its ability to govern itself, become economically prosperous and defend itself from hostile attacks – is in question. Also, there is the question of the ability of the small state to influence its immediate international environment. The literature commonly claims that small states have two broad options to compensate for this inherent weakness.

Firstly, a small state can make certain domestic arrangements in order to limit its vulnerability. Katzenstein (1984, 1985) argues that small European states form a domestic buffer in order to ease the constraints of the fluctuating international economy. He convincingly made a case for how small democratic corporatist states can buffer from within and become economically, politically and societally successful. Accordingly, small states need two things: fast-paced change and flexible adaptation (which is secured through short decision-making chains and corporatist, consensual decision-making); and a capacity to socialize risk by developing a comprehensive welfare state and active labour-market policies.

Secondly, the other option for a small state is to find a protecting power or to join an alliance in order to prosper, economically and politically (Keohane 1969). Historically, small states have always sought protection by larger neighbours. The post-Second World War order offered small states a new alternative, namely to seek protection through membership of regional and multilateral institutions. The United Nations provided small states with general recognition by the international community. Also, membership of international bodies such as the IMF and the World Bank has proved a crucial and generally positive factor for small states striving to cope with economic crises. These bodies have provided aid and economic shelter, albeit often at the cost of conditionality, imposing severe constraints on states' domestic policies. Many small European states have sought economic and political protection by regional organizations such as the European Union and the European Free Trade Association (EFTA). Some of them also sought military protection through membership of NATO, although a few smaller states preferred neutrality in order to preserve their independence (Bailes and Thorhallsson 2013) – even though many of them were unofficially sheltered by either of the two superpowers.

Others, notably the smallest European states in population (Iceland, Andorra, Monaco, San Marino and Liechtenstein), continued to seek economic and military protection preferentially from their large neighbours (Oxford Analytica 2010). Others, such as Scotland, chose to continue to be sheltered by their incorporation with their larger neighbours.

The case of Iceland indicates that it neither opted for Katzenstein's corporatist buffer nor sought external arrangements in order to minimize the risk of taking an active part in the neo-liberal economy. Iceland is characterized by sectoral democratic corporatism and not by an all-inclusive decision-making framework including key actors on the labour market or other powerful interests. Moreover, Iceland's membership of regional and international institutions did not serve to limit its risk before the 2008 economic collapse, mitigate the impact when the crisis hit with full force or assist the country to clean up after the crash – these being the three inter-related features of the shelter theory (Thorhallsson 2011). However, the IMF and neighbouring states came to Iceland's rescue 12 months after the crash, as is discussed below. The theory emphasizes the importance of economic, political and societal shelter for small states, owing to their more limited resources and means to withstand stress compared to larger states according to assumptions of the international relations literature. Furthermore, it argues that there is a need to distinguish between economic, political and societal shelter. The first may be in the form of direct economic assistance, a currency union, help from an external central bank, beneficial loans, favourable market access or a common market, provided by a more powerful country or a regional or international institution. Political shelter may consist of any of three different forms of cover provided by another state or a regional or international organization: military protection, diplomatic backing or the beneficial organizational rules and norms of the international system at any given time. The element of societal shelter, which is based on Rokkan and Urwin's (1983) account of centre–periphery relationships in state-building in Western Europe, refers to the importance of cultural relationships (transfers of messages, norms, lifestyles, ideologies, myths, ritual systems) between states or entities. In this connection, it is important to bear in mind that shelter may involve various costs, and the small state may be forced to pay a certain price for it. However, this price may never be higher than the gains it receives: otherwise one cannot refer to it as shelter.

According to Vital (1967), a small state such as Iceland provides an excellent case to study whether states can withstand stress and formulate their own policy, as it stood alone in the 2008 international economic downturn. Iceland was a small state that did not necessarily stand alone in all its affairs (to stand alone is not a necessary requirement for Vital), but it was thrown back on its own resources and did not receive external assistance to deal with the collapse until a year after the crisis event.

ICELAND'S DOMESTIC AFFAIRS: OPENNESS AND DISSENT

The question which needs to be answered is whether domestic arrangements such as economic management and administrative competence are more relevant than the opportunities and constraints associated with smallness. Does a small state like Iceland encounter, purely or partly, structural problems associated with its smallness, in the international system? Does an appreciation of Iceland's small size in terms of its economy and bureaucracy provide a better understanding of the economic collapse it suffered and the responses it made to deal with the crisis than do factors regarding economic management and administrative competence?

Iceland is closely associated with the Scandinavian states and has adopted many of their domestic characteristics. On the other hand, one of the important differences lies in the fact that social democratic parties dominated politics in the other Nordic nations for much of the postwar era, while coalitions consisting mainly of a right-of-centre party (the Independence Party) and a centrist agrarian party (the Progressive Party) prevailed in Iceland. Thus, Iceland did not develop consensual decision-making based on the corporatist model as in the other Nordic states. Instead, Iceland's decision-making continues to be based on sectoral corporatism (Thorhallsson 2010), since this emerged when agricultural interest groups gained a representational monopoly and privileged access to government in Iceland, as in many other European states, in the inter-war period (Lehmbruch 1984). Later, the rise in importance of the fishing industry gave it the same status as the agrarian lobby. These traditional leading sectors in the rural coastal regions could sideline other interests, and gained blocking power within the largest political party, the Independence Party, and the second-largest party, the Progressive Party. Rural coastal interests still prevail, partly owing to late industrialization (arriving only at the beginning of the twentieth century), export specialization (marine products) and over-representation of the rural areas in the national parliament. The aluminium sector (since the late 1960s) and the privatized financial sector (in the first decade of the twenty-first century) were granted the same status and influence as the fisheries and agricultural sectors within this Icelandic sectoral-corporatist framework (Thorhallsson 2010).

In addition, Iceland's sectoral corporatism has never been characterized by 'the voluntary, cooperative regulation of conflicts over economic and social issues through highly structured and interpenetrating political relationships between business, trade unions, and the state, augmented by political parties' (Katzenstein 1985, p. 32) as it has in the other Nordic states. Accordingly, the conditions for economic flexibility and political stability were absent. In other words, a culture of consensus did not prevail. For instance, Iceland has continued to have the highest level of strikes among the OECD countries (Aðalsteinsson 2006). With the Independence Party in government from early 1991 to early 2009, the structure of the Icelandic government's decision-making was more in line with what Katzenstein (1985) describes as the American trend towards exclusion (rather than the inclusionary nature of the small European states' corporatism). Social movements, such as the new environmental movement, were explicitly, and deliberately, sidelined in governmental decision-making processes. This was the perception of most, if not all, social movements, such as the Organization of the Disabled, which became openly very critical of the government's policies (Thorhallsson 2010).

Furthermore, the Icelandic government's quest for a neo-liberal agenda during this period made the Icelandic economy and society extremely vulnerable (see Chapter 10 on the case of New Zealand). It privatized the state-run banks, placed as few restrictions on the operations of the financial sector as possible within the EEA framework and was, in general, suspicious of surveillance authorities and failed to give them sufficient resources to carry out their work (Althingi 2010).

Economic mismanagement in the years prior to the crisis contributed to the scale of the downturn. The government fuelled the economic boom instead of addressing its overheating; it failed to curb the massive expansion of the banks, which further exposed the small economy to high risk. The Icelandic authorities took no notice of the general danger connected with closer engagement in the international financial system (Althingi 2010) or of the possible danger associated with the smallness of the Icelandic domestic market and the country's public administration (Prime Minister of Iceland's Office 2010).

The small economy has always been vulnerable to fluctuations in the international economy owing to its predominant reliance on marine product exports. Nevertheless, participation in the free movement of capital within the EEA, without attention given to the consequences for the small economy and the state's liability for its banks operating within the common market, made the country more than ever exposed to external risk. Moreover, the government's firm belief in the free market and limited interference it its operations – including those of the banks – was manifested in politicians' official and unofficial pressure not to restrain the 'outvasion' (Thorhallsson 2012). The Icelandic media invented the term 'outvasion' to describe the Icelandic bankers as brave Vikings. Their rapid acquisition of many foreign businesses was compared with a Viking invasion or raid.

Accordingly, Iceland fell into the trap of opening up the small domestic market without adopting the corporatist domestic buffer or any other form of domestic protective measures (see the final section of Chapter 1). The economy came to a standstill in the autumn of 2008.[1] Rescuing the banking system and guaranteeing creditors all their foreign liabilities was out of the question for the Icelandic government, as the Icelandic banks' loans and assets totalled more than ten times the country's GDP (Central Bank of Iceland 2010). Of all states affected severely by the financial crisis, Iceland is probably the only one not to have rescued its largest banks but to have placed them in receivership. The three banks that collapsed in the first week of October 2008 accounted for 85 per cent of the financial sector. Most of the remaining financial institutions fell soon after. Nevertheless, the total cost of trying to save the banks and re-establish them was about 22.5 per cent of Iceland's GDP (Statistics Iceland 2011).

The Icelandic Central Bank was unable to stand by the small currency, and in total the Icelandic króna depreciated by around 48 per cent between 2007 and 2009 (Ólafsson and Pétursson 2010). Moreover, a lack of consensual decision-making – which is of fundamental importance in Katzenstein's thesis – led to a dramatic decline of trust in politicians, violent protests and fall of the government.

Good economic management and the democratic corporatist model were in place in Katzenstein's seven small European states (Sweden, Denmark, Norway, The Netherlands, Belgium, Switzerland and Austria) during the latest international economic crisis. They managed far better in dealing with new domestic challenges associated with the global economy than did Iceland and the three Baltic states, which are also not characterized by corporatism (Thorhallsson and Kattel 2013).

In Iceland and Estonia, the neo-liberal agenda was a conscious political choice against corporatist developments in order to retain the sectoral corporatist features of the political and economic system (those of the financial sector, in the case of Iceland) and in order to drive economic liberalization further and keep the social partners weak, in the case of Estonia. The economic crisis was particularly deep in these countries because of their non-corporatist, neo-liberal political features. A lack of corporatist features also formed the basis for responses to the crisis in both cases. In the case of Iceland, the conflict-oriented political culture made it more difficult for the government to respond to and manage the crisis. The cases of Iceland and Estonia indicate that it makes a big difference whether a country enters the neo-liberal era with an already corporatist set of structures, or not (Thorhallsson and Kattel 2013) (see Chapter 10 on corporatism and the neo-liberal agenda in the case of New Zealand).

This leads us to the role of the public administration. The Icelandic administration was given insufficient resources to deal with the demanding task of supervising the banks. The absence of Icelandic politicians from the EEA/EU decision-making processes concerning financial rules left them unaware of the implications for the small economy and the capacity of the small-state entity. In addition, traditional features of the administration, such as little emphasis on long-term policy-making, a general lack of professionalism, outsourcing of projects, and political interference, led to insouciance about the threat posed by the so-called 'outvasion' to both state and society. The entire focus, by most politicians, public servants, researchers and the media, was on how to further boost the 'outvasion'. Virtually the entire society became engaged with the ongoing, non-negotiable 'outvasion culture' (Thorhallsson 2012).

On the other hand, we need to consider the original small-state literature regarding the small size of the public administration and the economy in order to understand fully the reasons for the Icelandic economic meltdown. Iceland's small administration did not have the resources needed to engage fully in comprehensive policy-making and legislation concerning the financial sector. The size of staff and lack of expertise within the administration led to a fundamental lack of supervision of the financial sector and assessment of the risks entailed in its expansion for the small community. The small bureaucracy was unable to deal properly with the complexity of the massive expansion by the banks; their operations in the new globalized international economy were too demanding (Thorhallsson 2012).

A small administration cannot be expected to engage in policy formation in as decisive a manner as larger administrations. Icelandic policymakers need to take account of the fact that the scope of the Icelandic administration will always be more limited than that of most other administrations in Europe. This has to be compensated for by seeking advice and assistance from others and by close engagement with supervisory bodies such as the EFTA Surveillance Authority (ESA) and its sister organization, the European Commission. Instead of expressing annoyance over alleged interference by ESA, Icelandic politicians and public bodies should have welcomed its efforts at supervision (Thorhallsson 2012).

Finally, the small domestic market, the small state budget and the small national currency could not sustain the Icelandic 'outvasion'. On the other hand, the question that remains unanswered is whether the small country would have had a chance to protect itself from the external shock by seeking protection by a more powerful neighbouring state or regional or international institutions. This is the subject of the following section.

ICELAND'S FOREIGN AFFAIRS: EXPOSURE TO RISK

Iceland's foreign policy still bears the hallmark of the past, of a small, insular, isolated society. Remoteness has had a profound influence on the traditional historical narrative, and politicians continue to play the 'national uniqueness' card with considerable success even though the country has been swept by globalization. The political discourse on foreign relations is dominated by nationalistic rhetoric and the concepts of sovereignty and independence. These are associated with Iceland's smallness and how important it is for such a small entity to protect its autonomy (Thorhallsson 2013).

Historically, Icelandic governments have pursued bilateral relations as a form of contact in the international system rather than multilateral relations within international institutions. The perception of Iceland being able to secure its core national interests bilaterally, without having to use international and regional institutions as a forum offering protection from larger and more powerful states, was particularly strengthened by its repeated success in extending its fishing zone despite vigorous protests and clashes with Britain. Moreover, Iceland's defence policy has been based primarily on its relations with the US since 1941. This has been manifested in the importance which Icelandic governments ever since have placed on the relationship with the US and limited activity within NATO. Furthermore, the legacy of the independence struggle, the idea that Icelanders were able to secure self-determination on their own without having to rely on multilateral cooperation, paved the way for an emphasis on bilateralism. This was also the case for the relationships between the Nordic states, based on bilateralism and cooperation within a loose institutional framework rather than integration (Thorhallsson 2013).

Icelandic politicians have managed to secure Iceland's economic and security interests through bilateral relations. As a result, they have hesitated to move towards a more multilateral international environment, and did not see much reason to participate actively in international organizations such as the UN, the OSCE, the Council of Europe and the World Bank. For instance, Iceland did not show much interest at all in playing an active part in the UN, despite the impressive example which the other Nordic states provided. The government did not develop functionally capable units within the central administration in order to become an active participant in these institutions. Also, from the 1950s until the late 1990s, the Icelandic government resisted pressure from the US and other NATO members to play a more active part in the decision-making processes of the alliance. Furthermore, the international approach of Icelandic politicians has been based on concrete economic advantages (markets for fisheries products and the extension of the fisheries zone) and securing the country's defence (building a long-lasting close relationship with the US). This is also manifested in the prioritization of the work of the IMF and limited interest in the activity of the World Bank. Thus, Iceland has been a member of most important post-war international institutions, but did not seek influence within them in the period under review (Thorhallsson 2005).

Icelandic politicians have been sceptical about their country's capacity to influence decisions taken in the international organizations mentioned above. They seem not to have believed that Iceland, as a small state, could influence decision-making and secure its interests within multilateral institutional frameworks. Though it is slowly changing, this perception has continued, and some politicians repeatedly claimed that, as a small state, Iceland would not have any influence within the EU (for instance, see Oddsson 2002).

In their political discourse, Icelandic politicians find it hard to admit that they have assigned considerable decision-making power to the institutions of the EU through the EEA and Schengen agreements. Iceland's step-by-step adaptation to European integration has been 'sold' to the general public as a means of securing better market access for Icelandic fisheries products in Europe. Governments have repeatedly rejected claims that Iceland has 'lost sovereignty' or 'pooled sovereignty' in the process of gaining access to these markets (Thorhallsson 2004). This was also the case with EFTA membership and the bilateral trade agreement with the European Economic Community. In the case of Schengen membership, the government joined in order to guarantee the continuation of free movement of Icelanders to the other Nordic states (Thorhallsson 2008) and claimed that Iceland's participation in the decision-making process had been guaranteed without the EU institutions being given authority over Iceland (Pétursdóttir 1999; Eiríksson 2004). Politicians find it almost impossible to admit or publicize this in view of the political discourse based on the importance of self-determination.

Accordingly, Iceland was exposed to the risk associated with the four freedoms of the Common Market – especially the free flow of capital – through its membership of the EEA Agreement without having the protective framework of the EU institutions. This framework includes financial back-up from the European Central Bank (as a lender of last resort) and the European Commission (though its Structural Funds, from which the hard-hit EU economies have benefited) and political backing to help it secure IMF assistance (such as Ireland and Greece enjoyed). Iceland was not a part of the EU or the Eurozone and thus could not seek the solidarity of its members. On the contrary, at the height of the financial crisis, the British government used its anti-terrorist legislation to take control of assets held within its borders by the beleaguered Icelandic banks and demanded full payback from the Icelandic government to British account holders. Tense relations followed between the two countries. To Iceland's dismay, all member states of the EU, including the Nordic states, stood by Britain, delaying much-needed external assistance from the IMF. Iceland was confronted with difficult bilateral negotiations with a few EU member states over the recovery of savings their citizens had lost in overseas branches of the Icelandic banks.

Iceland's struggle to obtain external financial assistance in order to deal with the crisis stands in sharp contrast with the case of the small states within the EU. Also, it would have been difficult to foresee that an EU member state would use its anti-terrorist legislation against another state and use its power to block IMF assistance to the country in question. Moreover, the IMF could not initiate its assistance until a year after the crisis hit, since the Nordic loans were part of the IMF's rescue package and they refused to lend Iceland money until the 'Icesave dispute' with Britain and the Netherlands had been settled (Strauss-Kahn 2009). In January 2010, IMF assistance was blocked yet again after the president of Iceland referred the Icesave deal to a popular referendum. The deal was rejected by 93 per cent of voters. A year later, a new Icesave deal was rejected in a second referendum by six out of every ten electors. These results indicate the nationalistic reaction to the economic collapse. The Icesave issue dominated political discussion in Iceland from the crash for nearly three years, until the second referendum, and raised nationalistic feelings against targets including IMF 'interference' and the European Union membership application. Interestingly, the lack of external support at the height of the crisis and in its aftermath came to be seen by many as a 'proof' that Iceland had to stand on its own (as it had 'always' done) owing to the uniqueness of the nation, its small size and the country's geographical location (Thorhallsson and Kirby 2012).

The case of the hard-hit economies of EU member states indicates that Iceland would not have been able to prevent the crisis even if it had been a member of the Union. An alliance, or membership of regional and international institutions, does not prevent economic crises from occurring in small states. The key to preventing deep economic downturns in small markets is, just as in larger markets, sound economic management and administrative competence (as is discussed in the previous section).

On the other hand, the case of Iceland indicates that a lack of economic and political shelter exacerbated the crisis. The Icelandic government and the Central Bank were unable to obtain external assistance during the months leading up to the crash. The European Central Bank, the Bank of England and the Nordic central banks were not willing to back up the overgrown financial sector in Iceland, though they offered some assistance and administrative assistance in scaling it down (which the Icelandic government neither initiated nor accepted). The US Federal Reserve was also unwilling to help out and did not offer Iceland dollar swap agreements of the type it offered, for instance, to Switzerland, Denmark and many other countries around the globe. The US is seen by many to have bailed out the Swiss financial sector (US Government Accountability Office 2011).

Hence, Iceland was not in any way sheltered by any external arrangements in order to limit the risk associated with its open economy and its large and international financial sector. It did not have any external means to prevent the collapse; the existence of measures to prevent crises is the first of the three inter-related features of the shelter theory. Furthermore, the small economy did not have any foreign backing when the ability of the bank to borrow in international markets completely dried up and the crisis hit with full force. The Icelandic government was left on its own while, for instance, the small hard-hit economies of the EU received assistance from the Union itself and its larger member states helped them to obtain assistance from the IMF. The EU and IMF provided them with joint rescue packages to prevent the collapse of their financial institutions and all the associated complications which follow such an event. These cases support the second claim of the thesis: that small economies are in need of external help during a crisis event. Furthermore, these regional and international organizations paved the way for the economic recovery in these markets – the small states within the EU received help in tackling the aftermath of the crisis, which accords with the third and final claim of the theory.

The Icelandic króna has been a mixed blessing for Icelanders. First, it may have contributed to the collapse of the financial sector (Ólafsson and Pétursson 2010, p. 13). The overvaluation of the króna, coupled with very high interest rates, made some of the investment opportunities offered by the Icelandic banks very appealing. After the market lost trust in the króna, the banks and the ability of the state to defend them, a large outflow of capital exacerbated the crisis. Second, the crisis became deeper because of the króna – particularly for those who had borrowed in foreign currency and for households and employees. Third, the country was not sheltered by the EMU's institutional framework and did not have access to its rescue packages. Finally, Iceland still faces a currency crisis. The consequences of lifting the capital controls are unknown, and this creates great uncertainty concerning economic recovery. That said, in the aftermath of the crisis, Icelandic entrepreneurs and the state, in general, benefited from the currency depreciation. The depreciation led to a quicker recovery than in Ireland (Thorhallsson and Kirby 2012).

Greater exchange-rate flexibility coincides with a smaller and shorter contraction. However, greater exchange-rate flexibility 'increases the probability of a currency crisis or a combination of a systemic banking and currency crisis' (Ólafsson and Pétursson 2010, pp. 25–26). Iceland's independent currency continues to impose a high risk regarding the country's economic recovery and future prosperity. It may have led to a smaller and sharper contraction than in Ireland, but at the cost of large and protracted consumption contraction and ongoing vulnerability. In our shelter terms, the króna increased the risk before the crisis event and deepened the crisis when it hit. Yet it helped the economy to recover, with enormous cost to consumers and, at the same time, makes it more difficult for the country to resolve the long-term effects of the crisis (Thorhallsson and Kirby 2012). Accordingly, the case of Iceland indicates that a lack of economic and political shelter magnified the crisis, though its national currency helped the economic recovery in the immediate aftermath.

CONCLUSIONS

Iceland neither opted for domestic buffers (corporatism and administrative competence) nor sought external arrangements (shelter) in order to minimize the risk of taking an active part in the neo-liberal economy. Katzenstein (1997) argues that small states will seek EU membership in order to limit their economic dependence on Germany; the more closely a small state is involved in the European integration process, the fewer direct costs are associated with engagement with the European project. This is clearly indicated by the case of Iceland. It is trapped within the European Economic Area without having the shelter inherent in membership of the European Union.

The small-state literature cannot take it for granted that multilateral cooperation within international institutions constitutes the best framework for small states to secure their interests. Politicians in Iceland and the most powerful interest groups in the country (those of the fishing industry and agriculture) have favoured the less restricted structure of decision-making within EFTA and the EEA compared to the supranational character of the EU. The present governing elite sees no reason to change its European policy and turn towards the growing supranational structure of the EU.

Small states in Europe still have considerable room for manoeuvre regarding the extent to which they are prepared to participate in European integration, as Katzenstein and Keating (see Chapter 1) argue. Iceland has used this room for manoeuvre to stay outside the EU. It also used the scope of the international system to take unilateral decisions, extend its exclusive fishing zone and strengthen its ties with the United States. However, it has been pressured by the ongoing integration process to follow its neighbours and take part in European integration in order to secure its key economic interests.

The pursuit of self-determination – over land, waters and resources – has structured the political discourse in Iceland. Also, the Icelandic political elite's first experiences of international relations were in the form of successful bilateral relations which secured core Icelandic national interests. This combination of a discourse based on the importance of self-determination and politicians' experience and ideas about how Icelandic interests would be best served led to an international approach based on bilateralism at the expense of multilateralism. Icelandic policy-makers were sceptical that Iceland's core interests, including self-determination, would be guaranteed within them. As a result, governments invested limited resources in building up a foreign service capable of taking an active part in these institutions.

The case of Iceland also indicates that small states' domestic policies cannot be placed in a uniform mould. Small states have room for domestic manoeuvre according to how they see their interests best served. Our case, Iceland, has not had the democratic corporatist means, identified by Katzenstein, to adjust to structural changes in the international economy – such as adapting to the free flow of capital. It kept its protectionist policies in the traditional economic sector intact, hindering their adaptation to the new global economy. Moreover, the state did not have the long-term capacity (partly because of its small administration, administrative incompetence and lack of long-term policy) to pre-empt the cost of change by structural transformation of the economy.

The small-state literature's key concepts, vulnerability and a lack of capabilities, which were developed from observations based on the world order of the 1960s, are still highly relevant today. Increased globalization and the neo-liberal international economy have reinstated their importance. Small states cannot simply be seen as smart, innovative, resilient and more flexible in responding to global competition, as was commonly claimed in the literature in the 1980s and 1990s (Katzenstein 1984, 1985; Briguglio et al. 2006; Cooper and Shaw 2009). The latest financial crisis has indicated that small states are more than ever hostage to the broader fortunes of the international economy. Small states need to acknowledge their limitations and take notice of them in their economic planning, the structuring of their public administration and their foreign policy. They have either to adopt comprehensive domestic arrangements and combine them with good economic management and central administrative competence or seek external economic, political and societal shelter in order to limit external shocks. The case of Iceland indicates that the importance of domestic arrangements and external shelter has never been greater than at present, with the growing reliance of small states on the world markets and free flow of capital.

NOTE

1. In 2009, Iceland's GDP decreased by 6.8 per cent, which was the largest drop in GDP recorded since measurements started in 1945, and unemployment rose to record annual averages of 8.0 per cent. General government debt increased from 28 per cent of GDP in 2007 to over 96 per cent of GDP in 2010. Real wages contracted during the height of the crisis, falling by 8 per cent in 2008 and 10 per cent in 2009. The depreciation of the króna had substantial inflationary effects, with inflation peaking at 18.6 per cent in January 2009 and the annual average standing at 12 per cent for the second year in a row. The price of imported goods rose enormously. For instance, food prices rose by nearly 40 per cent over a two-year period from early 2009 (Thorhallsson and Kirby 2012).

PART III

The small state in multi-level governance – new opportunities?

4. Small states in EU decision-making: how can they be effective?

Diana Panke

INTRODUCTION

The European Union is sometimes regarded as a system *sui generis*. While this characterization is appropriate in regard to some of the supranational institutional properties of the EU, in many other respects the EU is similar to other regional organizations (ROs), such as the Association of Southeast Asian Nations (ASEAN), the Economic Community of West African States (ECOWAS) or the Union of South American Nations (UNASUR), or to international organizations (IOs) such as the International Labour Organization (ILO), the World Trade Organization (WTO) or the International Whaling Commission (IWC) (Hix 2006; Cini 2007; Wunderlich 2012). In ROs, states cooperate with one another on a regional basis, while states cooperate on a functional basis in IOs in order to tackle common regional or policy-field-specific problems respectively through the creation of binding or non-binding norms. Moreover, the EU, just like each RO and IO, is composed of both big and small states, and, as in most ROs and IOs, there are many more smaller than bigger players.

Size is a social construct and context dependent.[1] Not only can the property that defines a state as big or small vary (e.g. economic power, military power, voting power), but size is also an inherently relational concept and therefore only meaningful in regard to a specific group (Panke 2012b, 2012e). For the purpose of this chapter, states are regarded as small if they possess less than the average power capacities. In the institutionalized context of the EU, it is not military power that matters most for a state's prospects of having a strong voice, but the share of votes that it has during day-to-day decision-making. Thus, all states that possess fewer than average votes in qualified majority voting in the EU's Council of Ministers as the venue in which states' interests are expressed during EU secondary law-making are regarded as being small.

In regard to the EU as well as other ROs and IOs, we know less about the prospects of successes of smaller states than about bigger ones. This is striking, not least since there are more smaller than bigger member states in most institutionalized forms of cooperation beyond the nation-state (Panke 2010b, 2013). Accordingly, this chapter sheds light on the role of size in EU decision-making. First, it illustrates that there are structural difficulties that smaller states face in pursuing their interests in negotiations beyond the nation-state, such as shortages in financial capacities, bargaining leverage and delegation size. On this basis it examines why some states are more effective in influencing EU policy than others. More precisely, it analyses how smaller states can optimize their influence in EU negotiations in order to ensure that the final policy outcome reflects their national interest as well as possible. The chapter ends with insights into how small states can best adapt to challenges faced in EU decision-making and international negotiations more generally.

EU DECISION-MAKING AND THE CHALLENGES ACCOMPANIED BY SMALL SIZE

In the day-to-day policy-making of the EU, secondary law in the form of regulations and directives is mostly passed via the co-decision procedure (since the Treaty of Lisbon this has been renamed the ordinary legislative procedure, OLP). In this procedure, the European Commission submits legislative initiatives to the European Parliament (EP) and the Council of Ministers simultaneously, who then decide on the final legal act in two or one reading. The EP starts each round with a reading, and the Council can accept, reject or amend the EP's changes to the Commission's proposal. Both legislative chambers, the EP and the Council, are equally important co-legislators. Thus, they both need to agree on the content of a directive or regulation before it is given legal effect.[2]

Previous rounds of EU enlargements increased the number of small member states. For example, looking at the EU-27, 19 countries have fewer votes in the Council of Ministers than the EU average. These are Malta, Cyprus, Estonia, Latvia, Luxemburg, Slovenia, Denmark, Finland, Ireland, Lithuania, Slovakia, Austria, Bulgaria, Sweden, Belgium, the Czech Republic, Greece, Hungary and Portugal. These small states all face structural difficulties in being successful in the day-to-day negotiations of the EU. First, by definition small states lack political power to shape EU law in the same manner as their bigger counterparts. When push comes to shove, they have less weight, since they possess a lower number of votes in qualified majority voting in the EU's Council of Ministers. However, this is not the only difficulty that small states grapple with when trying to upload their national preferences to the EU level and shape European directives and regulations in line with their own interests. Owing to their more limited economic capacities (GDP) and often smaller population size, the amount of financial and administrative resources necessary for building up policy expertise and broad networks to other states and EU actors are more limited than in bigger and economically better-off states (Panke 2012d).

One might argue that the considerable political and economic size differences between EU members are not very important. The group of small states is relatively heterogeneous, encompassing old and new members with high and low GDP per capita and different rates of support for EU integration. In addition, there are hardly any structural cleavages between small states on the one side and big members on the other, with institutional issues such as voting rights in the Council of Ministers being the only notable exception (Magnette and Nicolaidis 2005, p. 83). Most issues on the European political agenda are cross-cutting in character. Thus, small states might have more difficulties in exerting political influence, but this poses no structural governance dilemma according to which they have to implement EU law that systematically does not reflect their political interests. Such a line of argumentation, however, overlooks that (in the EU) all member states usually already have domestic rules in place in regard to the policy field to which an EU regulation or directive on the negotiation agenda of the Council of Minister relates. Thus, each state – no matter how big or small – has specific ideas about which domestic rules should be kept and which should be changed, as well as specific problems and ideal solutions at least in regard to some aspects of the draft EU regulation or directive.[3] As a consequence, the positions of any two states hardly ever fully overlap, and a small state that would free-ride on the negotiation efforts of another state would not be able to completely accommodate its preferences. Moreover the more limited shaping capacity in the agenda-setting and decision-making stages of EU policy-making is important, because of its implications for the effectiveness and legitimacy of EU governance. Small states face strategic disadvantages vis-à-vis bigger states in successfully furthering their interests on the EU level (Panke 2010b). This lower shaping capacity does not necessarily, but can easily, translate into a misfit between EU and national policies, which, in turn, brings about high costs of adaptation and implementation for already less wealthy states (Börzel and Risse 2000; Knill 2001; Börzel 2003). Thus, they face the risk of more easily running into capacity shortcomings in timely, correct and complete legal transposition and practical implementation of EU law (Chayes and Handler-Chayes 1993). Since compliance is the very precondition for the effectiveness of EU law, non-compliance hampers an effective community order. Shaping disadvantages could also have negative consequences for the legitimacy of the EU, since stakeholders in small member states might be disappointed by failures of their states to effectively safeguard their interests. Despite these potential implications, there is a gap in the literature to which this chapter seeks to contribute. There are numerous excellent case studies on small states in the policy-shaping process of the EU,[4] but rarely comprehensive empirical overviews on how small states perform in exerting influence in EU decision-making (Hanf and Soetendorp 1998). Hence, the subsequent sections discuss how states use prioritization strategies to cope with size-related difficulties, how effectively they negotiate in regard to the issues that are important to them and why some states are better than others in influencing EU policies of importance to them.

HOW SMALL STATES RESPOND TO SIZE-RELATED CHALLENGES

Smaller states in the EU have not only fewer votes in the Council, but also considerably fewer financial, staff and administrative resources. This poses a challenge for ministries back home to swiftly develop national positions for all draft resolutions and draft directives that are at any one time on the EU's negotiation agenda (Panke 2010a). Thus, the attachés posted in the national missions of smaller states in Brussels receive instructions only at the last minute or not at all; the instructions tend also to be less detailed than those of their counterparts from larger states (Panke 2010a). At the same time, the national missions in Brussels differ in size. Larger member states have more attachés and diplomats posted at the EU headquarters than smaller member states. Thus, the missions cannot systematically compensate for the negative effects caused by capacity shortcomings in the ministries back home, as they also suffer from a small number of staff, small budgets and limited administrative capacities (Panke 2010b). What can small states do to optimize their work under these conditions? How can they make the best out of being a member in the multilevel system of the EU?

In a nutshell, the answer is 'prioritization'. Smaller states cannot cope with the same amount of draft policies, in the same detail, as bigger states (Laffan 1998; Maes and Verdun 2005; Panke 2010a, 2011b).[5] As a consequence, they need to pick and choose. In general, setting priorities allows smaller states to concentrate their limited capacities on the issues that are most important to them, while they do not spend much time, personnel and administrative resources or budget on less important regulations or directives. If extremely low priorities are not dealt with at all, the overall workload can be reduced and scarce resources can be saved and redirected to the important highly prioritized dossiers. Shortly after having been admitted into the European Union in the two big rounds of Eastern enlargement, many of the new member states tried to cover all EU policies that the Commission put on the negotiation agenda simultaneously; over time they shifted to a system of selective engagement (interview, PermRep#68, 18 June 2009; interview, PermRep#21, 22 July 2008).[6]

Thus, the essential question that this chapter addresses is the following: Are smaller states equally effective in influencing these EU policies that are of high importance to them than bigger states? How can differences in the ability of states to influence EU policies be explained? Are some smaller states better at shaping EU directives or regulations than others?

NEGOTIATION SUCCESS: THE PATTERN

Negotiation success is commonly defined as the degree to which member states achieve their goals (Bailer 2004, p. 100) or, put differently, the extent to which a final negotiation outcome reflects the preferences of a state (Thomson and Hosli 2006; Koenig 2008). This chapter does not deduce success from a match between outcomes and initial positions, but regards success as the extent to which states manage to influence the negotiation outcome in line with their positions. The chapter presents data from a survey. In three selected policy fields (environment, agriculture and economics) the survey conducted in 2009[7] asked staff from both ministries and permanent representations in Brussels who participate in day-to-day EU negotiations about their perception of the average frequency of negotiation successes for issues of importance for their state. They were asked: 'How often do you successfully change parts of the text of a European directive or regulation according to your positions?'[8] The question did not focus on the general or the overall success of a state in EU negotiations, and it also did not inquire into the level of congruence between a state's initial position and the final outcomes. Instead, the survey asked precisely for the frequency with which the negotiator of a state successfully changed parts of secondary EU law according to instructions. The survey indirectly controls for the high salience of the subject matter, as states do not have positions on each and every issue under negotiation, but only on those elements of a directive or regulation that are important to them (see below).

Figure 4.1 shows the average success rates of the 27 EU member states (see Panke 2012c). It illustrates that the average extent to which states influence policy outcomes for issues that are of importance to them varies between states. Negotiators from the UK, Sweden, Ireland and France are most successful in regard to influencing EU policies in line with their

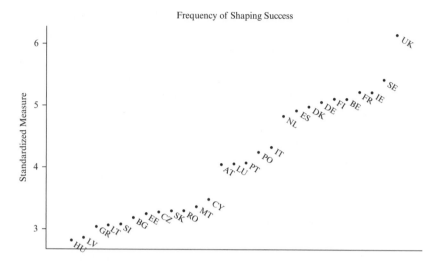

Figure 4.1   Differences in shaping success of the EU-27 states

national positions, while Hungary, Latvia and Greece are less able to influence EU directives and regulations concerning the issues that are important for them. Also, some of the smaller EU member states are more successful in uploading their policy preferences to the EU level than others. Sweden, Ireland, Belgium, Finland and Denmark are more successful in getting what they want than Hungary, Latvia, Greece and Lithuania.

THEORETICAL CONSIDERATIONS AND EMPIRICAL ANALYSIS

How can differences in the ability of states to influence EU policies be explained? Are smaller states equally effective in influencing these EU policies which are of high importance to them than bigger states? Are some smaller states better at shaping EU secondary law than others?

If states are silent during negotiations, they cannot exert influence over policy outcomes: 'The EU delegation that does not take the floor is practically overruled by the others' (interview, PermRep#43, 13 January 2009). Hence, the more actively they participate in negotiations, the more states should be able to shape EU policies in line with their positions. Moreover, the extent to which a specific shaping strategy contributes to negotiation success is likely to be contingent upon scope conditions for its effectiveness.[9] A state could frequently apply a multitude of different shaping strategies, but might still be unable to influence the major points in the directive or the regulation if the applied strategies do not meet the scope conditions for its effectiveness.[10] The effectiveness of a strategy and consequently its contribution to negotiation success might depend not only on the frequency with which states use a particular strategy, but also on the availability of strategy-specific resources.

Effective arguing requires not only that states voice arguments, but also that the arguments are of high quality (Panke 2010c). Compelling arguments are inter-subjectively valid and resonate with the prior beliefs of the recipients, whereas unconvincing arguments are not regarded as scientifically true, normatively appropriate or factually correct by the participants of an interaction (Habermas 1992, 1995a, 1995b; Panke 2008). Accordingly, states are more successful the more frequently they use expertise-based arguing strategies in negotiations and the more EU-specific expertise they possess.

The effectiveness of bargaining depends not only on the voicing of national concerns, but also on the credibility of direct or indirect threats accompanying the red lines and the extent to which they are regarded as damaging (Elster 1992; Fearon 1998; Panke 2006). Accordingly, states with more bargaining resources (more political power) are likely to be more successful than states that apply bargaining strategies equally frequently, but have considerably less bargaining resources at their disposal, because the chance that a bargaining act is perceived as threatening and, therefore, effective is much lower.

Moreover, states can exert influence in line with their position through lobbying other actors (Panke 2012d). In the EU, states can contact EU actors (Commission, Council presidency, European Parliament) and other member states. To be able to further their own interests through third-party contacts requires that states as lobbying activists systematically build up and maintain networks to the lobbying targets. Thus, in order to be effective in lobbying, the state in question needs to possess sufficient staff in the relevant policy section of the mission in Brussels to build up and maintain the essential networks. Thus, states are more successful the more frequently they use lobbying strategies in negotiations and the more staff their permanent representation has in the respective policy area.

On the basis of these considerations we expect that states are increasingly able to influence negotiation outcomes in line with their positions, the more voting power (H1a), argumentative power resources (H1b) and staff as networking resources (H1c) they possess and the more often they use argumentative strategies (H2a), bargaining strategies (H2b) and lobbying strategies (H2c) during negotiations.

In order to test these theoretical expectations, this section draws on the survey conducted in 2009. The dependent variable 'shaping success' is ordered count data, ranging from 1 (lowest) to 7 (highest). Thus, the method used is ordered logit regressions (ologit). The independent variable data on the usage of argumentative, bargaining and lobbying strategies (targeting EU actors; targeting other member states) stem from the 2009 survey.[11] Bargaining power resources are operationalized by the number of votes a state has under qualified majority voting in the Council of Ministers. The variable 'EU-specific expertise' is operationalized through the proxy 'duration of membership in the EU' in years. The number of staff in the three policy fields in the permanent missions was obtained from the respective homepages (see Panke 2010b).

Table 4.1 reveals that states tend to be more successful at exerting influence over EU policies for issues that are of importance to them, the more resourceful and the more active they are. This is in line with the theoretical expectations. The more bargaining resources a state possesses (H1a) and the more often it uses bargaining strategies (H2a), the greater are the odds that this state is influential for the prioritized issues (Table 4.1, model 1). Also,

Table 4.1   Accounting for varying shaping success

	Model 1	Model 2	Model 3	Model 4
H1a Voting resources (number of votes)	0.040** (0.012)			
H1b Ideational resources (EU expertise)		0.025*** (0.006)		
H1c Networking resources (staff in permanent representation)			0.026 (0.014)	0.035** (0.013)
H2a Usage of bargaining strategy	0.848*** (0.092)			
H2b Usage of arguing strategy		0.671*** (0.083)		
H2c Lobbying EU actors			1.276*** (0.098)	
H2c Lobbying MS actors				0.949*** (0.087)
Number of observations	334	335	336	335
LL	−536 204	−533 228	−493 872	−532 618

Notes:
*** = p<0.001; ** = p<0.01; * = p<0.05.
LL = log-likelihood.
To avoid problems arising from multicollinearity between resources (votes and staff in permanent representations correlate with 0.5475) and between strategies (EU actor lobbying and member state actor lobbying correlate with 0.6944), four different models are presented.

the more EU expertise a state possesses and the more often it uses arguing strategies, the greater its odds of being influential (Table 4.1, model 2). As expected, using lobbying strategies significantly increases the odds of a state influencing EU policies in line with its own positions (H2c). As models 3 and 4 illustrate, this holds true for lobbying EU actors (Parliament, Commission and Council presidency) as well as other member states. In line with the resource hypotheses H1c, states increase their odds of policy shaping the more staff work in the respective policy areas in the permanent representation of the state in Brussels. While this effect is robust, it is highly significant in model 4 and less significant in model 3 ($p=0.057$). These findings suggest that the smaller states are (the fewer votes they possess) the less able they tend to be in successfully influencing EU policies in line with their positions. While smaller states have a disadvantage in respect of bargaining, models 2 to 4 of Table 4.1 indicate that states can be influential if they make use of EU expertise in argumentative shaping strategies and if they establish networks to EU actors and other states and use lobbying strategies. Is this a window of opportunity for smaller states, or do they face difficulties in effective arguing or effective lobbying as well? To shed light on this aspect, the following questions need to be addressed: Which strategies do states use? Are bigger states more prone to engage in bargaining, arguing and lobbying? Do smaller states use bargaining strategies less frequently and instead resort significantly more often to arguing or to lobbying?

Which states tend to use which strategies? Do bigger and better-resourced states make different choices from smaller states? Do the strategies of older member states differ from those of states that have more recently become members of the EU? In general, bigger states should be more inclined to use bargaining strategies than smaller states, as the latter lack the resources to make bargaining equally effective (H3a). Likewise, states that have a large number of staff working in the policy sections of the national missions in Brussels are likely to have larger networks and should accordingly more frequently resort to lobbying strategies (H3b). Finally, states that have acquired substantive EU-specific expertise should be more inclined to use these ideational resources in choosing strategies of arguing (H3c).

Size (measured through the number of votes a state has in the EU's Council of Ministers) correlated highly with staff resources in a state's permanent representation in Brussels. Bigger states are financially better off and therefore able to maintain larger missions with more policy-sector staff (the correlation is 0.5475). Thus, the models in Table 4.2 test H3a and H3b in separate models.

As expected, the odds that a state uses bargaining strategies increase significantly the more bargaining power it possesses (H3a). Likewise, the odds that a state uses argumentative strategies increase significantly the more

Table 4.2 *Endogenizing strategy choices*

	Usage of bargaining strategies	Usage of bargaining strategies	Usage of arguing strategies	Usage of arguing strategies	Usage of EU actor lobbying	Usage of EU actor lobbying	Usage of state actor lobbying	Usage of state actor lobbying
H3a Size	0.025*** (0.005)	0.070*** (0.012)		0.054*** (0.011)		0.065*** (0.011)		0.055*** (0.011)
H3b Expertise			0.044*** (0.005)		0.040*** (0.005)		0.030*** (0.005)	
H3c Staff	0.044** (0.014)		−0.001 (0.014)		0.022 (0.013)		0.013 (0.013)	
N	336	336	337	337	337	337	336	336
LL	−550070	−551964	−560662	−586919	−920760	−94471	−790504	−799780

Notes:
*** $= p<0.001$; ** $= p<0.01$; * $= p<0.05$.
LL = log-likelihood.

expertise it possesses (H3b). However, it is not the case that states are significantly more inclined to use lobbying strategies the more staff resources they have for networking. All lobbying models feature the expected positive sign, but staff size is not significant in regard to the frequency with which actors choose to lobby EU institutions or other member states. Moreover, Table 4.2 illustrates that size is always an advantage. The larger a state is, the greater the odds that it frequently uses bargaining, arguing and lobbying strategies. Size is an advantage in EU negotiations, since bigger states are simply in a position to do more. This is in line with the observation that smaller states need to set priorities and focus their negotiation activities only on a limited number of issues. Similarly, it is always an advantage if a state knows the EU well. The longer a state has been in the EU, the more expertise it can gather about EU policies and about cleavages between the actors and possible threats or compromises. In addition, older member states have had more time to build up networks to EU and state actors. Thus, EU expertise is not only a positive for effective arguing, but also has positive effects on the prospects for bargaining and for lobbying.

CONCLUSIONS

Not all EU member states are equally able to actively participate in EU negotiations. Owing to limitations in budget, staff and administrative capacities in the ministries back home and the missions in Brussels, smaller states cannot cover all items on the EU's negotiation agenda in the same depth as the bigger member states. Thus, smaller states prioritize. As a consequence smaller states tend to have fewer national positions and positions in regard to fewer aspects of a draft law than bigger member states. Also, smaller states focus their negotiation activities on those regulations or directives or aspects thereof that are most important for them. As a result, smaller states are overall less active in EU negotiations than larger states (Panke 2010b).

This chapter did not focus on negotiation activity per se, but analysed how well states are able to influence EU policies in regard to the positions that their states developed. This revealed that not all states are equally effective in changing the aspects of EU secondary law for which they have national positions. For example, the UK, Sweden, Ireland and France are most successful with regard to influencing EU policies in line with their national positions, while Hungary, Latvia and Greece are the least able to upload their preferences to the EU level. How can differences in the ability of states to influence EU policies be explained? Are smaller states as effective as bigger states in influencing those EU policies that are of high importance to them? Are some smaller states better at shaping EU directives or regulations than others? Compared to negotiators from larger states, those from smaller states tend to be less successful in influencing EU policies in line with their positions. This is mainly due to the disadvantage that smaller states have with respect to the bargaining strategy. Smaller states simply have fewer votes in the Council of Ministers and are therefore less able to exert influence over EU policies via bargaining. However, the size of states is not the only factor with an impact on the propensity of negotiators to be influential. Apart from bargaining strategies, states can resort to argumentative and lobbying strategies, both of which significantly increase the chances of shaping outcomes of EU negotiations as well. Both strategies are supported by strategy-specific resources. In the case of argumentative strategies, having EU expertise positively influences the ability to influence policies. In the case of lobbying strategies, having a large number of staff in the national missions in Brussels supports the scope of a state's network that can be activated for lobbying. This suggests that smaller states can be especially influential in the EU if they do not use bargaining strategies but instead engage in lobbying and arguing. Moreover, the more EU expertise a small state possesses, the better position it is in to influence EU policies. Finally, the larger the missions in Brussels, the better a small state is equipped to effectively make its positions heard.

But do small states use argumentative and lobbying strategies more frequently than larger states? Do smaller states use bargaining strategies less frequently than bigger states? The answers are 'no'. Bigger states are simply in a position to negotiate more actively, and states use all negotiation strategies more often the larger they are. At the same time, size is not the only driving force for the choice of which strategies states employ frequently. In general, states are more active in regard to bargaining, arguing and lobbying strategies the longer they have been members of the EU. Irrespective of whether a state is small or large, the more time it has had to gather expertise about EU policies and about cleavages between the actors and possible threats or compromises and the more time it has had to build up networks to the EU and state actors, the more frequently it engages in arguing, bargaining and lobbying respectively and the greater the prospects that these endeavours will lead to influence over policy content.

Thus, smaller states face disadvantages in EU negotiations. But, if they set priorities and concentrate only on the most important issues and use not only argumentative strategies but also lobbying strategies, they can be quite successful in uploading their positions to the EU level. Expertise and networks matter. In both respects small older states have an advantage over equally small states that joined the EU only recently.

Thus, especially for newer, smaller member states it is essential to establish an institutional memory about how the EU works and about EU policies, so that expertise from previous negotiations concerning similar policies can be activated for argumentative and lobbying strategies when needed. Moreover, newer, smaller member states could potentially benefit from investing in resourcing the missions in Brussels. Having more staff tends to be an advantage as well. However, it is not the sheer number of attachés and diplomats per se that matters, but it is important that the staff in the missions are highly qualified and possess a large source of EU expertise.

NOTES

The author interviewed permanent representatives at the EU. The interviews were given on condition of anonymity; thus they are coded simply by numbers and the shorthand 'PermRep'.

1. For this very reason, there is no consensus on how to define a small state (Magnette and Nicolaidis 2005; Thorhallsson 2006; Thorhallsson and Wivel 2006).
2. In cases where the Council and the EP disagree after the second EP reading, a conciliation committee is set up, which develops a compromise that the Council and the EP have to agree with in order to pass a legal act. If no agreement can be reached, the act fails (see Panke 2010b).
3. For example, the pesticides negotiations had eight very important conflicts, in which almost all member states had positions and interests at stake, and hundreds of less important ones in which only some member states had strong positions (Panke 2010b).
4. For example, Raunio and Wiberg (2001); Raik (2002); Bunse et al. (2005); Maes and Verdun (2005); Sepos (2005); Galbreath (2006); Laffan (2006); Tiilikainen (2006); Björkdahl (2008).
5. As a member of a small state reported, 'You cannot cover everything' (interview, PermRep#44, 16 January 2009). For example, an official stated: 'The capital develops positions when there is a need to, when they have a special interest. But most of the time in the trade area we are just fine. None of the countries intervene at every item that is being discussed' (interview, PermRep#25, 23 July 2008). Another official stated: 'we are often quite short on resources . . . That basically means that we are forced to focus on what is most important' (interview, PermRep#9, 29 May 2008). A colleague from another small state reinforced this point: 'I think you have to be somewhat selective in what it is that is really important to you. I mean, unlike some of the bigger member states, you will not be able to have an input into each and every issue that is discussed, and you have to choose the topic that you really want to have an impact on, but then you have to put all your effort into that one' (interview, PermRep#47, 5 February 2009).
6. Some states, such as Hungary, Estonia and Lithuania (interview, PermRep#5, 5 February 2009; interview, PermRep#7, 26 May 2009; interview, PermRep#22, 22 July 2008), disseminate governmental priorities developed in response to each new Council presidency's programme to the line ministries, which communicate priorities all the way down to the negotiators. Others, such as Austria, Ireland and Bulgaria, rely to a greater extent on ad hoc prioritization, leaving greater margins for the setting of priorities with the policy units in the ministries or even the individual negotiators (e.g. interview, PermRep#19, 21 July 2008; interview, PermRep#20, 21 July 2008; interview, PermRep#21, 22 July 2008; interview, PermRep#43, 13 January 2009).
7. For more information on the survey, see Panke (2010b, 2012c).

8. The answers ranged from 1 to 7, with 1 resembling the lowest and 7 the highest shaping success. The survey findings of the 338 respondents are reliable, since a triangulation (own and third-party assessment) by interviews confirmed the variation in shaping success observed by the survey. For more information, see Panke (2010b).
9. In addition, the predispositions, preferences and strategies of other actors matter, as case studies have illustrated (see Panke 2010b, 2011a, 2012a). Yet information on these variables can only be obtained on a case-by-case basis. Therefore, this chapter exclusively focuses on the usage of specific strategies and the possession of the strategy-specific resources (Panke 2012c).
10. Likewise, a state is likely to be ineffective in shaping EU policies in line with its own positions if it does not target all the crucial actors in the decision-making process and remains in a minority position (see Panke 2010b). However, information on the distribution of positions as well as the actual usage of negotiation strategies can only be obtained for specific case studies on the basis of document analysis, triangulated in-depth interviews and process-tracing techniques (see Panke 2010b).
11. A proxy for the usage of bargaining strategies is the question 'On average, how often do you voice *national concerns* in negotiations?' (emphasis in the survey), and a proxy for the usage of argumentative strategies is the question 'How often do you *provide expertise* to other states in negotiations?' (emphasis in the survey). The answer categories ranged from 1 (never) to 7 (very frequently). There are two types of lobbying strategies, those targeting EU actors or those targeting other member states. Lobbying EU actors is captured via the following questions: 'During the negotiation of a file, how often do you contact the European Commission in order to influence the Commission?', 'During the negotiation of one file, how often do you contact the European Parliament in order to further your own interests?' and 'During the negotiation of one file, how often do you contact the Presidency in order to influence the Presidency?' Lobbying other member states is captured through these two questions: 'How often do you contact big member states in order to further your own interests?' and 'How often do you contact small states in order to further your own interests?' The variable 'EU actor lobbying' is the average of the first bundle, and the variable 'third state lobbying' is the average of the second bundle of questions.

5. Small if needed, big if necessary: small member states and the EU's diplomatic system in Kiev

Jozef Bátora

INTRODUCTION

Traditionally, small states in international relations face the danger of dominance by large states. Hence, in general, small states thrive in international orders based on rules, norms, institutions and international regimes which tame large states in their potential of arbitrary power projection (Katzenstein 1985; Thorhallsson 2006; Steinmetz and Wivel 2010; Baldersheim and Bátora 2012b). Being small has also several advantages. As Michael Keating argues in Chapter 1, small states are more agile in adapting to a changing international environment than large states. This has to do with their ability to gather relevant stakeholders and policy makers more effectively than large states; there may also be less distance between societal groups, and it is more likely that a small state society is characterized by a shared sense of a common destiny. In foreign policy, this sense allows a small state to develop joint positions on international issues more readily than many large states. This capacity of small states as such does not outweigh the challenges of potential dominance by larger entities in international relations, as the latter usually have larger power resources at their disposal.

One of the ways in which small states in Europe outweigh the relative disadvantages of their small size while keeping the advantages has been membership in the EU. The Common Foreign and Security Policy (CFSP) framework, along with other institutional arrangements including the setting up of the European External Action Service (EEAS) after the Treaty of Lisbon, has provided small EU member states with opportunities to multiply their influence well beyond what their relative size would allow. This is particularly relevant for small EU member states with limited resources for diplomatic representation outside of Europe. Some of them have only a handful of embassies in sub-Saharan Africa,

Latin America or South-east Asia. The EU, with its network of 139 diplomatic missions – the so-called EU delegations – in 163 countries around the world, provides a cost-efficient resource for small member states, enabling them to gain a degree of presence on the ground, collect relevant information and wield influence in places where they have no embassies of their own (EEAS 2013, p. 3). While the benefits seem clear, more profound questions arise when considering diplomatic representation in capitals in which both the EU and the member states have diplomatic missions. The Treaty of Lisbon states that the EU delegations represent the Union. Yet diplomatic representation remains one of the core tenets of state sovereignty, and EU member states and their diplomatic services cling to this prerogative quite strongly (Adler-Nissen 2014). The parallel nature of diplomatic representation via the EU delegations and via national embassies creates numerous ambiguities and tensions regarding the question of who represents which interests, and how. Hence, the diplomatic system of the EU (see Spence 2002), consisting of joint rules, procedures and structures at the EU level and the level of the member states for conducting diplomatic relations with third states, constrains the independent conduct of foreign policy of member states. As a number of recent case studies of the EU member states' interactions with EU delegations in third countries and in international organizations show, the patterns vary in different locations (see case studies of the EU delegations to international organizations in New York and Geneva, and bilateral interactions in Beijing and Washington, DC in Spence and Bátora forthcoming).

The current chapter focuses on the internal dynamics of the EU's diplomatic system on the ground, and the interactions between the EU Delegation and the member states' embassies, in Kiev, Ukraine. With about 70 foreign embassies and 25 EU member states present with their own diplomatic missions, Kiev is a dense diplomatic milieu. The chapter focuses on practices and processes that form interaction patterns between the EU Delegation and the embassies of member states. Most studies of the emergent system of EU diplomacy focus on the systemic, legal and institutional features of EU-level diplomacy, notably the EEAS. Only a few studies have explored relations between EU-level diplomacy and the national diplomatic services of the member states so far (Balfour and Raik 2013; Adler-Nissen 2014; Spence and Bátora forthcoming). By presenting empirical material gathered in interviews in Kiev and through study of official documents, the current chapter provides a picture of emerging patterns of interactions between key components of the EU's diplomatic system in third-country capitals.

The rest of the chapter is ordered as follows. It first presents three paradigmatic views of the interaction patterns within the EU's diplomatic system in third-country capitals – market, hierarchy and network. It then presents empirical findings on the relations between the EU Delegation and selected embassies of small member states in Kiev. The material provides insights into how small member states working with the EEAS to achieve cost-efficiency, modes of how they preserve sovereignty, and how they seek to maintain a degree of democratic control by their national constituencies. Finally, the chapter sets out its conclusions.

THE EU'S DIPLOMATIC ACTORNESS: COMPETING INTERPRETATIONS

The EU's diplomatic actorness has been ambiguous so far. Some see the EU as acting more or less like a state (Bretherton and Vogler 1999; Hettne and Söderbaum 2005). Others see it as incapable of doing so and, instead, seek diplomatic actorness in the member states. They argue that member states have been strongly reluctant to give up control of foreign affairs capabilities, and participate only in initiatives that provide them with direct benefits with no strong commitments for future participation in other diplomatic and defence-related actions (Milward 1992; Moravcsik 1999; Menon 2008). Still others suggest there is a need to study the EU's actorness as a combination of EU-level capabilities with those of the member states. The argument here is that EU integration in external affairs emanates from growing socialization over time, sharing mutual commitments and obligations and a willingness to partly give up individual preferences in return for the benefits of maintaining a common policy framework (Keukeleire 2000; M.E. Smith 2004; Bátora 2005, 2013; Lewis 2005; Mérand 2008).

These three interpretations of the EU's diplomatic actorness are all plausible and consistent with three leading meta-types of organization – markets, hierarchies and networks (Powell 1990). Based on this, one can envision at least three paradigmatic models of an EU diplomatic system: a) *a diplomatic market*; b) *a diplomatic hierarchy*; and c) *a diplomatic network*. Each of the models implies different levels of integration and principles of interaction, different mechanisms of coordination, and different modes of determining who are legitimate participants in the respective institutional constellation. Indeed, each of the models also implies different modes of interaction with third parties.

MODELS OF THE EU'S DIPLOMATIC SYSTEM: MARKET, HIERARCHY, NETWORK

In recent decades, debates among scholars in organization studies and organization sociology have focused on the relations between three paradigmatic organizing principles – markets, hierarchies and networks (Granovetter 1985; Powell 1990; Greif 1994; March 1999).[1] The debate has focused on the role of formal and informal organization in structuring the nature of transactions, roles and resources of participants. A key dichotomy identified by Williamson (1975), building on Coase's (1937) work, is to be found between 'markets' and 'firms' (hierarchies). A market structure is usually characterized by transactions that are straightforward and non-repetitive and require no transaction-specific investments. Market exchange is based on prices, which are the single most important factor determining the nature of relations between actors and the potential of the reoccurrence of such relations. In markets, trust is low and opportunism is high. Markets provide for flexible relations, and simple and fast communication. There is in principle no expectation of long-term commitment and no guarantee of repeated transactions. Opportunism is the rule, as actors seek to maximize their own profits. Markets have low integrative effects on actors, as they provide for non-coercive coordination of exchanges.

Hierarchy is a preferred way of ordering transactions when knowledge specific to a particular kind of transaction builds up and it is no longer cost-efficient to conduct relations within a market structure. Establishing a hierarchy is also a way of dealing with: a) 'bounded rationality' in the sense of the inability to anticipate all kinds of contingencies – in a hierarchy the roles of actors and their interrelations are formalized and there is no need for complex contracts covering all kinds of potential contingencies; and b) 'opportunism' – actors' attempts to ruthlessly achieve benefits by all means available are tamed by authority relations and possible identification with the organization. Hierarchical organization has clear boundaries and internalizes transactions within the boundaries through clean lines of authority, detailed reporting mechanisms and formal decision making. Relations between actors are shaped by their respective positions within the hierarchy.

Network forms of organization are distinct from markets and hierarchies. They arise when items exchanged between actors are not easily measured and when transactions between them are recurrent and long-term. Actors in a network are bound by a sense of mutual obligation rather than formal legal frameworks, and sanctions are usually normative rather than legal. A core principle in a network is that one actor is dependent on the resources of other actors and that there are benefits to be had from the pooling of resources. Individual units in a network exist not by themselves but in relation to other units. In a well-developed network, it makes more sense to exercise voice rather than exit, as the latter may be more costly in losing the benefits of long-term commitments of fellow members of the network. Reciprocity is hence a key principle informing interactions either through mutual expectations of benefits or by creating indebtedness and thereby continuity in relations. Deepening of relations among actors within a network may, however, also restrict access to actors from the outside. Networks hence may be less open than markets but more open than hierarchies.

Using the three organizational paradigms, the following models of the EU's diplomatic system can be derived.

The EU's Diplomatic System as a Market

The key principle of joint EU diplomacy would be lowering the transaction costs for member states; only those diplomatic initiatives of the EU that would be more costly for the member states to pursue on their own would be supported. Loyalty of member states to the EU would be limited to individual external actions, and there would be no obligation for further cooperation beyond a given action and the negotiated mandate. Structures of the EEAS would be focused on providing services to member states, which would cost less than the services provided by the respective national foreign affairs administrations. Moreover, the EEAS could serve as an agency facilitating the provision of external affairs services by individual member states to other member states.

Member states would compete in providing foreign affairs expertise and services in more or less any given geographical and functional area in the EU's external affairs. In this situation, small member states would seek to develop niche competences that could be competitively sold to other member states and/or to the EU's foreign affairs apparatus. Possessing a particular regional or cultural competence could provide the market advantage. Member states could use their specific niche competences and/or other kinds of specific advantages to pursue their own interests in an instrumental way. Opportunistic behaviour would hence not be ruled out, but rather would be a systemic element of this kind of foreign policy-making system. Relations and cooperation with outside (non-EU) actors would be based primarily on cost–benefit assessments, and the EU foreign policy-making system would hence be relatively open with no clear boundaries between the inside and outside.

The EU's Diplomatic System as a Hierarchy

In a hierarchical system, the standard state-based model of foreign policy making as an activity aimed at promoting unified positions and interests on given foreign policy issues would apply. EU foreign policy making would follow the patterns of federal states such as the US, Canada or Germany. This would imply that member states would continue to conduct their own external relations, but the federal level would be responsible for streamlining and external representation of the Union as a federal entity. The high representative and the EEAS would play a standardized role of a 'federal' foreign affairs administration with all that it entails for the need to find proper ways of externally representing the interests of all units of the federal entity and the ability to streamline and coordinate these interests internally.

The roles and competences of actors (the EU-level foreign affairs administration, the foreign affairs administrations of member states) would be formalized and relatively stable and would not be re-negotiated in relation to each specific issue and/or according to assessment of costs and benefits. There would be clear hierarchical lines of authority and reporting, where member states would be reporting to and supporting the EU-level foreign affairs administration. Opportunism of member states would be limited by the authority relations and by their identification with the Union. The boundaries of what is inside and what is outside would be relatively clear.

The EU's Diplomatic System as a Network

In this model, EU foreign policy making would be based on a pattern of recurring interactions, where the foreign affairs administrations of member states and of the Union would be bound by a sense of mutual obligation. The key principle of cooperation would be pooling of resources, sharing information and a sense of common purpose. Influencing partners in the EU foreign policy network would be more beneficial than pursuing individual initiatives in an opportunistic manner. The latter kind of behaviour would be normatively sanctioned.

The EU-level foreign affairs administration would play the role of a key node in a network of 28 foreign affairs administrations. Interactions would be characterized by a sense of mutual obligation, reciprocity in the promotion of 'interrelational goals' (Keukeleire 2003) and an agenda of maintaining a 'sense of togetherness' (Spence 2009). Readiness to cooperate with non-EU actors would be determined based on compatibility of these actors' goals with the goals of the EU foreign policy network. The

EU foreign policy-making system here would hence be less open than in a market model but more open than in a hierarchy model.

The three models are not mutually exclusive. In reality, dynamics related to each of the models are likely to coexist across institutions, foreign policy agendas and situations. One might even find that the same actors shift between patterns depending on the foreign policy situation and agenda. Nevertheless, the models are helpful in constructing meaningful explanations of the developments of the EU's foreign policy-making system. They are ideal typical heuristic devices in the sense of Weber (1970) – they allow for a structured ordering of an otherwise highly complex empirical reality and hence for elaboration of meaningful explanations of empirical developments.

The following section explores the dynamics of coordination and interaction between the EU Delegation and embassies of selected member states in Kiev.

EU DIPLOMACY ON THE GROUND: EMPIRICAL OBSERVATIONS FROM KIEV

This section presents empirical findings from the study of cooperation and coordination processes between the EU Delegation and embassies of member states in Kiev. The analysis is based on study of official documents and a set of interviews with representatives of the EU Delegation, the Ukrainian Ministry of Foreign Affairs (MFA) and Parliament, and senior officials from the embassies of the Czech Republic, Hungary, the Netherlands, Slovakia and Sweden conducted between February and May 2012.[2] All the interviewees were senior officials at the level of ambassadors or deputy chiefs of diplomatic missions and/or directors-general and/or directors in the case of Ukrainian officials.[3] Information from the interviews was then evaluated in light of information available from official strategic documents and reports, as well as websites. While the limits of interviews as sources of qualitative data are well known, one of the key strengths in using this data collection technique in analyses of practices of diplomatic representatives on the ground is in the nature of the insights on processes of coordination and cooperation that can hence be generated. Compared to information available in official documents and/or strategic documents, data from interviews provide a more organic picture of actual dynamics on the ground.

In what follows, I first briefly present the diplomatic environment in Kiev and then address processes of coordination and the nature of interaction between the EU Delegation and the selected member state embassies.

The Diplomatic Environment in Kiev

At the time of writing, 25 member states were represented in Kiev by embassies, with only Ireland, Malta and Luxembourg not having an embassy in town. This makes Kiev one of the top five capitals in the world in concentration of EU member states' embassies, with only Washington, Moscow and Tokyo scoring higher (Austermann forthcoming). In addition to embassies from EU member states, there are altogether around 70 bilateral embassies in Kiev, with 70 national days to celebrate annually. Hence there are receptions and other kinds of gatherings where members of the local *corps diplomatique* meet every two or three weeks, which provides for plenty of opportunities to discuss matters informally.[4] Cooperation among member states' ambassadors is based on informal communication, and ambassadors are reported to call each other by first names. Collaboration is also facilitated by participation of member states' representatives on trips out of town, where diplomats of various ranks get to know each other and later use these informal contacts in their daily work and in information exchange.[5]

The EU Delegation as a Coordination Hub

The EU Delegation in Kiev is the main coordination hub of the EU's diplomatic presence in Ukraine, in charge of coordination of diplomatic initiatives and organization of meetings. The role of the Delegation has changed compared to the time before the adoption of the Lisbon Treaty. While previously the Delegation was more or less only a 'secretariat' of the member state embassy holding the presidency of the Union, it is now much more in charge of coordination.[6] One of the positive effects of this change is that there are greater continuity and improved institutional memory in relation to the EU coordinated diplomatic processes. One of the interviewees considered the EU Delegation 'the leader of the band'.[7] This was considered particularly visible in areas such as negotiations of the Deep and Comprehensive Free Trade Area (DCFTA) with Ukraine, where the EU was clearly in the lead and member states followed, so that the relationship between the EU Delegation in Kiev and the member states' embassies here could be considered hierarchical.[8] The view communicated to us by senior officials in the Ukrainian MFA confirms this; they pointed out that they communicate more or less exclusively with the EU Delegation when it comes to issues related to the Association Agreement.[9]

One of the core tasks of the Delegation is to organize coordination meetings of representatives from the member states. There are various formats and various frequencies of meetings. The heads of mission meeting is held at least once a month, but, when particular issues flare up, the frequency is higher. Deputy ambassadors meet on a bi-monthly basis. Various issue-based working groups also meet several times a year. The format of these groups sometimes comprises representatives of all member states, but there are groups (such as an energy working group with a focus on gas or an elections group) which comprise only selected representatives. So working groups are organized based on variable geometry. As one of the national embassies reported to us, the working groups are a way of 'resource sharing'. Because small member states have limited resources to cover all aspects of a particular issue area, being part of a working group enables the national diplomats to gain access to information and insights that they otherwise would not have.[10]

As some embassies reported to us, networking with the EU Delegation is facilitated by informal contacts with nationals of the respective member state working in the Delegation. In this way, member state embassies get information on EU initiatives, gain analytical insights from an EU perspective and enhance their ability to promote their own point of view.[11] Hence, formal networking opportunities in meetings and lunches organized by the EU Delegation are enhanced by networks of informal relations between member states' embassies and their nationals in the EU Delegation.

The nature of coordination by the EU Delegation is not considered hierarchical. As one of the ambassadors argued, 'there is no top-down steering by the Delegation. I am a bilateral ambassador. We are a part of the EU and, naturally, we coordinate our positions, but we report to our headquarters, which is the Ministry of Foreign Affairs, not Brussels.'[12]

Information Sharing between the EU Delegation and National Embassies: Asymmetric Networking

The EU Delegation uses various channels to share information with national embassies of the member states. There are standard e-mail lists set up in various formats, mostly in relation to working groups. There is a high degree of asymmetry in how information is shared. The general pattern confirmed by most interviewees is that, while the EU Delegation shares high volumes of information with the member state embassies as a matter of course and on a regular basis, this practice is not reciprocated by the member states. This is partly related to the fact that there is no duty to share information with the EU Delegation. Also, as two embassies reported, there is still a lack of trust between the EU member states.[13] As one of the senior national diplomats reported to us, 'there is no genuine exchange of views on important issues; everyone is a bit careful; agenda is more about following the events and not predicting or preparing – in other words, heads of mission and deputy heads of mission meetings are more reactive than proactive'.[14] Some member states do, however, share information with the EU Delegation on an informal basis and in cases when they do not want to involve all the other member states.[15]

The quality and analytical value of information provided by the EU Delegation may be higher than information gained by national channels in Kiev. This concerns, for instance, the practice of the EU Delegation of inviting leading politicians and other Ukrainian actors to discuss particular issues. As several embassies reported to us, in this way they can gain valuable information and insights that they would not be able to get on their own.[16]

The embassies of small member states also rely upon the EU Delegation for information concerning particular agendas and legislation negotiated in relation to requirements of EU accession (such as changes in the criminal law). When there is a need for these kinds of information, member state embassies take the initiative and contact the EU Delegation, which is considered an authoritative source of information on EU policies. Hence, the EU Delegation may be playing the role of an *information bank* for the member states when it comes to local political information as well as information related to various aspects of the EU accession process of the host country.[17]

Finally, some member states use the EU Delegation as a secretariat of sorts when they need to reach out and share particular information with a host of stakeholders. The EU Delegation is hence useful and effective, as it has a broad network of contacts throughout the political and economic spheres in Ukraine.[18]

In sum, information sharing in Kiev is mostly conducted as asymmetric broadcasting from the EU Delegation to the member states. Some of our interviewees pointed out that the information sent out by the EU Delegation is a way of streamlining positions of member states in relation to particular issues. As one ambassador put it:

> [Information sharing by the EU Delegation] is helpful for us. It is helpful also in taking clear stances, in being united in these stances. It would look very bad if one [state or group of states] said something completely different from another one [state or group of states]. I would say that the coordination role of the EU Delegation 'normalizes' us as well as our relations [of national embassies]. It keeps us informed and protects us from a situation when someone would move in one or another direction.[19]

It could be considered an instrument of standardization or normative isomorphism (DiMaggio and Powell [1983] 1991) in foreign policy making among the EU member states.

National Approaches and the EU Approach: Coordination and Autonomy

The processes of information sharing among member states' embassies and the EU Delegation provide an important procedural and structural foundation for coordination of foreign policies and the diplomatic approaches used in promoting them. As one ambassador put it, 'we are one twenty-seventh of the EU–Ukraine relations. It is a complex of bilateral relations comprising a framework of overall [EU] relations with Ukraine.'[20] However, two tendencies undermining such unity and coordination stand out in the accounts given to us by our interlocutors in Kiev. First, while there are efforts at coordination, it was reported to us that the member states retain their national bilateral approaches to Ukraine and only coordinate with the EU when they deem this is useful and necessary.[21] The EU Delegation confirms this also from its point of view.[22] Somewhat paradoxically, maintenance of the focus on national approaches and bilateral priorities may be fostered by the fact of EU membership of countries. This tendency towards greater 'self-centredness' of countries such as the Czech Republic, Slovakia and Hungary in the post-accession period recorded on the level of foreign policy strategies is also reflected in the continued preference for promoting bilateral national priorities in relation to Ukraine. As one of the ambassadors argued:

> Today we are more 'ourselves' than we used to be during the pre-accession negotiations. We are freer within the EU but we are also more accepted and recognized by countries in the EU framework. Simply put, we have stabilized ourselves; no one can 'trifle' with us. Our positions are accepted and we are a component of something that has a certain geopolitical weight, so our standing has been fortified.[23]

Hence, membership in the EU seems to be prompting some member states to take on more autonomous views of foreign policy issues. The standpoints in relation to the crisis events and violence in Ukraine in February 2014 differed quite substantially if we compare such close countries as the Czech Republic and Slovakia. While the former took a firmer view condemning the actions of President Yanukovich and his regime against the protesters in Kiev and elsewhere in Ukraine,[24] the Slovak foreign ministry, conscious of the country's energy and other forms of economic dependence on Ukraine and Russia, used a more conciliatory tone in its public statements.[25]

The second tendency, which is also quite paradoxical, is the increasingly common practice of the EU Delegation of making statements on political developments in Ukraine, often quite harsh ones, without prior consultations with the embassies of the member states. Such autonomy of the EU's diplomatic actorness in Kiev is perceived as problematic by some of the national embassies. As one national diplomat argued:

> The [EU] ambassador has his own view . . . He very much pushes the line that he stands for. Of course, it is not a revelation of a secret to say that this is not completely in line with what [my country] thinks of Ukraine, and I think this is also the case of [other countries]. In this respect, I feel that the head of the EU Delegation here does not even pretend to act as a common voice of the EU 27. He has his own agenda and keeps it. And, if there is no consensus against it among HoMs [heads of missions], then it is difficult to influence or change the official position presented by him.[26]

Potential efforts to challenge the views of the EU Delegation are difficult in light of the fact that the head of the EU Delegation presides over the heads of mission meetings, where s/he can shape the agenda and conclusions. The shift from rotating presidency of these meetings towards more permanence seems to have brought about more coherence and continuity as well as greater autonomy for the EU Delegation to shape policy.[27] Moreover, the personal skills and character of the head of the EU Delegation also play a role. The often highly critical tone in the public statements on developments in Ukrainian government and governance by Ambassador Teixeira, who held the post of head of the EU Delegation in Kiev at the time of our data collection, was not always perceived as diplomatic enough. As some of the interviewees reported to us, his statements were often far harsher and more critical than the lines that the national diplomats were instructed to take on particular issues.[28] A somewhat different angle in the criticism regarding this was voiced by a senior official from the Ukrainian MFA, who argued that Ambassador Teixeira's statements concerning the internal affairs of Ukraine were inappropriate 'because he is a diplomat', implying that diplomats should not be commenting on the internal affairs of the host country.[29] Nevertheless, as a number of interviewees from member states' embassies argued, the statements by the head of the EU Delegation, even if harsh and concerning internal affairs, are useful and enhance the leverage of member states.[30] One of the senior national diplomats even argued that the entrepreneurial approach of the EU Delegation in making statements going far beyond what any individual member state would officially state allows member states to 'hide behind' the EU when it comes to the criticism of internal affairs that needs to be voiced. Some of the national embassies are actually quite happy with such 'dirty work' being done by the EU Delegation, leaving the national diplomats the comfort of avoiding public criticism of Ukrainian internal affairs.[31] Finally, from the point of view of the EU Delegation, the need to make public statements on various issues stems from the changes in the Lisbon Treaty. As a senior official in the EU Delegation pointed out:

Following the creation of the EEAS, Ukrainians perceive us, in a way, that we represent the member states and we are invited by them to meetings with ministers, the prime minister or the president. Before the EEAS was set up, this function was performed by the presidency, and the Delegation was often not invited. I have participated in a couple of such meetings. Now they expect us to make statements on every occasion. This is a difference between us and national diplomacy. [Some national] diplomats are used to sleep through it, meaning 'I do not have to perform; I will put something on paper afterwards . . .' As regards the EU Delegation, we are there on behalf of 500 million citizens, so we have to be heard and visible; we have to take a stance and defend policy. Here, one has to be very visible; we call it 'in lead'.[32]

Such a role for the EU Delegation is a challenge to the ability of the member states to conduct independent bilateral relations with third countries. In the Ukrainian context, where the member states have varying opinions on numerous issues, this is a particular challenge in coordinating joint policies. But it is also a challenge for what may be termed the diplomatic logic of appropriateness, a sense of what the proper role is of a national diplomat representing her country. As one of the national ambassadors in Kiev put it:

Of course, we still live in conditions of bilateral diplomatic relations as well, so some ambassadors, taking themselves still as a bilateral ambassador, are more or less unconcerned about what is happening and being discussed at the coordination meetings. Some ambassadors are thus interested first and foremost in bilateral relations, and are rather disinterested in the EU–Ukraine relations. Nevertheless, I always assert and address it to those who claim that 'We have excellent relations with Ukraine' that 'No, you do not, because your bilateral relations are part of general EU–Ukraine relations – and those are not excellent.' So the [member state diplomat] who claims that she has good bilateral relations with Ukraine in the current circumstances is contradicting herself.[33]

The current institutional set of EU foreign policy making fostering both the maintenance of national autonomy in diplomatic actorness and the increase in autonomy of the EU-level diplomatic apparatus built around the EEAS and EU delegations on the ground is likely to lead to proliferation of such ambiguity about the appropriateness of roles performed by national and EU diplomats.

Sharing Diplomatic Resources and Services

The EU Delegation in Kiev was seen as a useful service centre by most of our interviewees in national embassies as well as in the EU Delegation.[34] It provides information and facilities to the member states. One embassy representative characterized the relations as a 'hub-and-spoke system with the

EU Delegation as a service centre and information provider in the centre and member states embassies using it to support their work'.[35] A senior official from another national embassy characterized the EU Delegation as a 'secretariat' which they all use frequently to distribute information and invitations to colleagues as well as to acquire particular kinds of information which they do not possess.[36] The senior official we interviewed in the EU Delegation confirmed this view by presenting the role of the Delegation as being 'at the disposal' of the member states' embassies and providing them with information and premises for meetings as well as diplomatic officials as speakers for particular events upon request.[37]

Member states use the services of the EU Delegation when needed, but not all services can be provided by the Delegation. This concerns most notably consular services, which continue to be the domain of the member states (Fernandez-Pasarin forthcoming). National embassies in Kiev hence cooperate with other national embassies in consular matters and issuing visas. France and the Czech Republic have a bilateral agreement on consular cooperation, where Ukrainian citizens can apply for French visas in the Czech consulate in Donetsk. With the aim of cutting costs, some member states have also opted for the outsourcing of visa services to VFS Global – a London-based globally active private enterprise operating visa application centres in major cities around Ukraine.[38] While the visa application centres handle the application process from the administrative side, the visa decisions are taken by the authorities of the respective countries concerned. The need for outsourcing these administrative tasks is considerable, as our interviewees estimated the numbers of visas issued per year is around 50 000 in the case of Hungary, 25 000 in the case of the Netherlands and 11 000 in the case of Sweden.[39] The market principles and cost-efficiency concerns seem to prevail here over the principles of cooperation with other EU member states and/or the EU Delegation in consular matters.

In some cases, there is a degree of reciprocity in sharing resources in support of diplomatic work, and the EU Delegation is not always the main service provider, as member states take on that role. An example of this in Kiev was the meeting of the working group on energy security, which was meeting in the Slovak embassy. The reasons for this were practical. While heads of mission meetings would usually be held in the EU Delegation, this particular working group needed a large enough meeting room which would be, at the same, secure against eavesdropping by outsiders. It turned out that the EU Delegation did not have such a room, and the Slovak embassy was the only one in town able to provide a room with sufficient size to allow all the interested participants from member state embassies to be seated around the same table.[40] Another form of reciprocity in sharing diplomatic resources with the EU Delegation was situations when member state embassies would invite the EU Delegation to join meetings they had set up with Ukrainian counterparts.[41]

In general, while market principles inform some aspects of relations between the EU Delegation and the embassies of member states, the pattern is rather that of reciprocity in sharing resources and services, which matches with the network type of relations outlined earlier in the chapter. As one of the ambassadors put it:

> There is definitely no hierarchy here. The EU Delegation is not in a superior position vis-à-vis national embassies. In general, when we are talking about the EU, we are the EU . . . So we perceive it rather as a network. To describe the relations of EU Delegation and national embassies specifically, it is about cooperation, coordination and mutual help.[42]

There are also various regional sub-networks at play, such as that formed by the regular interactions and coordination, sharing of information and division of tasks among the Visegrád countries (Poland, the Czech Republic, Hungary and Slovakia).[43]

CONCLUSION: COEXISTING AND SHIFTING PRINCIPLES OF DIPLOMATIC COORDINATION AND THE IMPLICATIONS FOR SOVEREIGNTY AND DEMOCRATIC CONTROL MECHANISMS

The chapter shows that there are shifting patterns of how small member states interact with the EU Delegation in Kiev. In some issue areas where their national interests are particularly well defined and they can achieve better results on their own owing to political, economic or historical ties, small member states prefer to remain small and go it on their own. In other areas, where their interests are less pronounced or less clearly defined, they are happy to join ranks with the rest of the EU's diplomatic system and 'go big', as it were. Paradoxically, going big means subjecting one's own decision making to a higher degree of hierarchical or network coordination within the EU's diplomatic system. Remaining 'small' means that a state is selective, goes it alone and approaches coordination in the EU's diplomatic system in an opportunistic market-like fashion.

A broad pattern that can be discerned is that interaction patterns and practices vary across areas of competence and expertise. In areas where the EU has competences (exclusive or not), such as negotiations of the Association Agreement with Ukraine, relations between the EU Delegation and member states' embassies resemble a hierarchy. Small member states prefer to let a bigger entity of which they are part determine interests and call the shots. In political matters relating to various policy agendas such as energy security, relations evolve in network-style interactions. And yet in other areas, where the EU Delegation and/or member states provide each other with services arranging meetings and information upon request, relations are more market-like. This then has implications for how democratic control should be performed. In areas where the EU takes the lead and primary responsibility, it should be primarily EU-level mechanisms such as the bodies of the EU Parliament and/or the administrative control mechanisms of the European Commission that should ensure control and accountability. On the other hand, in areas where member states remain firmly in control of their respective diplomatic approaches, it remains the task of the national parliaments and other control bodies on the national level to perform control. The most elusive area seems to be the network-coordination patterns, which may be highly effective but may also be challenging in terms of determining who is actually responsible for initiatives and the various steps taken. This is in line with some of the research on network forms of administration, where it has been a challenge to discern clear accountability relations of the actors involved (Kickert et al. 1997). This ordering of modes of democratic control may also be used as a guiding principle when assessing which agenda falls under whose responsibility.

The case study of the EU's interaction patterns in Kiev also shows that sovereignty of member states is not challenged *tout court*. In certain policy areas, member states prefer to promote their own agenda and do so without comprehensive coordination with other member states. They prefer to remain small, as it were, and enjoy the capacity for action that smallness provides them with. Moreover, it is important to note that the constellation of actors and the nature of interaction patterns are likely to vary in relation to the importance of the host capital (i.e. how many EU member states maintain their own diplomatic presence) as well as the location of the host capital. It may be hypothesized that the higher the density of member states' presence the less likely there are to be challenges to member states' sovereignty. Further research is needed to explore these issues.

NOTES

Work on this chapter was supported by the Slovak Research and Development Agency grant no. APVV-0484-10.
1. In the account of the three paradigms of organization I build on the arguments of Powell (1990).
2. Interviews in Kiev were conducted by Veronika Pulišová, then a Ph.D. candidate at

Comenius University. The reason for selecting these five countries is that they are all small or medium-sized member states, and the interviews were conducted as part of the above-mentioned research project focusing on the changing role of such states in the emerging foreign policy-making system in the EU post-Lisbon.

3. The appendix to the chapter includes a list of interviews but does not include names, as interviewees spoke under conditions of anonymity. The interviews were based on semi-structured questions; they were recorded and transcribed. Transcripts of interviews were then used as a basis for the analysis.
4. I9.
5. I9.
6. I2, I4, I6, I9.
7. I9.
8. I1, I6, I9.
9. I8.
10. I6.
11. I4, I5.
12. I1.
13. I1, I5.
14. I5.
15. I4.
16. I1, I4, I5.
17. I5, I6, I9.
18. I9.
19. I1.
20. I4.
21. I1, I5, I6.
22. I2.
23. I1.
24. See the statements on the website of the Czech MFA, www.mzv.cz, from February 2014.
25. See the statements on the website of the Slovak MFA, www.mzv.sk, from February 2014. The causal effect of economic concerns and the resulting conciliatory tone in public statements regarding the crisis in Ukraine were also confirmed by a senior official from the Slovak MFA in a conversation with the author on 31 March 2014.
26. I5.
27. I5.
28. I1, I5.
29. I3.
30. I4, I6, I9.
31. I4, I6.
32. I2.
33. I4.
34. I1, I2, I4, I5, I6, I9.
35. I5.
36. I9.
37. I2.
38. VFS Global is owned by Kuoni Group headquartered in Zurich – offering visa and other services to diplomatic establishments worldwide – and served 45 governments in 107 countries in late 2013. For more see http://www.kuoni.com/group/vfs-global.
39. I6, I9.
40. I1, I4.
41. I1, I4, I6, I9.
42. I1.
43. I1.

APPENDIX

List of Interviews

I1, senior diplomat, Slovak embassy, Kiev, 14 February 2012.

I2, senior diplomat, EU Delegation, Kiev, 1 March 2012.

I3, senior diplomat, Information Department, MFA of Ukraine, Kiev, 19 March 2012.

I4, senior diplomat, Czech embassy, Kiev, 21 March 2012.

I5, senior diplomat, Hungarian embassy, Kiev, 24 March 2012.

I6, senior diplomat, Swedish embassy, Kiev, 28 March 2012.

I7, senior member of the Ukrainian Parliament, member of the Parliamentary Committee on European Integration, Kiev, 28 April 2012.

I8, senior diplomat, Department for the EU, MFA of Ukraine, 8 May 2012.

I9, senior diplomat, Netherlands embassy, Kiev, 23 May 2012.

6. Political mechanics of smallness: the Baltic states as small states in the European Parliament

Allan Sikk and Licia Cianetti*

The impact of state size on macroeconomics, political economy and international politics is well established in academic literature. When it comes to domestic politics, the received wisdom is that nearly all contemporary democracies are too big to benefit from the advantages assigned to small political communities, following the conclusion from Dahl and Tufte's seminal *Size and Democracy* (1973). However, there is evidence on the impact of country size on the size of parliaments, democratic endurance, civil conflict, electoral turnout and party membership levels.[1] Still, much of the research is exploratory in nature, and the mechanisms by which state size affects political variables remain understudied.

Anckar (2002) is among the few to break the mould, as he argues that smaller country size means smaller distances between elites and citizens and, as a result, interest articulation is filtered through fewer intervening structures and agents. This chapter analyses the working of such intermediate institutions in the Baltic states. More specifically, we look at the members of the European Parliament (MEPs) by analysing patterns of representation in the committees and political groups of the European Parliament and on national party boards. Small country size in conjunction with party system fragmentation has led to MEPs being scattered among the organs of the European Parliament (EP) and to their negligible representation on party boards. This can reduce the influence of the Baltic states within the EP, but also the influence of MEPs within their parties and, by implication, reduce the EU-related policy expertise and even the overall importance of the political relevance of the EU in domestic politics.

At the same time, we discover that the MEPs from the Baltic states are politically more experienced than MEPs from larger countries, despite their arguably more marginal position. We find that in general country size is negatively correlated with national political experience of MEPs, so that the levels of experience are higher in smaller member states, and particularly in new member states – such as the Baltic states. We propose a theoretical model for the relationship and also discuss additional factors (shorter length of political career paths and attractiveness of MEP status) that can further strengthen the relationship in the Baltic states.

This higher level of national parliamentary and cabinet experience may compensate both for the small numbers of representatives in the EP and for the small number of MEPs on party boards. Particularly, those MEPs who have served in national cabinets have, as ministers, interacted with the national parliaments and the EU (both the European Commission and the EU ministerial-level meetings). Hence, such MEPs and, by implication, their countries and national parties are *ceteris paribus* at an advantage when it comes to using argumentative and lobbying strategies (see Chapter 4) in asserting influence in the European Parliament.

THE BALTIC STATES AND THE POLITICAL IMPACT OF SIZE

Estonia, Latvia and Lithuania are often included in studies on European small states and have also been the subject of many case studies focusing on the political and economic effects of country size. Interest in the Baltic states intensified after their accession to the EU and NATO and in the wake of the Great Recession, which hit them particularly hard. While the small size of these countries has often been used as an explanatory or intervening variable, the specific mechanisms through which size affects politics – especially domestic politics – are relatively uncharted.

Most studies that include the Baltic states have concerned political economy or foreign policy – including studies of all European small states and those that focus specifically on one or more Baltic states (most frequently Estonia). Although they define smallness in various ways, they generally tend to assume that it leads to vulnerability and limitations and look at the economic, political or defence implications. Studies on foreign policies have focused particularly on international security and negotiations in the EU. In international and security studies, size is typically related to a country's capacity to project power and defend itself. These studies argue that we need to take small size into account in order to understand Baltic foreign policy, especially as it entails specific vulnerabilities and limits international capabilities (Trapans 1998; Männik 2004) and influence on agenda-setting in international organizations (Galbreath and Lamoreaux 2007; Lamoreaux and Galbreath 2008; Archer 2010; Crandall 2014). The effects of smallness are often intermingled with the effects of other factors, such as proximity to Russia (Archer 2010), membership in regional organizations (Männik 2004; Lamoreaux and Galbreath 2008), or international political economy (Kattel et al. 2010). As a consequence, country size is often seen as an important, but fuzzy, background condition.

Some of the same themes surface in studies on negotiating strategies in the EU. Especially after the 2004 enlargement, size differences in the EU and their implications for decision-making practices have attracted academic attention. Estonia, Latvia and Lithuania are typically included in comparative studies of European small states (Bunse et al. 2005; Thorhallsson 2006; Panke 2010b, 2012c; Steinmetz and Wivel 2010; this volume, Chapter 4). Like the literature on foreign policy and security, studies of EU decision-making assume that smallness limits the negotiating strategies of small states. Opportunities and possible ways to overcome those limitations are also highlighted; for example, Diana Panke looks at how small EU states can under certain conditions 'punch above their weight' in EU negotiations (Panke 2010b, 2012c).

These studies provide useful insights into small states' negotiating capabilities and strategic possibilities within the EU. Smallness is seen as an important constraining factor, but the mechanisms through which small size actually affects the political process are often not considered in detail. One exception is a study commissioned by the EU Affairs Committee of the Estonian Parliament, which focuses specifically on Estonia's officials and their strategies vis-à-vis EU institutions (Made 2010). Made posits small size as one of the main factors in Estonia's EU policies, because of limited resources, perception of the country's own potential, and strategic constraints. Through his close focus on Estonian officials, he provides useful insights into the differences between Tallinn-based and Brussels-based officials, their perceptions of country size and influence, and their strategies for dealing with size-related limitations. He argues that the small number of EU policy experts can result in a high workload and multi-tasking, which can affect the quality of decision-making.[2]

The analysis of Estonian party politics after EU accession by one of the authors of this chapter is another attempt at uncovering the mechanics behind the influence of size (Sikk 2009a). The effects of EU membership on party politics were found to be mediated by the small size of the country. The small number of European policy specialists and of MEPs means that they have limited presence in the decision-making bodies of political parties, which can contribute to the sidelining of European issues in favour of domestic concerns. However, a broader comparative framework is necessary for clearly identifying the specific effects of smallness beyond the case of Estonia.

In this chapter, we focus on the effects of country size on EU politics by looking at the numbers and role of MEPs from the Baltic states. MEPs are arguably the most prominent European specialists – party politically speaking – and a crucial link between (national) political parties and European politics. Through a comparative analysis and theory building on the impact of size on the numbers, distribution, status and background of MEPs, this chapter complements findings from other studies to uncover some of the elementary mechanisms through which size matters. Our theoretical arguments and those stemming from the quantitative comparative analysis are complemented and tested by an in-depth look at the MEPs from the Baltic states. For the most part, we use size as a continuous rather than a dichotomous variable, as that allows us to develop more general theoretical models and alleviates the need to come up with (potentially arbitrary) cut-off points. We look at the Baltic states as countries at the extreme low end of the scale and use the specific detail to illustrate the general effect of size.

We show that, even though small countries are overrepresented in the EP relative to their size, the small absolute number of MEPs has implications both for coverage of issue areas in the EP and their involvement within party organs. However, country size also has an effect on the level of national political experience of MEPs. MEPs from small member states tend to have more experience in national politics than those from larger member states. This can imply stronger linkages to national politics and can compensate for the small numbers in terms of the quality of representation.[3] We also propose an underlying theoretical model for the relationship between size of representation and national political experience and finish with a discussion of intervening and additional factors, some of which can be independently linked to country size.

COUNTRY SIZE AND REPRESENTATIVE INSTITUTIONS

The size of national delegations in the EP is linked to country size by the principle of 'degressive proportionality', where some of the specifics have been influenced by historical bargaining (see Corbett et al. 2011, pp. 27–29) (see Figure 6.1).

The average ratio is three MEPs per million people, but it is much more favourable for smaller member states than large member states. Hence, there are 4.5 MEPs for 1 million Estonians, yet only 1.2 per million Germans; Luxembourg and Malta have the most favourable ratio of about 12 MEPs per million. Taagepera and Hosli (2006) develop a logical model linking the size of a country's population and national representation in the EP (or any other international organization):

$$S_i = \frac{SP_i^n}{\sum P_k^n}$$

where S_i is the number of seats for country i, S stands for the total number of seats available, P_i is the total population in country i, and n is an exponent equal to:

$$n = \frac{\left(\dfrac{1}{logN} - \dfrac{1}{logS}\right)}{\left(\dfrac{1}{logN} - \dfrac{1}{logP}\right)}$$

where N is the number of member states, S the total number of seats and P total population (of the EU). The line based on the logical model in Figure 6.1 fits the line well (close to the empirical linear OLS fit, not shown), but the two smallest member states as well as Germany (the biggest member state) are clearly overrepresented.[4]

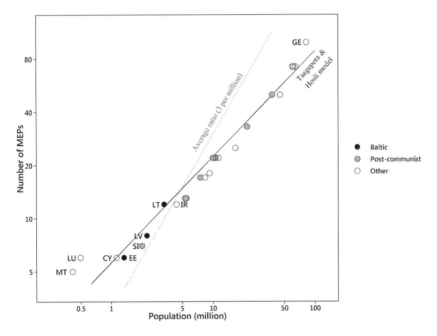

Figure 6.1   Number of MEPs per million people

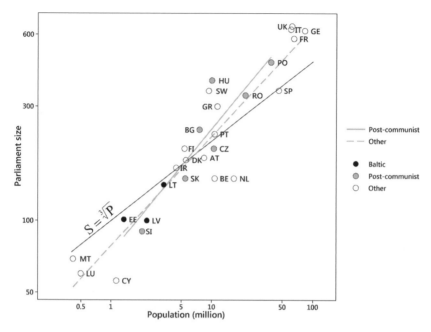

Note: Grey lines show empirical OLS fits.

Figure 6.2   Country size and size of parliament (lower houses)

A similar relationship holds for the number of seats in national parliaments. For an obvious reason it is less strong than that between the country size and the EP delegation – the size of national parliaments has been decided independently by individual countries. As argued by Rein Taagepera and his colleagues, the total number of seats in national assemblies approximately follows the cube root of total population. They argue that the cube root formula minimizes the workload of representatives by optimizing the number of communication channels between representatives and constituents and representatives themselves (see Taagepera and Shugart 1989, p. 175; Taagepera 2007, ch. 12). The size of national parliaments in EU member states follows the cube root function very closely, with parliaments in larger member states being slightly 'oversize' and those in smaller member states slightly 'undersize' (see Figure 6.2).

Finally, cabinet size is also related to country size. It is positively, albeit weakly, linked to total population ($R^2 = 0.26$), with relatively smaller cabinets in post-communist countries, controlling for country size (see the lower empirical OLS fit line in Figure 6.3). However, there are many outliers – such as Hungary, Malta and the Netherlands with undersized

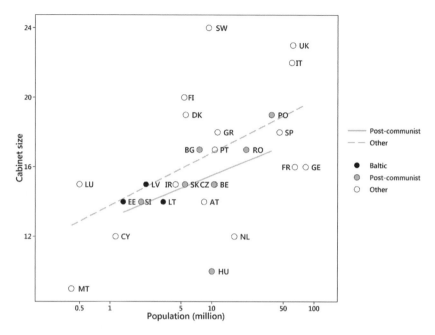

Source: Number of cabinet members from S. Andersson et al. (2014).

Figure 6.3 Country size and cabinet size

and Sweden and Finland with oversized cabinets. The reasons why larger countries tend to have larger cabinets are not immediately clear and remain beyond the scope of this chapter. At this point, we can only speculate that it may be related to more limited resources and a smaller number of significant issue areas in smaller countries; the variation also partly stems from different institutional arrangements and notions of what constitutes a cabinet.

EUROPEAN PARLIAMENT PARTY GROUPS AND COMMITTEES

Small state MEPs can sometimes punch above their weight and wield disproportionate influence in the Parliament. Regardless of their background and even the size of delegations, MEPs from small countries can enjoy more power by being 'kingmakers'. One example is the establishment of party groups. A party group needs to have at least 25 representatives from at least a quarter of member states (Corbett et al. 2011, p. 78). Baltic

MEPs have been highly sought after at times in recent years. For example, the Europe of Freedom and Direct Democracy (EFDD) group led by the United Kingdom Independence Party (UKIP) and the Italian Five Star Movement disintegrated on 14 October 2014 when a Latvian MEP (Iveta Grigule of the Union of Greens and Farmers) decided to leave the group but was soon reinstituted when an MEP from the Polish Congress of the New Right (Robert Iwaszkiewicz)[5] decided to join. In 2009, the establishment of the European Conservatives and Reformists (ECR) group hinged upon recruiting members from a sufficiently large number of member states. Out of this necessity, ECR joined forces with a nationalist Latvian party (TB-LNNK) with just one MEP among other, often controversial, parties from Central and Eastern Europe (Bale et al. 2010).[6] In the same year, Indrek Tarand, an anti-party independent candidate, was successful in his bid to become an MEP for Estonia. Before eventually joining the Greens–European Free Alliance (Greens–EFA) group, he was courted by no less than four other groups – the Alliance of Liberals and Democrats for Europe (ALDE), the Party of European Socialists (PES), ECR and the group of the non-attached (Sikk 2009b; Ehin and Solvak 2012).[7]

EP committees have been growing in importance as the significance of the EP itself has grown. It has been shown that committee members possess high levels of expertise on the policy areas of the committees (McElroy 2006). Owing to the high number of committees (20 as of 2014–15), only bigger member states can have representatives in all committees.[8] The Baltic states are very far from that, given their very small number of MEPs. One strategy for overcoming the problem of small size could be cooperation. Between them, the Baltic states have 24 MEPs, and if the choice of committees were carefully coordinated they might just be able to cover all the committees between them. Such coordination is only hypothetical because of partisan divides and an at best limited sense of common identity. Toomas-Hendrik Ilves, the most popular candidate in the 2004 European elections in Estonia (former foreign minister and later the country's president), made his views on 'Baltic unity' clear in a 1999 speech entitled 'Estonia as a Nordic country': 'it is time to do away with poorly fitting, externally imposed categories. It is time that we recognize that we are dealing with three very different countries in the Baltic area, with completely different affinities' (cited in Lehti 2006, p. 71).

In practice, there is little evidence of coordination across national delegations. Indeed, even coordination among Baltic representatives belonging to the same EP group can be difficult if they come from parties that are adversaries in national politics. The Baltic delegations in the ALDE group are particularly notorious in that regard. Its Lithuanian members belong to the Labour Party (centrist, often characterized as populist and marred by corruption scandals) and the Liberal Movement (the most economically and socially liberal Lithuanian party). Both have at times been included in the governing coalitions, but always avoided each other. The Estonian members of the EP group belong to the free market-eer Reform Party and the centre-left Centre Party, with a controversial dominant leader and a particular stronghold among the Russian-speaking minority, which have in recent decades been foes in Estonian party politics. Even stranger bedfellows can be found when looking at MEPs from all three Baltic states together. The Greens–EFA have three members from the Baltic states: Bronis Ropė (Lithuania), Tatjana Ždanoka (Latvia) and Indrek Tarand (Estonia). Ropė is the vice-chair of the agrarian and Eurosceptic Lithuanian Peasant and Greens Union. Tatjana Ždanoka is a co-chair of the hard-line Russian Union and was once barred from running for the national parliament because of continued membership in the Communist Party after it had called for a coup against the democrati-cally elected pro-independence government in 1991. Yet Indrek Tarand (an independent) used to be the secretary-general of the Ministry of Foreign Affairs during the EU membership negotiations and is also known for his fervent anti-communism – infamously for a controversial public prank against former communist top politicians in Estonia.[9]

Therefore, because of the combined effect of small numbers of MEPs and lack of coordination between them, two committees (Development and Constitutional Affairs) were without any Baltic representatives – even when including substitute members.[10] A further three (Economic and Monetary Affairs, Fisheries and Legal Affairs) only included substitute members from the Baltic states. In addition to coordination problems, a key reason for the uneven distribution of MEPs in committees is the popularity of some committees.

The Foreign Affairs Committee, in particular, has for a long time been the committee of choice for Baltic MEPs, as it included five full members from the Baltic states – with three from Latvia alone. Together with the sub-stitutes, seven Baltic MEPs were involved in the work of the committee – nearly a third of all Baltic MEPs. The situation has been similar since at least 2008 (Sikk 2009a), when the Foreign Affairs Committee included as many as nine members (four members and five substitutes). In 2008, the Security and Defence sub-committee was particularly popular among Baltic MEPs – it also had vice-chairs from Latvia and Lithuania.[11] In 2015, the committee on Industry, Research and Energy was also popular, with five full members and one substitute.

The concentration on some committees (and absence from others) may be a sign that Baltic MEPs chose to focus on issue areas more significant to them and their constituents, hoping to make a difference there. This corresponds to the strategy of prioritization in the European Commission discussed by Diana Panke in Chapter 4. The focus on Foreign Affairs is expected, as the membership in the EU was to a great extent seen as a foreign policy project and part of the grand turning away from communist history by 'returning to the West' (see Tulmets 2014). High membership in Industry, Research and Energy is explained by the relevance of EU energy policy for all states, but for Lithuania in particular. Following the EU accession the country had to close its nuclear power station in Ignalina (Ivanov 2008), and the future of sustainable electricity production has since been a preoccupation for the country. Typically, three Lithuanian MEPs (27 per cent of the national delegation) have been sitting on the committee as full or substitute members.

The size of individual party delegations from the Baltic states is further affected by the fragmentation of party systems. The average size of a party delegation in the EP is four – even theoretically far beyond the reach for almost all Baltic parties. Indeed, Estonia has the lowest average size of party delegations (1.2). Note that Italy has the highest average party delegation (10.3) despite a fairly fragmented party system, which shows how much more difficult it is for parties from small member states – even with lower fragmentation – to have anything but a niche presence in the EP. In 2014, 16 parties from the Baltic states – four from Estonia, five from Latvia and seven from Lithuania – entered the EP, ten of them with only one representative. Only Unity from Latvia managed to send a 'delegation' in a meaningful sense of the word by winning four seats. However, this is generally highly unlikely, given the multi-party systems and proportional electoral systems in the Baltic states.

MEPS AND NATIONAL PARTY ORGANS

Owing to the small overall number of Baltic MEPs and rather fragmented party systems, the representation of MEPs on party boards is very low. As of 2015 Unity (V) in Latvia is an exception, as three out of its four MEPs are members of the party board – a respectable fifth of all members.[12] However, that was only made possible by the surprisingly strong performance by the party in the 2014 European elections; its support more than halved in parliamentary elections only five months later. No other Baltic party has as many MEPs, the maximum among all others being two – limited to four Lithuanian parties and one Estonian party. Hence, numerically speaking, the MEPs are bound to remain a tiny minority on party boards.

When looking at Baltic MEPs from the perspective of national delegations in the Parliament, their profile within their (national) parties has generally been high. Typically, more than half of them have been either party board members or in an even more senior position. Hence, in January 2015, 16 out of 25 Baltic MEPs (64 per cent) had been elected to their party boards, and seven (28 per cent) of them were either vice-chairs or leaders of their parties – the Lithuanian MEPs Rolandas Paksas (Order and Justice) and Valdemar Tomaševski (Electoral Action of Poles). Another Lithuanian MEP – Viktor Uspaskich – is the honorary chairman of the Labour Party, which he set up in 2003, but he stood down from leadership in 2013 after he was found guilty of fraudulent bookkeeping. Two other MEPs from Estonia (Marju Lauristin) and Lithuania (Algirdas Saudargas) are former ministers and very eminent politicians highly respected by their parties.

The MEPs who do not have leadership positions in their parties are mostly people who do not have prominent party political careers behind them and owe their success to other factors. These include an independent (Tarand, see above), a well-known former professional poker player (Antanas Guoga from Lithuania) and a 33-year-old grandson of Vytautas Landsbergis, one of the most eminent Lithuanian post-independence politicians (Gabrielius Landsbergis). Two of the Latvian MEPs benefited from the open list system (used in all three Baltic states) and a high number of personal preference votes. Andrejs Mamikins (a prominent journalist) and Iveta Grigule (who ran an expensive personal campaign funded by unnamed benefactors) were successful despite their relatively low standing on their parties' candidate lists (fourth and third, respectively). Grigule had been a member of the national parliament since 2010, but had left the Green Party after irregularities in her campaign funding, which had financial consequences for the party; she joined the Latvian Farmers' Union (the second party in the electoral coalition) in the run-up to the European elections.

COUNTRY SIZE AND NATIONAL POLITICAL EXPERIENCE OF MEPS

The previous section painted a rather bleak picture of atomized small country MEPs who can cover only a limited number of issue areas – even between all MEPs from the three Baltic states – and whose voice is weak in national party organs. However, these limitations can partly be compensated for by their national political experience – which can, in turn, also be a function of small size.

The Baltic MEPs have among the highest levels of previous experience in a national parliament and cabinet among all EU member states. In 2009,

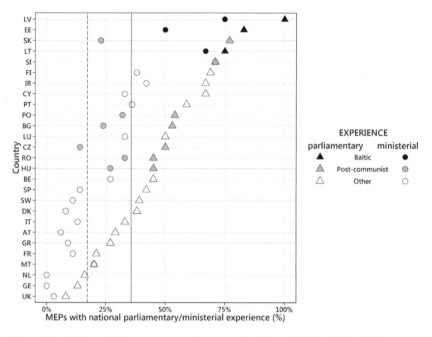

Note: Vertical lines indicate average parliamentary (solid) and ministerial (dashed) experience.

Source: Based on Corbett et al. (2011, pp. 56–58).

Figure 6.4   *MEPs with national parliamentary and ministerial experience by member state*

nearly a third of MEPs (31 per cent) had been former prime ministers or presidents (see Figure 6.4).[13] Overall, small and post-communist countries seem to have higher levels of experience – Slovakia and Slovenia are close to the Baltic states, and nearly all post-communist countries have a higher-than-average score on both of the indices.

It is obvious from Figure 6.4 that MEPs from smaller member states tend to have more experience in national politics. We study the relationship in more detail below, but first propose a very basic theoretical model to outline our expectations. In short, we argue that political elites tend to be more concentrated in smaller countries, and the effect is not only due to the smaller population but mediated by the effect that size has on intermediate institutions – specifically, the size of the EP delegation, the size of the national parliament and the cabinet size.

A THEORETICAL MODEL

Before looking at the empirical relationship between country size and MEPs' experience in national parliaments, it might be useful to discuss our theoretical expectations. That can be done by logical models as proposed by Taagepera (2008). We can argue that the relationship is anchored at 100 per cent for a (hypothetical) single MEP (for a discussion on anchor points, see Taagepera 2008). If there was a tiny member state that had only a single MEP, it would be extremely likely to be someone who has also had a chance to serve in the national parliament. On the one hand, such prominent national politicians would have an electoral advantage and, on the other hand, such a candidate must have been a political 'talent' who would have been an MP at some point in her career.

An anchor point is much more difficult to establish at the other end of the scale. We can expect the share of former MPs to decrease with the increasing size of the national delegation in the EP. Some MPs can choose not to continue their careers in the European Parliament. For the sake of argument, let us consider a national parliament in a hypothetical huge country with 500 MEPs – roughly what a country the size of China would get under the current formula. If the parliament of that massive country followed the cube root law (see above and Taagepera 2007), it would have around 1000 members. Hence, the EP delegation would come to challenge the national parliament in terms of its size. Consequently, it would be likely that many MPs would not aim to become MEPs, and others would be building up their careers focused on the European rather than the national parliament, as there would be almost an equal amount of opportunities.

It is difficult to suggest an exact shape for the function. We can only speculate that it would decrease constantly as the number of MEPs multiplies (hence the use of the logarithmic scale below) and establish the rate of change empirically. When fitting a constrained regression (which forces the best fit line to go through the anchor point), 0 per cent is reached at about 300 MEPs (see Figure 6.5).[14]

Figure 6.5 shows that there is a broad negative relationship between the number of MEPs and their experience in national parliaments, and by extension between the country size and experience. Overall, the number of MEPs (logged) explains 36 per cent of the variation in their parliamentary experience, the percentage predicted by ordinary least squares regression decreasing from 70 per cent (for countries with five MEPs) to only 22 per cent (for countries with 95 MEPs). However, there is a fair amount of scatter around the statistically modelled relationship – much of it is explained by the history of member states. On average, the parliamentary experience of MEPs from the formerly communist member states is some

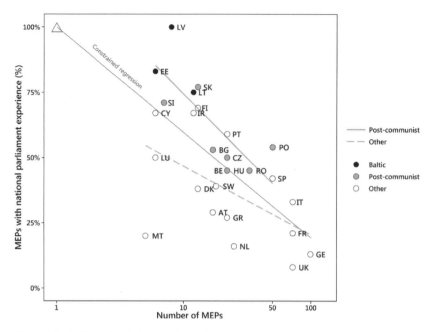

Note: The hollow triangle is an anchor point (see text).

Source: Based on Corbett et al. (2011, pp. 56–58).

Figure 6.5 *Number of MEPs and MEPs' experience of a national
parliament*

23 percentage points higher compared to West European (not formerly
communist) member states, when controlling for the effect of country
size – indicated by the raised linear fit line for post-communist countries
in Figure 6.5.

Some of the outliers may be explained by very small national parliaments
relative to the population (for example, the Netherlands; see Figure 6.2).
Interestingly, nearly all states above or near the line are new (or newish)
member states – the post-communist countries, but also Spain, Portugal,
Finland and Cyprus – as well as Italy, with its newish party system largely
created around the time of communist breakdown in Eastern Europe.
However, the same does not apply for Sweden, Austria or in particular
Malta, whose MEPs have unusually low parliamentary experience for such
a small country.

The empirical relationship between the number of MEPs and their
national ministerial experience is nearly as strong, as the (logged)

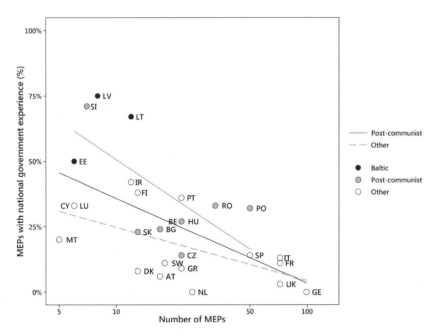

Figure 6.6   Number of MEPs and MEPs' national ministerial experience

number of MEPs explains 33 per cent of the variation in experience (see Figure 6.6).[15] Again, the MEPs from post-communist member states carry more ministerial experience (some 20 percentage points higher on average). Unsurprisingly, the overall level of previous ministerial experience is lower than national parliamentary experience – the number of cabinet positions is more limited both in available seats and in parties that win seats in national parliaments yet have seldom or never been in government (see below).

It is easy to see why MEPs from small member states could be relatively experienced. Even though cabinets tend to be smaller in small member states, they are bigger relative to the number of MEPs. For example, Luxembourg has 2.5 cabinet members per MEP, while at the other end of the spectrum Germany has more than six MEPs per cabinet member. In other words, that increases the probability of any MEP having sat in the national cabinet.

This effect is amplified in countries where governments change more often, as it gives more politicians a chance to serve in the cabinet. Notably the Baltic states – like nearly all small member states – tend to have relatively short-lived cabinets.[16] However, several large member states have also had rather short-lived cabinets – such as France, Romania, Poland and most notoriously Italy, which may explain the relatively high levels of experience given the size of EP representation. The *combination* of large cabinets with high cabinet turnover (i.e. low duration) particularly gives even more politicians a chance to serve as ministers.[17]

Another important intervening variable is the presence or absence of parties permanently excluded from national governments – some of which may be particularly or even only successful in European elections – such as the Danish June Movement, which was represented in the EP until 2009, or the United Kingdom Independence Party, which has had a sizeable representation in the EP since 2004 yet did not win representation in the national parliament until 2014. Furthermore, the success of parties that have failed to enter national government further contributes to the low levels of ministerial experience among MEPs (most notably the French Front National or Danish People's Party). Among the Baltic MEPs, those from Latvia and Lithuania have high levels of ministerial experience. The countries combine medium-sized cabinets with very high levels of cabinet turnover – hence, the levels of ministerial experience are not surprising, especially as the governments in these countries have been fairly inclusive of most major parties (with the exception of the predominantly Russophone Harmony Centre).

Additional potential explanations of the higher levels of national political experience among MEPs from smaller and, in particular, newer member states include the typical length of political career paths, electoral systems and factors particular to new member states, principally post-communist countries. MEPs from smaller member states can also have more national political experience because of more limited political career opportunities on a national level. These tend to be more limited in smaller countries, as the potential career ladder in national politics is shorter. People can become ministers at a younger age,[18] as the ladder from junior political roles to the apex of national government is shorter owing to a less complex political hierarchy with fewer levels. Note that the argument here is close to the proposed tentative theoretical model for national parliamentary experience presented above.[19]

In theory, electoral systems might also affect the levels of national political experience among MEPs. In particular, we could speculate that the presence of preference voting might raise the profile of MEPs by giving an advantage to candidates tried and tested in national politics. Preference voting is used in all three Baltic states[20] and may explain the particularly high levels of experience among Baltic MEPs. The absence of preference voting may explain the low levels of national experience in some of the member states (the UK, France, Germany and Greece) and low levels for post-communist countries (Romania and Hungary).[21] However, some countries with closed lists (Portugal and Spain) have fairly high levels of national political experience. Closed lists can, in principle, either allow the parties to enlist lesser-known candidates or lead to stronger control over who can become an MEP, protecting the party elites against internal challengers.

The higher levels of experience among MEPs from post-communist countries (and other relatively new member states) may also be explained by the fact that the accession only took place recently and by lower living standards in the countries. For the political elites of new member states it was impossible to build up their careers focusing on the European level from early on, and all aspiring politicians had to focus entirely on careers in national political institutions. Finally, service at the EP can be more coveted for politicians from new member states, because the remuneration (including expenses) is better compared to national salaries for MPs or ministers. That may, yet again, lead to top spots on electoral lists being reserved for senior ranks within political parties.

CONCLUSION

This chapter discussed the political mechanics of country size by looking at the patterns of representation in the European Parliament and national political experience of MEPs. We found that the potential influence of Baltic MEPs in the European Parliament is severely constrained by low numbers. It can also contribute to the separation of mainstream domestic politics and European issues (see Sikk 2009a), as MEPs are bound to remain a small minority among the leadership of national parties – an effect amplified by high party system fragmentation.

Furthermore, given the small number of MEPs from all three Baltic countries, the countries are unlikely to be represented in all EP committees. It can be argued that national expertise in certain European policy fields would suffer as a consequence even if the MEPs enthusiastically interacted across party and country lines. However, cooperation is scarce, often even between MEPs belonging to the same EP party group. Less pessimistically, the MEPs from the Baltic states have been prioritizing issue areas that are perceived to be particularly relevant or where they see an important role for the EP (a strategy for countries to overcome their smallness mentioned by Panke in Chapter 4). This mostly applies for external affairs, as the Foreign Affairs Committee has constantly seen a steady representation of Baltic MEPs. Additionally, Lithuanian MEPs have been focused on energy policies, explained by particular issues in the country.

However, we also show that the small numbers are partly compensated for by the relatively high profile of Baltic MEPs, indicated by high levels of national political experience (as ministers and MPs) and leadership roles within national parties. We argue that there is a general negative correlation between such expertise and country size, further amplified in new member states, which has led to very high levels of national political experience among the Baltic MEPs. In particular, the MEPs who have previously served as ministers have high levels of expertise on European policies and on executive–legislative interactions, acquired while negotiating between the European Union institutions as well as nationally between the executive and legislative institutions. Overall, the combination of higher-than-average expertise and prioritization help to alleviate the problems resulting from small numbers and problems of coordination between Baltic MEPs.

NOTES

*   The authors wish to thank the editors of this volume and Rein Taagepera for helpful comments on an earlier draft of this chapter.
1.   See on size and parliaments: Taagepera and Shugart (1989); Taagepera and Recchia (2002); Taagepera (2007); small size conducive to democracy: Ott (2000); Srebrnik (2004); *large* size conducive to democracy: Clague et al. (2001); Gerring and Zarecki (2011); Erk and Veenendaal (2014); civil conflict: Fearon and Laitin (2003); Hegre and Sambanis (2006); Collier and Hoeffler (2009); Brückner (2010); turnout: Blais (2000, p. 59); Geys (2006, pp. 642–643); party membership: Weldon (2006).
2.   Still, given the study's aim to provide policy recommendations, it does not clearly distinguish between effects related to size and other factors (such as the short period of EU membership).
3.   Possibly, it also alleviates the disconnect that may result from the physical distance between Brussels and national capitals.
4.   The reasons why Germany is overrepresented are discussed in some detail in Corbett et al. (2011, pp. 27–29). Malta and Luxembourg benefit from a legally stipulated minimum number of seats per member state – according to the Taagepera and Hosli model, their delegations would include three and four MEPs, respectively. Please note that the seat distribution refers to *pre-Lisbon Treaty allocation*, as data from Corbett et al. (2011) used later in the chapter refers to that period. Post-Lisbon Treaty seat allocation would fit the Taagepera and Hosli model even better, as the total number of seats increased, while the numbers of German and Maltese MEPs were reduced.
5.   See 'Farage's Eurosceptic group collapses, Sakharov prize winner postponed', *EurActiv*, 16 October 2014, available at http://www.euractiv.com/video/farages-eurosceptic-group-collapses-sakharov-prize-winner-postponed-309257, and 'Farage's Eurosceptic group saved by Polish MEP', *EurActiv*, 21 October 2014, available at http://www.euractiv.com/video/farages-eurosceptic-group-saved-polish-mep-309367 (accessed 15 January 2015).
6.   ECR only narrowly met the requirement to include MEPs from at least seven member states.
7.   Also see 'Nädala Tegija', *Radio Kuku*, 10 July 2009 (in Estonian), available at http://podcast.kuku.ee/2009/07/10/nadalategija-2009-07-10/ (accessed 12 January 2015), where Tarand discussed his negotiations with various groups openly and in rich detail.
8.   Substitute members have few disadvantages over full members (Corbett et al. 2011, p. 146), and we look at them in the following discussion.

9. See Sikk (2009b, p. 4).
10. The data here and below refer to the situation as of January 2015.
11. In 2008 the distribution was generally more even, as there was at least one Baltic representative in all committees (three with substitute members only). However, the total number of Baltic MEPs has decreased by three since then.
12. The 'European' connection is further strengthened by the presence of Andris Piebalgs, a former EU commissioner.
13. After the 2014 elections the share of MEPs from the Baltic states with ministerial experience dropped to levels common in countries of similar sizes; the share of Latvian MEPs with parliamentary experience dropped somewhat from the extremely high level. Note, however, that owing to the small number of MEPs from these countries a change in the background of just one MEP can change the percentages considerably.
14. However, such an extrapolation carries dangers, especially as we ought to assume that the share with national parliamentary experience approaches 0 per cent asymptotically but never falls below that. Such a more sophisticated model is beyond the scope of this chapter.
15. We have not used constrained regression here, as it is difficult to determine the anchor point. A similar logic to that used under parliamentary experience ought to apply, but forcing the regression through the same anchor point would fit the empirical data very poorly. The intercept for (non-constrained) linear regression is at 68 per cent only. A more advanced theoretical model should also take into account the actual size of cabinets or parliaments – these are correlated to country size (and the number of MEPs), but there is significant variation at similar country sizes (see Figures 6.2 and 6.3).
16. Luxembourg is an exception: the mean cabinet duration has also been slightly above the EU average in Ireland, Denmark and Finland (see S. Andersson et al. 2014).
17. Further evidence on the combined effect of cabinet size and duration is available on request.
18. There is evidence that the average age of ministers in democracies is positively correlated to country size and was particularly low in Estonia and Latvia (44.6 and 43.6, respectively, in 1999–2012). More detail is available on request from the authors.
19. Interestingly, extrapolating the empirical fits leads to intuitively sensible model predictions for hypothetical nano-countries. A society of 92 would have a cabinet with a single member on average (societies significantly smaller than that would lack formal institutions altogether). That is a reasonable expectation considering the nature of socio-political organization. The average age of ministers in such a country would be 36.6. That is, again, a rather reasonable expectation for a sole leader, on average. Note that we are assuming democracy – otherwise the person might hold on to power, and the mean age would increase significantly.
20. The 2009 election in Estonia was an exception that may partly explain the relatively lower levels of experience there. The levels are lower than those in Latvia and Lithuania even when discounting the independent Indrek Tarand, whose campaign strongly attacked the adoption of closed party lists (which were scrapped soon after the election).
21. Data on electoral systems are from Corbett et al. (2011, pp. 17–18).

PART IV

The modern small state – the social
investment state? On 'getting to Denmark'

7. Small-state Scandinavia: social investment or social democracy?

Nik Brandal and Øivind Bratberg

INTRODUCTION

The concept of a social investment state is often presented as a way of reconciling economic productivity with social equality. From this perspective, social investment implies that welfare policies (and regulation of the economy more generally) may be designed so as to encourage high-skilled labour and social mobility and thereby a reasonable extent of redistribution. Thus, the state invests in its citizens, who respond with enhanced productivity, and equality is enhanced as a fortunate side effect. However, there may be good reason to discuss whether social investment as a development model is in fact capable of maximizing productivity and equality without any trade-offs being involved. Social investment evidently requires state intervention with the aim of encouraging a competitive economy. Investment is not, however, informed by a moral argument for redistribution or egalitarianism and is likely to yield different priorities in rough economic weather. The present chapter takes this line of argument as a point of departure and discusses social investment against the concept of social democracy. Social democracy, as we will contend, requires more than a state that invests in its citizens. Here, state intervention goes beyond maximizing the return on human resources to ensure that other aims are pursued, such as the protection of precarious groups in society or financial support to uphold a viable civil society. Furthermore, social democracy is also reliant upon collective organization and negotiated settlements, elements that do not feature in the social investment model.

The thesis that we wish to investigate is hence that social democracy can be clearly demarcated from a social investment model and that the distinction between the two is best displayed at times of economic difficulty. Analysing how state action is designed to address an economic crisis may thus help establish a conceptual border between them. The economic difficulties encountered across the western world from late 2008 onwards offer an excellent opportunity to examine such borderlands between social investment and social democracy. In the present chapter, this is pursued through the study of three small-state social democracies. If our thesis is plausible, it should be borne out with clarity in states that are 1) strongly imbued with social democratic ideas and 2) small and homogeneous and therefore possess a certain leeway for political elites to redirect the course of policy. These characteristics should then be 3) exposed to a moment where egalitarianism is put to the test against pressures to maximize productivity and scale down redistribution. We will therefore address the question through an analysis of developments in what is conventionally considered the heart of present-day social democracy – the Scandinavian small states of Norway, Denmark and Sweden.

A brief assessment should be added here of whether these could be considered typical small states at all. In terms of economic and military power, they are currently certainly minnows on the world stage, wholly dependent on the support of allies. In certain areas such as human rights and foreign aid, however, they aspire to gain a global impact beyond what their economic and military capacity would imply. It might therefore be instructive to approach the question of Scandinavian small-stateness through a sketch of their history.

When Denmark had to cede the territory of Norway to the King of Sweden in 1814 as a fall-out from the Napoleonic wars, it opened an unprecedented period of Scandinavian peace. The peaceful dissolution of the union between Sweden and Norway in 1905 was seen as further evidence that Scandinavia was somehow set apart from the rest of Europe, a view which was strengthened when the Scandinavian countries managed to stay out of the First World War. The sense of Scandinavian 'otherness' became the catalyst for a Scandinavian small-state ideology, as it left the three states with a newfound sense of vulnerability, which they at various points since have tried to counter through Scandinavian cooperation. In the mid-nineteenth century, it even gave birth to its own ideology: Scandinavism, which paralleled the unification movements in Germany, drawing upon the idea of Scandinavia as a unified region based on its common linguistic, political and cultural heritage. This was an ideology born of a sense of vulnerability faced with a growing Germany. However, the various schemes, with the exception of trade agreements and the rather non-committal Nordic Council, have inevitably floundered, from the currency union (1870–1914) to the Nordic defence union suggested after the Second World War. Rather the countries have preferred to seek security through international organizations and agreements, thus tying major powers to the maintenance of their security and stability (see Chapter 3 on Iceland for an interesting deviation from this pattern).

The difficulties in establishing Scandinavian cooperation stem from the different geopolitical positions of the individual countries as well as from differences in their economies. Whereas Sweden had many of the largest industrialists, typified by the Wallenberg family, who were also considered social entrepreneurs in a healthy cooperation with the state (Bergh 1981, p. 32; Pryser 1988, p. 534; Olstad 2010, p. 144), Danish industry was multifaceted with fewer large-scale enterprises. Norway, on the other hand, relied disproportionately on certain raw materials and easy access to hydroelectricity, making fish, timber and aluminium the primary exports. In all three countries, the post-war years were characterized by strong state intervention, but only in part through the expansion of public ownership – as, unlike Britain, public utilities, transport and infrastructure were already under state control (Brandal et al. 2013).

Our empirical focus in the chapter is the trajectory and immediate aftermath of the financial crisis, that is, the four-year period from 2008 to 2012, which pushed economic priorities to the forefront in all European economies and prepared the ground for a struggle of priorities between growth and redistribution. By investigating how the three Scandinavian countries have responded to the recession, we address the dilemma between *competitiveness* (typically seen as resulting from social investment) and *solidarity* (seen as emblematic of social democracy). How is this dilemma played out in the Scandinavian countries post-recession, and what do developments there suggest about social investment and social democracy in small states? Conceptually, is it possible to draw a clear dividing line between social investment and social democracy as we contend? And, in political practice, what might the scope conditions be for social investment with an egalitarian outcome in small-state Europe?

SOCIAL INVESTMENT AND SOCIAL DEMOCRACY

In his book *The Third Way*, the British sociologist-cum-political strategist for New Labour Anthony Giddens (1998) held that, while the old welfare state had sought to protect people from the market, the social investment state should enable individuals to maximize their potential in it. By investing in human capital, the state would enhance its citizens' capacity for skilled work in a more flexible and internationalized labour market. Social investment was seen as a successor to the post-war welfare state in Europe. The latter, particularly where it was based on universally accessible services, was understood as a mode of de-commodification – a countermechanism to the distributive consequences of the market. In Northern Europe, this largely took the form of universally accessible services amounting to a form of 'social citizenship', while in continental Europe the evolving welfare state was to a larger extent conservatively disposed, protecting existing hierarchies in the workplace and between the genders (Marshall 1950; Esping-Andersen 1990). The social investment state contrasted with both these varieties of the post-war welfare state: its aim would be to prepare the citizen for prosperous survival in the same market that previous versions of the welfare state had sheltered against. It would do so by investing in supply-side measures such as first-class education, infrastructure and public services (see Lundvall and Lorenz 2012).

The rise of the social investment state as a composite of welfare state and labour-market reforms thus 'result[ed] from the joint legacies of post-1945 welfare regimes and of their encounter with neoliberalism, particularly its critiques of the state' (Jenson 2012, p. 62). The social investment state was presented both as a counter-argument to neo-liberal critiques and as a response from first-world countries to the added competition from low-cost economies in the second and third world. Its tenets could be swiftly summarized. Contrary to the neo-liberal assumption, an extensive welfare state (funded by high taxes) was not necessarily a barrier to economic growth. Clever use of state funding could help create more skilled labour with more productive time at their disposal, for example through better schools, 'up-skilling' in the workplace, and public childcare which enables highly educated parents to work full time. *Vis-à-vis* developing economies, the social investment argument suggested a revised position for Europe in the global division of labour. Unable to compete with Brazilian wages or Chinese supply of labour, Europe's position would have to be further up the value ladder: higher wages enabled by higher productivity, drawing on skilled and flexible labour that would be nurtured by the social investment state.

Furthermore, the new and modernized version of the welfare state could be seen to address not only the requirement for higher productivity, but also the demographic challenge of an ageing population, by bringing more people into skilled (and tax-paying) jobs. Finally, an improved gender balance and social mobility would be other features of a society thus transformed. Social investment thus suggested an optimistic view of European sustainability; Giddens himself asserted that the change in the global order could be accommodated to produce both solidarity and prosperity if the welfare state and labour markets were successfully reformed (Giddens 1998, p. 1; Jenson and Saint-Martin 2003).

The essence of the social investment model is state provision of services that *prepare* rather than *repair* (Morel et al. 2012, p. 1). Human investment can thus be seen as analogous to other forms of state investment, what the Swedish sociologist Jenny Andersson (2004) refers to as productive social policies. Here, social policies are not primarily driven by a wish to redress injustice through redistribution and protection of the vulnerable in society. Rather, the ambition is to maximize the capacity of each and every individual and thereby ensure the most efficient return on welfare-state expenses. When the state invests in excellent schools and universities it is also a strategy to ensure skilled labour and good citizens; and, when generous funds are directed to maternal leave and childcare, the expected consequence is a sustained birth rate as well as employees who maintain their productive capacities whilst establishing a family.

Such social policies may represent a new social contract between the state and its citizens. The state invests in people by delivering sound and efficient services. In return for the investment, the populace delivers skilled labour, civic participation and tax revenue (Jenson and Saint-Martin 2003). In political terms, social investment has been raised on the political agenda since the 1990s. Associated in an early phase with the Third Way thinking of Giddens, its use has widened within Anglophone social theory to encompass a wide range of reforms favouring an 'enabling' or 'smarter' state: interventionist but well aware of the lessons learnt about market efficiency.

Social investment is a strategy that is assumed to be particularly capable of accommodating a globalized and knowledge-based economy where technological development, open borders, flexible labour markets and the 're-skilling' of workers are essential features. In recent years social investment has become a guiding principle, first for Third Way thinking and then for reform packages within a range of European countries and from the European Union. The Lisbon Strategy of 2000, aiming to make the EU 'the most competitive and dynamic knowledge-based economy in the world capable of sustainable economic growth with more and better jobs and greater social cohesion' (European Parliament, Committee on Employment and Social Affairs 2010), is but one example. Social investment also reflects a strong emphasis on the responsibilities of the citizen. Social policies that pacify rather than activate are shied away from. Arguably, this is in contrast with a Keynesian welfare-state strategy, where cash transfers outside of the labour market were accepted to a higher degree. Moreover, where Keynesianism is oriented towards the here-and-now in terms of balancing demand, social investment is concerned with future returns. Skills development, for example, points to life cycles and inter-generational social mobility as measures of success (Morel et al. 2012, pp. 10–11).

The social investment state is considered in this chapter as a development model, establishing a foundation for balanced and sustainable economic growth. Our use of the concept is therefore broader than what is often encountered in the literature, where social investment is addressed within the frame of welfare-state development. From our perspective, it is inaccurate to delimit social investment to welfare-state provision and public services more generally (Vandenbroucke and Vleminckx 2011). The welfare state, macro-economic policy and labour-market regulation are three requisite components of an economic development model broadly conceived. Not only does that reflect its theoretical groundings in a wider scholarly debate following Giddens, but a broadening of the concept also prepares the ground for addressing social investment alongside the other key concept we wish to address, social democracy.

We perceive social democracy in this context not primarily as a political philosophy but rather as a set of principles suggesting a specific development model, in this sense essentially comparable with social investment. For Roger Scruton (2007, p. 642), social democracy reflects '[t]he theoretical and practical attempt to reconcile democracy with social justice, through the use of state power'. Democratically elected governments should intervene in the economy whenever necessary, not primarily to ensure productivity but to nurture the capacity for growth *and* a fair allocation of the wealth thus created. Social democracy thus implies a sustained commitment to individuals, groups, economic sectors and geographic areas that lag behind.

The social democratic approach to liberty is based on the idea that it does matter how liberty is distributed between individual members of society, and that a key quality of a decent society is that access to basic social services be ensured for all. Poverty and deep-seated inequality are thus viewed as threats to personal freedom, perhaps even more so than the excesses of state regulation that are criticized by liberal theorists on the right. So both civil liberties and a minimum of material wealth and opportunities must be provided to everyone by a democratically elected government if one is to avoid liberty becoming the exclusive property of a privileged minority. This points towards an extensive welfare state: the state takes on responsibility to ensure that nobody is seriously afflicted by poverty, bad health or accidental market fluctuations. However, social democracy involves more than a universal welfare state and a progressive tax system. When perceived as a development model, it arguably rests on three equally important pillars: *concertation*[1] (rather than confrontation) between the social partners – state, employers and trade unions; the *comprehensive welfare state*; and an *activist industrial policy* with the aims to sustain a skilled labour force and a favourable fiscal environment (Brandal et al. 2013, ch. 5; Dølvik 2013; Vartiainen 2014).

Historically, the Scandinavian countries come close to this ideal-typical conception of a social democratic model. Concertation in the form of a negotiated economy is a key feature of small-state Scandinavia, noted by

Peter Katzenstein's landmark study of *Small States in World Markets* in 1985. Centralized negotiations between employers and trade unions help ensure an equitable distribution of profit. They also provide for moderate wage settlements, which in turn help keep inflation low and thus contribute to a competitive private sector. Participation in the labour market is high, its tax base thereby helping to fund an extensive system of social security. This welfare state reflects the aim for productive social policies, which keep the workforce skilled and mobile. Risks entailed by competition are mitigated by social policies aimed at ensuring that aid is provided when jobs are lost or change hands. Finally, the labour market is more flexible than its continental counterparts but complemented by a safety net consisting of not only cash transfers but activation strategies and 're-skilling'.

Another key characteristic of the political economy in Sweden, Denmark and Norway is the comparatively small wage differentials. Restraining inequality, rather than effecting a root-and-branch redistribution from capital to labour, has been a dominant goal for the Scandinavian labour movement. A side effect of this approach is that productive enterprise is supported (since salaries for skilled labour are linked to general tariffs and thus not allowed to rise disproportionately), while less successful companies are left to wither away (since there are also barriers against extensive reduction of salaries).

RESOLVING THE COMPETITIVENESS VERSUS SOLIDARITY DILEMMA?

The overall social democratic compact outlined above reflects a dual strategy of safety and competitiveness, expressed through the Norwegian Labour Party's classic slogan 'To Create and to Share'. The order of the two components – creating wealth, which is thereafter distributed – is no coincidence. It also allows for a macro-economic strategy that, following Keynes, enables the state to save in periods of private-sector growth in order to increase spending in economic downturns. As a governing strategy it captures the essence of the social democratic vision of society, but in Scandinavia it emerged and evolved to some extent through cross-party compromise. Its foundation was laid in the interwar era, when the accommodation between the labour movement and the agrarian parties in each of the Scandinavian countries paved the way for political stability. This is tied to a key characteristic of the Nordic Model, that the Scandinavian historians Bo Stråth and Øystein Sørensen (1997) have labelled 'the Nordic Sonderweg', in which protracted processes of negotiations involving the affected parties are preferred to rapid and/or revolutionary changes. Perhaps as important from a small-state perspective, especially in times of crisis, would be the extensive learning involved in these processes, producing different ideas and solutions.

The literature on the social investment state rarely differentiates social investment from social democracy. What is typically compared and contrasted with social investment is the assumedly adverse alternative, what Keating and Harvey (2014) refer to as the market liberal model (see also Chapter 9). Here, the drivers of development are low levels of taxation and light-touch regulation, not least in the labour market. This is expected to attract inward investment and spur development through individual opportunities for wealth creation.

As a model for development and for welfare-state reform, these ideas had particular traction during the 1980s. Social investment could thus be perceived as a re-justification of state intervention following the neo-liberal interlude. Yet it is an activism that first and foremost seeks to heighten productivity rather than pursuing redistribution as a goal in itself. Social investment may be concentrated on the most competitive sections of the population or privilege certain geographical or economic areas more than others. Investments are normally directed to targets where the higher returns are expected. This seems to contrast with common notions of social democracy, where individual liberty is seen as best pursued through redistribution and greater social equality. One variety of this difference of thought is found in the scholarly exchanges between proponents of Third Way thinking and welfare-state researchers following Danish sociologist Gøsta Esping-Andersen. To the latter, the social investment state leans too heavily on active labour-market participation and therefore tends to penalize those unable to take part. Social *investment* has come to be seen as superior to social *protection* and, as a result, may fail not only on a normative fairness criterion but also when it comes to mobilizing all the productive forces of society.

To sum up, social investment reflects an underlying tension between 'a social democratic' approach, inspired by the Nordic welfare states, and a 'Third Way' approach, which represents an '"Anglo-liberal" view of social policy' (Morel et al. 2012, p. 19). Both represent attempts to define a sustainable development model that integrates welfare-state provision with societal needs. However, whereas, with social investment, equality seems to be a (potential) by-product of high productivity, with social democracy equality is given a higher priority. Following from this argument, it is perfectly possible to pursue social investment without a commitment to equality or social and geographical redistribution.

DEVELOPMENT MODELS AND STRATEGIC CHOICES FOR SMALL STATES

The idea that social investment could help sustain the welfare state in light of neo-liberal critique and globalization was by no means new at the time of Giddens's publication in 1998. Its origins were intertwined with the literature on the political economy of the Scandinavian countries. During a limited period of the 1990s, the two strands – reflecting a Third Way form of social investment and a social democratic form of the same – could easily be conflated. In 1996, Esping-Andersen (1996, p. 25) noted as a distinctive feature of Scandinavia that, rather than continuing the growth of public employment, 'policy is directed to active labour market measures, such as training and mobility, and wage subsidies'. Common ground can also be detected in the literature on 'flexicurity', referring to social models which successfully combine a flexible labour market and extensive social security, a dynamic that is underscored by active labour-market policies intended to ensure a rapid bounce-back through re-skilling for the unemployed. Here, numerous small states in Northern Europe have acted as role models, particularly Denmark and the Netherlands (Jørgensen and Madsen 2007; Hendrickx 2008).

To what extent are these policy debates particularly relevant to small states? Being a small state is not a prerequisite for social investment, which has become a commonplace strategy across Europe. Similarly, social democracy can be practised in countries large and small. However, as argued in Chapter 1, small states are characterized in particular by vulnerability to market fluctuations and the ability to adapt swiftly and cohesively in response to external challenges, given the proximity between rulers and ruled. Social investment and social democracy may therefore seem to be particularly appropriate in small states, since these are typically required to combine international competition with internal cohesion, by maximizing human resources and securing domestic peace. These requirements can be addressed most effectively by a state that is able to harness the productive capacities of the economy, and on this account small-stateness may be an advantage. A key quality of small states is that they are sufficiently governable to allow for coherent development strategies based upon a broad political consensus. This does not require social or ethnic homogeneity but an underlying agreement on the basic features of the development model. Indeed, *governability* and responsiveness could be seen as the key characteristic (or asset) of small states, in addition to the vulnerability that is inherent to small and outward-oriented economies dependent on international trade and security (Brandal et al. 2013).

Social investment is furthermore a strategy that has inspired several small-state governments with centre-left credentials. According to the Scottish Government's (2013, pp. 160–161) White Paper on *Scotland's Future*, welfare should be considered 'a "social investment" . . . designed at all stages [of a person's life] to promote equality, fairness and social cohesion' (see also Chapter 9). Such investment was expected to yield 'specific returns, such as learning and development in early years, employ-ment and health gains in adult life, and for older people, increased independence and ability to be active in their communities'.

In fair economic weather the distinction between the social investment state and social democracy may be of merely theoretical interest. Social investment broadly corresponds to the governing strategy proffered by social democracy, and whether or not you trace the causal chain back to its ideological inspiration is unimportant. An economy which invests con-sistently in human capital is likely to experience high social mobility and general economic growth to the benefit of all. There is, however, reason to think that this is to a lesser extent the case in adverse economic circum-stances. The financial crisis and its aftermath could serve to draw a wedge between strategies for investment (and expected returns) on the one hand and pursuit of equality on the other. How has this potential friction played out in Scandinavia since 2008?

SCANDINAVIA AND THE FINANCIAL CRISIS 2008–2012

The 2008–2012 crisis has had different consequences in the Scandinavian countries, especially within labour markets. The number of employed has continued to grow, albeit somewhat more slowly than before, in both Norway and Sweden, but has seen a marked fall in Denmark. Unlike the crisis in the early 1990s, however, the total unemployment rate in Scandinavia has been rather stable. Between 2008 and 2012, employ-ment dropped by 6 per cent (165 000) in Denmark, while increasing by 110 000 in Sweden and 65 000 in Norway. In comparison, in the 1980s and 1990s crises, employment fell by more than 570 000 in Sweden, 130 000 in Denmark and 115 000 in Norway (Dølvik et al. 2014, p. 58). The unem-ployment rate was highest in Sweden (8.2 per cent) and lowest in Norway (3.6 per cent), with Denmark in the middle (7.1 per cent). By 2013, the Scandinavian countries appeared to have emerged from the crisis as more robust economies with stronger public finances and a better balance on foreign trade than most other countries in Europe.

Denmark was the Scandinavian country most afflicted by the crisis, as a loose fiscal policy and liberalization of the credit markets in the 2000s had instigated a spiralling private mortgage debt, similar to the situation in Norway and Sweden in the early 1980s. When the property and financial bubbles burst, the large private debt and subsequent deleveraging resulted in a drop in private consumption and investment. Added to by cuts in public consumption, the consequence was a substantial downturn in overall demand (Pedersen and Andersen 2014). Denmark thus entered a period of stagnation and witnessed among the highest increases in unemployment in Northern Europe; in fact the unemployment rate did not drop below 7 per cent until 2013–2014.

Even though Sweden, because of its large industrial export industries, was hit hard by the collapse in international trade following the outbreak of the financial crisis in 2009, its economy recovered quite rapidly in 2010–2011, and its GDP growth from 2008 to 2014 was even higher than Germany's (Kangas and Saloniemi 2013; Berglund and Esser 2014). Unlike the case for Germany, though, registered unemployment saw an increase from 6.1 to over 8 per cent in 2014, despite a steady growth of people in work. In Norway, a significant drop within the export and building industries in 2009 was more than offset by an all-time high within the country's offshore industries, and it was the Scandinavian country least afflicted by the financial crisis (Berge 2009; Hippe et al. 2013).

The conservative government in Denmark chose to tighten its budget, which delayed the upturn compared to the other two countries. Also, the centre-right governments in Denmark and Sweden preferred tax relief to increases in public consumption and investments to stimulate the economy, whereas the centre-left government in Norway chose to follow a more traditional Keynesian crisis policy. While both strategies had as their aim an increase in public consumption, they represent differing views of the exact role of the state in the economy. As much of the tax relief went towards private savings and down payment of debts, it did little to increase domestic consumption and largely failed to stimulate employment. The more traditional social democratic strategy pursued by the Norwegian centre-left government would thus appear to have been more effective in promoting job creation, whereas the centre-right strategies of Denmark and Sweden to a large extent benefited those already employed (Dølvik et al. 2014, p. 37).

While it is possible to analyse the differences between Norway, Sweden and Denmark and the different ideological strands of the parties in government, what is more prominent when looking at the responses to the financial crisis of 2008–2012 is the broad consensus underpinning the policies enacted. This would then appear to be a heritage from the handling of the crisis of the 1980s and 1990s, which led to a realignment of the centre-left and the centre-right in their views on the welfare state.

When entering the crisis in 2008, the conservative parties had to a large extent put aside the radical critique of the welfare state that was so prominent in the early 1980s, and instead they, as well as the populist right, now accepted the basic principles of the Nordic welfare model. While the social insurance schemes have been tightened in economic downturns, this has happened independently of the political colour of the party in government. There has been a broad agreement to emphasize the 'work policy', that any policy should have as its basic aim an increase in employment and a countering of exclusion from the workforce. Similarly, there has been hardly any ideological conflict over either the family policy, of which the opportunity to combine work and family life has been the cornerstone, or the pension reforms, aimed at raising the retirement age. In most of the reforms, the social partners have played a crucial role. In the Norwegian pension reform of 2011, they took part in the political negotiations in advance of the eventual settlement (Hippe et al. 2013), while at other times they have influenced policy through participating in expert committees laying the foundations for reforms, such as the Danish Zeuten committee (Pedersen and Andersen 2014).

To understand the Scandinavian responses to the 2008–2012 financial crisis, it is therefore instructive to look at how the three countries responded to the previous crises in the late 1980s and early 1990s. While all the Scandinavian countries introduced reforms which reduced the rates of income and corporate tax, and expanded the tax base through tax settlements reaching across party political divides (Dølvik et al. 2014, p. 31), the crisis also led to a tightening of the budget policy through the introduction of a more rules-guided fiscal policy, with a clear emphasis on long-term budget balance. The new policies were supported by extensive pension reforms aimed at increasing workforce participation and strengthening the financial sustainability of the welfare state. There was also an agreement among the social partners that ensured moderate increases in wages in order to strengthen competitiveness through new forms of sector-based agreement coordination in Denmark and Sweden, as well as a strengthening of negotiated wage settlements in Norway (Andersen et al. 2014).

While the radical left-wing welfare-state critique of the 1970s was put aside by the social democrats in all the Scandinavian countries, the 1990s reforms by and large were adjustments and reorganization of the welfare system, rather than cuts or a dismantling, and the reforms were implemented in combination with an extensive development of the secondary and higher education systems, as well as an escalation of the labour activation policy (Dølvik et al. 2014, p. 85). As the social democratic parties returned to office during the 1990s, economic consolidation was combined with resuscitation, and in some areas even strengthening, of the traditional features of the Nordic Model. Tripartite concertation was revitalized and further developed, the trade unions kept their strong position within the system, and the need for 'belt tightening' was by and large met with understanding by the general public, as was illustrated by the electoral victory of the Social Democratic Party in Sweden on a promise to tighten fiscal policy, increase taxes and reform the pension system in 1994. Similarly there was public approval of the Norwegian wage regulation law of 1988 and 'Solidarity Alternative' in 1992–1997, where the social partners in concertation with the government agreed to moderate wage increases in combination with public policies for increasing employment, de-bureaucratization of the public sector, new on-the-job training schemes and currency stabilization.

Unlike the case in countries such as Britain and Germany, where there was substantial deregulation, weakening of social agreements and cutbacks to the welfare system, Scandinavian politicians in cooperation with the social partners were able to stabilize and grow their economies, strengthen the coordination of wage negotiations, preserve the welfare state, increase the investments in human and social capital, and maintain the compressed wage and income structure throughout the 1990s (Fløtten et al. 2014). Welfare reforms have continued under changing governments throughout the 1990s and into the 2000s. These reforms thus included means for facilitating participation, toughening of the welfare policies, and increased emphasis on the role of economic incentives. In most cases, the policies adapted have been a combination of all three, as the reforms have been shaped by stricter requirements for participating in work experience training, job courses and so on, rather than cuts to the benefit payments.

Another common feature has been the prioritization of social investment policies as part of a broader social democratic model, best illustrated by family policies and the heightened focus on education and qualification towards social groups at a disadvantaged position in the labour market. This has been paralleled by sustained efforts to integrate immigrants into the labour market (Djuve and Grødem 2014). The welfare reforms of the past decade have thus been based on an increasingly interconnected relationship between work, social and education policies, which today, in combination with regional policies, would appear to be the most prominent feature of the Scandinavian social investment policy. While the welfare policies have seen cutbacks and adjustments, family and education policies have by and large been expanded (Dølvik et al. 2014, p. 91).

As social investment policies have had a prominent position within the Scandinavian countries, the education system has become their cornerstone, and a high level of education among the general population has been a priority in times of both crisis and prosperity. A particular emphasis has been put on schemes aimed at continuing education within the workforce, and the right to such education has been an important element of the tripartite concertation. As illustrated through the Danish concept of 'mobication', a combination of mobilization and education, continuous updating of workforce competence is seen as an important means for reducing the risk of unemployment (Andersen and Pedersen 2010, p. 3).

The crisis of the 1990s also had two important long-term structural consequences for handling the crisis of 2008–2012. First, the renewal of the compressed wage negotiations and tripartite concertation on welfare and labour-market reforms resulted in the social partners actually strengthening their positions and legitimacy at the end of the twentieth century (Andersen et al. 2014). Second, the economic consolidation of the 1990s and the growth of the early 2000s gave the Scandinavian countries greater leeway for implementing counter-cyclical policies than the countries within the Eurozone when the financial crisis of 2008–2012 erupted – even if the conservative government in Denmark chose not to use the window this opened for a Keynesian response to the crisis (Cameron 2012; Lindvall 2012).

DO POLICY CHOICES SUGGEST A SOCIAL INVESTMENT/SOCIAL DEMOCRACY DIVIDE?

There are two important lessons to draw from this account of the Scandinavian trajectory through the financial crisis. First, it is evident that the broader development model does matter, not least in setting the stage for how unexpected economic challenges are met. In the Scandinavian countries, social investment policies have been accompanied by the negotiated economy, where settlements between trade unions, employers and the state have balanced the goals of growth, employment and equitable distribution. This institutional infrastructure is a definitional criterion of the social democratic development model, and its significance was amply illustrated by the crisis. Second, the crisis did exhibit a contrast between social investment and social democracy in strategic choices and their consequences. This is not the same as the distinction between austerity measures and Keynesianism in macro-economic policy. Rather, investment in human capital is a strategy whose success is context-dependent. The social investment state befits fair economic weather, a situation of stable economic growth with international trade at its heart. That small-state Scandinavia, characterized precisely by the vulnerability to shifting international currents described in Chapter 1, has developed a more robust scaffolding than that assigned by social investment is not by coincidence. Institutions are at the centre of this.

Did the Nordic Model, which we would argue is basically a social demo-cratic model, develop by happenstance or by luck? Did decision-makers select policies that fitted together into a productive system or did some invisible political-economy hand operate? What has led the Scandinavian countries to avoid crony capitalism with welfare-state pay-offs to particular interest groups? The decrease in inequality that began around the mid-1930s was related to wage compression, which presumably reflected in part the activities of unions beyond pure market forces. Also, as Abramitzky et al. (2012) have noted, the distribution of income for workers in Norway in the 1890s does not support the notion that the Nordics developed greater equality at the beginning of the twentieth century without insti-tutional interventions. Unlike today, Norway had a more unequal income distribution in the nineteenth century than did the United States. Moene (2005) identifies the key innovation of the model as a shift from market determination towards institutional determination of wages, as evident in the Saltsjöbaden Agreement in Sweden and the Main Agreement in Norway in the mid-1930s.

History has shown that the small-state character of the Scandinavian countries has served to their advantage when it comes to addressing swift changes in their environment, requiring a refitting of the policy toolkit. Moreover, this refitting has permitted the underlying structure of the model to remain. The position of the social democratic develop-ment model in Scandinavia illustrates what Pierson (2000) refers to as the increasing returns of a given institutional settlement. The trajectory of a given model – be it in the form of market liberalism or social democracy – may be exceptionally difficult to change, since the actors involved adapt to the model and established policies are expanded rather than reversed. The social democratic model in Scandinavia has been threatened by reforms induced in the wake of the financial crisis – but, in Pierson's terminology, the path pursued has yet to meet a critical juncture, despite the changes incurred in recent years. However, although the institutional features may be seen as path-dependent, they are not permanent or perennial. Within Scandinavia, there has been a tendency to weaken the direct influence of social partners in shaping policy, as tripartite concertation has given way to expert committees, often without the social partners. The technocra-tization of policy making also reveals some ideological differences, as it has been the preferred mode of conservative governments more than of social democrats (Dølvik et al. 2014, p. 42). While it is still unclear what the result of this will be for the Nordic Model, it would seem that, com-bined with a growing number of rules and regulations being negotiated at a supra-national level, it entails the risk of a decline in democratic participation.

CONCLUSION: SOLIDARITY BY DEFAULT

The events of 2008–2012 have illustrated a point that has been raised previously in analyses of the Scandinavian countries: centralized wage-setting removes decisions from both the market and the local unions, so that increased demand for labour increases employment rather than the wages of incumbent workers or the profits of owners (Moene and Wallerstein 2006, p. 18). An evident virtue of constraining wages in a recession is that it increases the efficacy of deficit spending and monetary policy in boosting employment and thus allows policy-makers to stimulate the economy at a lower cost of increasing national debt. A distinctive feature of the Nordic response to the Great Recession of the 1930s was the use of labour-market policies as a macro-economic tool to buffer employment. According to Moene and Wallerstein (2006, p. 19), productivity growth was accelerated at the level of the individual citizen through

> industries with low levels of productivity [being] prevented from staying in business by paying low wages . . . [and] workers in industries with high level of productivity are prevented from capturing much of the productivity differential in the form of higher wages. By reducing profits in low-productivity firms and increasing profits in high-productivity firms, labour and capital would be induced (or coerced) to move from low productivity to high productivity activities, increasing aggregate efficiency as well as improving equality.

The optimal performance of an economy depends on finding the right balance between institutions and markets at any point in time. In a world subject to diverse shocks, that balance is likely to change frequently, so that decision-makers will always be adjusting against a moving target, something which small states with low corruption and accessible political elites may be more capable of doing. When the Swedish banking system verged on collapse in 1993, conservatives and social democrats united around the same policy. In the 2007–2009 crisis, statements by the Ministry of Finance on restoring full employment were far stronger than any comparable policy pronouncements in the United States, where diverse other issues seemed to dwarf the weak employment recovery and the problems of joblessness (Freeman 2013, pp. 24–25). Three factors seem to contribute to this consensual and evidence-based approach to policy: population size, as people living in small open economies are likely to be connected through short networks of links, smaller degrees of separation and thus a greater sense of community than persons in larger countries; compressed income distribution, which creates shared economic interests, which in turn makes people more likely to come to similar conclusions about policy; and a dense web of institutions that influences decisions. Interacting through institutions means that decision-makers on one side deal with people on the other side of the issue, in contrast to dealing through impersonal markets (Freeman 2013, p. 25).

Twenty years ago, conservatives argued that a large welfare state was incompatible with a dynamic, successful market economy. Social democrats feared that a more market-based society was incompatible with an egalitarian income distribution and low levels of poverty. The argument today is different. Rather than viewing small states with extensive public sectors as inhibited, analysts look for reasons why these states have succeeded in combining extensive welfare states and a large public sector not only with high productivity but also with social equality. While the Scandinavian countries had divergent experiences in the Great Recession and ensuing recovery, all maintained higher employment population rates and lower unemployment rates than the United States and most EU countries and, with the exception of Iceland, whose banking system collapsed, maintained strong government financial balances and relatively low debt-to-GDP ratios.

To return to the argument proffered by this chapter, we see social investment first and foremost as a strategy for maximizing productivity by way of strategic state intervention. Where social investment results in greater social equality, it is thus a fortunate rather than logical outcome – owing first and foremost to a more consistent equality of opportunities. By contrast, the social democratic model represents a form of solidarity by default: the negotiated economy ensures a degree of social equality through equitable conditions in the labour market at the same time as social investment is encouraged through the welfare state. The model is robust across party political divides: it is supported by social democrats because they subscribe to equality and by conservatives and liberals because they promote the productivity that is inherent in the model.

This conclusion also chimes well with the assumption that social investment is itself most effective if supplemented by a social structure with limited inequality and strong social actors. In order to capture such dynamics between policy and institutions, research on social investment could benefit from a re-reading of Katzenstein (1985) to highlight the political economy and institutional infrastructure in European small states.

NOTE

1. The term is drawn from the literature on corporatism, a system of governance where interest groups are organized in national, hierarchical organizations. Concertation implies that interest groups influence policy formation and implementation. See Lijphart and Crepaz (1991).

8. Small nation versus small states: the case of Quebec

Stéphane Paquin

Quebecers have historically lived in a vulnerable political situation that involves a form of political, economic and financial dependency vis-à-vis the Canadian central government. The power and resources of the government of Quebec have always been limited. Faced with this situation, the government and civil society in Quebec have developed strategies and practices to create room for manoeuvre or an internal buffer in the federal system. They have developed since the 1960s the 'modèle québécois', or Quebec model, in order to cope with some of these difficulties. The first strategy was the construction of a Quebec national state at the provincial level. The government of Quebec became the 'national government' of the Quebec nation. The fundamental goal of this state is to promote and develop the nation of Quebec. The second strategy was to become directly involved in international affairs through identity paradiplomacy, the aim of which is to construct and reinforce Quebec's national identity by undertaking international actions abroad. The government of Quebec became a strong supporter of free trade in the 1980s in order to facilitate its exports to the United States but also to limit the power of the Canadian government to intrude in its field of jurisdiction. The last strategy was to structure Quebec society through the creation of concerted action mechanisms to develop a unique development model in Canada, the 'modèle québécois'. The Quebec model is a soft form of corporatism to facilitate collective bargaining and adjustment to various vulnerabilities.

Since 1965, the road travelled by Quebecers is amazing and may be unique in the western world, but many worry about the viability of the 'modèle québécois' in the future. The goal of this chapter is to explain the evolution of the Quebec model since the 1960s and its challenges for the future.

WHAT IS QUEBEC?

With a population of 8 million, Quebec is comparable in size to many small states, somewhere between Sweden and Denmark. Yet Quebec is not a small sovereign state but a Canadian province within a federal regime. It thus does not have access to the same public policy tools, for example monetary and formal foreign policy, that other small states might enjoy. It has access only to about half of the tax revenues collected in the province. But still, the Quebecers do have a 'national state' or a 'government' of their own with a budget close to 100 billion dollars a year.[1]

Neither is Quebec a small nation without a state, like Scotland prior to devolution (see Chapter 9), since the government of Quebec is chiefly responsible within the province for education and culture, healthcare and social services, the economy and the environment, natural resources, agriculture, transportation and justice. Quebec also has important financial autonomy, since it collects directly around 80 per cent of its income through income, business or sales tax. The rest comes from the Canadian government for social transfers or equalization policy. In 2006, the Canadian parliament recognized Quebec as a 'nation' but 'in a united Canada', as it has its own distinctive language and culture and has held a specific public space distinct from Canada since the country's creation.

Quebec is also considered to be a 'global society' within Canada. This society is based on associative pluralism, a strong network of businesses and an intense economic life that contribute to community-building. Civic life is an anchor in a specific territory, that of Quebec, which favours the institutionalization of a distinct democratic space. Quebec has woven a network of institutions and non-governmental organizations of which Quebec is the first, if not the only, reference point (Dieckhoff 2000, p. 123).

STATE-BUILDING IN QUEBEC SINCE THE 1960S

Before the 1960s, the dominant ideology in Quebec opposed vigorous state intervention. In the post-war years, Quebec was a 'liberal society' in the sense that the state intervened little in the economic field and preferred to leave social and educational policies to religious communities, essentially the Catholic Church (Bourque et al. 1994). Even before 1960, it became clear that these non-interventionist policies were not sustainable. The demographic boom necessitated the intervention of the state in healthcare and social services, while the modernization of the economy required a more professional and better-funded education system (McRoberts and Posgate 1983).

Table 8.1   *Average number of years of schooling in 1991 of men born in 1926, 1946 and 1966 in Quebec, Ontario and the United States*

Year of birth	Quebec	Ontario	USA	
			White	African American
1926	9.0	10.9	12.1	9.4
1946	11.7	12.8	13.5	12.2
1966	14.0	13.9	12.9	12.7

Before the Quiet Revolution of the 1960s, French Canadians were behind in schooling and higher education. The level of education in Quebec was behind not just the Ontario average but also that of the US white *and* African American population. If you were a male born in Quebec in 1926 you had, on average, 9 years of schooling compared to 10.9 for Ontarians, 12.1 for white Americans and 9.4 for African Americans. If you were born in 1946, you had on average 11.7 years of schooling, compared to 13.9 for Ontarians, 12.9 for white Americans and 12.2 for African Americans (Lemieux 1999; see Table 8.1).

On top of that, French Canadians also faced discrimination within Canada. A study presented by the Royal Commission on Bilingualism and Biculturalism supported this. According to the commission, male French Canadians had in 1961 an average employment income 35 per cent below that of anglophones in Montreal; during the same period, anglophones held 83 per cent of management positions in the metropolis. The Glassco Commission came to the same conclusion in 1962 in regard to the federal public administration. They found that 'the number of French Canadians holding key positions in the government administration is insignificant' (quoted in Fraser 2007, pp. 34–35). These factors strengthened the idea that French Canadians were 'nés pour un petit pain' ('born for a small loaf', meaning destined to be second-class citizens).

The rise to power of Jean Lesage's Liberals on 22 June 1960 marked a significant paradigm shift in the history of state intervention in Quebec. The Quebec government would progressively become highly interventionist. Leaving behind their hostile attitude towards the state, Quebecers developed a sense of trust in government intervention in the economic, social and political spheres (Pelletier 1992). The slogans of the Quebec Liberal Party in 1960 and 1962 would mark the tone: 'C'est le temps que ça change' ('It's time for a change') and 'Maîtres chez nous' ('Masters in our own house'). The Quebec government took on responsibilities in areas such as education, the economy, energy, healthcare, social services and culture. The government's strategy had two major components. First, the government would use the powers of the state to ensure the economic growth of the province; second, it was decided that the fruits of economic activity would benefit francophone Quebecers first by improving their financial situation (Bourque 2000).

In addition to the expansion of the state and its intervention in the social sectors, the Quebec government sought to consolidate a francophone business class. The government took various initiatives from the 1960s on to support Quebec industry and to encourage exploitation of its natural resources and transformation in Quebec. It completed the nationalization of hydroelectricity in 1963. In 1965, the Lesage government created the Caisse de dépôt et placement du Québec, a Quebec pension fund that is now the biggest investor in Canada.

Nowadays, the Quebec government is quite large compared to other provincial governments in Canada. The cost of the public administration of Quebec represents 29 per cent of its GDP, with close to 550 000 civil servants (including education and healthcare);[2] this is much more than in any other Canadian province.[3] Public services and social expenditures financed by the government of Quebec are much higher than in any other Canadian province or in the United States. The population of Quebec gets CAD 17.5 billion (12.5 billion euros) more in public services than the population of Ontario, for a difference of 26 per cent. Quebec has a unique (in Canada) affordable childcare system, Scandinavian-style family policies, unique prescription drug insurance and the lowest university tuition fees in North America. In many ways, Quebec has some characteristics of the social investment state (see Chapter 1).

IDENTITY PARADIPLOMACY

In the 1960s, the Quebec government became much more active on the international scene. For over half a century, it has pursued its own international policy parallel to that of the Canadian federal government, a practice that we call 'identity paradiplomacy'. The fundamental aim is to construct and reinforce Quebec's national identity by undertaking international actions abroad. Identity paradiplomacy is distinct from protodiplomacy in that it does not aim for political independence (Paquin 2004). The twofold purpose of Quebec's international strategy is to galvanize Quebec's development and to achieve international recognition of Quebec as a nation. The distinction between paradiplomacy, identity paradiplomacy and protodiplomacy is important. It helps to make sense of Quebec's international activities abroad and explain the relative continuity of action between the Quebec Liberal Party and the Parti Québécois, which have alternated in office since the 1960s. It also helps one understand why Quebec international activities are very institutionalized – the province seeks to imitate the degree of institutionalization of sovereign states, but on a smaller scale.

Panayotis Soldatos, who coined the term, defines paradiplomacy as the 'direct and, in various instances, autonomous involvement in external-relations activities' of federated states (Michelmann and Soldatos 1990, p. 37). We can talk about paradiplomacy when a subnational or non-central government, like the government of Quebec, mandates an actor, often a minister, to negotiate or enter into relations and defend its interest directly with other actors abroad. These actors may be sovereign states, federated states, NGOs or private sector actors. Paradiplomacy is thus similar to normal diplomacy, with the major difference that non-central governments are not recognized actors in international law. They cannot become full members of international organizations or sign an international treaty (with some exceptions in the case of Belgium). However, they often participate in international negotiations and in the work of international organizations but within the national delegation – in the case of Quebec, within the official Canadian delegation. Protodiplomacy is when a non-central government actively seeks international recognition to become independent.

Although nationalism in Quebec dates far back, something changed in the 1960s. An unapologetically nationalist discourse emerged in Quebec during the Quiet Revolution to justify stepping up international relations. Premier Jean Lesage, in his speech inaugurating the Maison du Quebec in Paris, stressed that Quebec is more than just another Canadian province. He presented the 'state' of Quebec – not the province – as a lever against the threat of assimilation in North America. For Lesage, the Maison du Quebec in Paris 'is an extension of the work we have undertaken in Quebec' (our translation, quoted in Bernier 1996, p. 30). This is not to suggest that Lesage intended to work clandestinely to achieve Quebec independence. The Quebec Liberal Party's federalist leanings are beyond doubt. Lesage was a former Liberal minister in Ottawa under Louis St-Laurent. For Claude Morin, a deputy minister in the Quebec government under Lesage, Quebec's international actions were not the work of politicians or civil servants discreetly laying the groundwork for independence. Rather, the desire to play an active role on the international stage served domestic ends: international policy decisions were 'related to concrete problems or needs felt in that time' (our translation, Morin 1987, p. 35). One significant factor, for Morin, was the strong desire felt by politicians and officials for Quebec to have an international presence. Thereby the new wave of 1960s

Quebec nationalism sought to break with traditional nationalism, particularly the policies of the Union Nationale and the 'Grande Noirceur'
period.

It has often been claimed that Quebec diplomacy emerged to make up
for the under-representation of francophones in the Canadian diplomatic
service. Studies presented during the Royal Commission on Bilingualism
and Biculturalism supported this view. The Department of Foreign Affairs
even attempted to stonewall the work of two Quebec academics officially
mandated by the commission to study whether Canada's biculturalism was
upheld in the Department of Foreign Affairs. In his report on the matter,
Gilles Lalande wrote: 'It is surprising that the law of numbers has not
allowed a single French-speaking career officer to be head of mission in
the vast majority of countries where Canadian interests are considered the
most important' (our translation, quoted in Patry 1980, p. 79).

In 1960, as Quebec was building its state apparatus, France–Quebec
rapprochement was seen as an important nation-building tool. Quebec
faced difficulties that could be more easily solved with the help of a
country like France. This led to the first international agreements on cooperation and education. The education system had been overhauled since
the arrival of Jean Lesage's Liberals, who created the first-ever Quebec
department of education. Understandably, Quebec's needs were great in
this area – particularly in terms of labour and technical expertise (Mesli
2014). Policies fostering cooperation with France would allow Quebec to
catch up more quickly, responding to what were felt to be accrued deficien-
cies. France had the financial and human resources to lend Quebec the
specialists it needed to develop its own system (Morin 1987, p. 37).

From the early 1960s on, Quebec would establish a set of cooperation
policies with France and other French-speaking countries to strengthen the
status of the French language and bolster the development of Quebec as a
nation (Bélanger 1994, p. 425). In 1965, Paul Gérin-Lajoie, Quebec's deputy
premier and minister of education, would also use nationalist arguments to
justify developing an international policy for Quebec: in his view, Quebec
was inadequately represented by the federal government, and the Canadian
foreign services ignored the French-speaking world. Gérin-Lajoie felt
it necessary for Quebec to forge closer ties with the countries of the
Francophonie, because federal diplomacy was not doing the job.

International relations are, in theory at least, a matter for sovereign
nations. Becoming an international actor able to meet with heads of state
was a giant symbolic leap for Quebec – and a highly attractive prospect
for identity builders. Branching out into the international scene can also
be a strategy to strengthen identity domestically. Appearing in an international setting raises the Quebec premier's profile and prestige at home.

Developing strong bilateral relations with sovereign states like France is also critical. Quebec, a sub-state entity, has managed to cultivate closer ties with France than Canada, a sovereign nation, has forged with the UK. With General Charles de Gaulle recognizing Quebec in his 1967 speech (*Vive le Québec libre*) and Quebec taking a seat alongside sovereign nations at international conferences, the psychology of nationhood in Quebec was utterly transformed in the 1960s.

Other factors also led Quebec to chart its own international course. Even in the 1960s a fair number of international treaties were dealing with both international and domestic issues, and it was becoming harder to determine the boundary between the two. In the context of international organizations and international conferences, themes are dealt with that relate to education, public health, cultural diversity, the environment, business subsidies, the treatment accorded to investors, and the removal of non-tariff barriers, barriers to agriculture, barriers to services, and so forth. The enlargement of the stakes on the international scene means that, at the level of taking decisions concerning foreign policy, all ministries, from the least to the most important, have at least part of their activities internationalized. This implies that ministries of foreign affairs no longer have the ability to centralize decision-making and representation and to control functions concerning foreign affairs. It also means that the fields of jurisdiction of the Quebec government were affected directly. If Quebec failed to act on international relations it would be left to the federal government to negotiate international agreements in Quebec's fields of jurisdiction. In the context of the 1960s Quiet Revolution, that was simply not an option.

Sovereign states generally seek to fully exercise their constitutional jurisdictions. The same applies to federated states like Quebec, which are, at least in theory, sovereign within their fields of jurisdiction. It is in the interest of Quebec governments to protect their fields of jurisdiction against federal interference, and sometimes even to seek greater independence or autonomy from the central power. Consequently, Quebec is not inclined to yield matters of provincial jurisdiction to the federal government when they extend to the international arena. Quebec generally feels that these matters are its responsibility.

In the decades following Confederation, the international interests of Quebec, like those of the Dominion of Canada, were essentially limited to attracting immigrants and forging commercial ties (Beaudoin 1977). Since then, however, the scope of Quebec's interests has broadened to the point where today the government of Quebec is as concerned with free trade and environmental issues as its federal counterpart. Quebec maintains an international presence to protect its interests in a number of fields, such as its business interests, cross-border relations, environmental issues, and even security since 9/11 (Michaud and Ramet 2004).

Within Canada's federal system, the province of Quebec has many constitutional jurisdictions (the economy, natural resources, labour, health, education and culture), large civil services and important financial resources. The division of power in relation to foreign affairs is a subject of debate in Canada. Some authors, like Grace Skogstad (2012, p. 202), talk about a 'de facto shared jurisdiction'. Two major reasons explain this situation. First, although the Canadian government can negotiate international treaties in the fields of jurisdiction of the Canadian provinces, it does not have the power to force the provinces to implement a treaty (Skogstad 2012, p. 204; Paquin 2013). International treaties have to be implemented at the proper level of government through a law of incorporation. In Canada, international treaties thus have to be implemented by the federal government but also by the provinces and even by municipalities. Because of that situation, Quebec has become more active in international negotiations in the past 50 years. This issue is very important, since, according to de Mestral and Fox-Decent (2008), 'roughly 40 per cent of federal statutes implement international rules in whole or in part' (p. 578).

Emerging in the 1960s, Quebec's desire to take its place in the world was also bolstered by globalization: Quebec nationalism now favoured developing international strategies (Keating 1997). Quebec nationalism, once a protectionist, autarkic impulse, today champions free trade and international expansion. For Alain Dieckhoff (2000), Quebec nationalism cannot be reduced to a simple shift in mood or the awakening of a primitive tribal force, but is rather a fundamental manifestation of modernity. Quebec's leaders used nationalism to justify support for regional integration and free trade with the United States. Pierre Martin (1995, p. 2) explains that 'Quebec has not endorsed free trade (with the United States) despite its nationalism, Quebec chose free trade because of its nationalism.'

In Quebec, the big fear was the resurgence of protectionism in the United States and, as the US market was already very important for Quebec exports, a consensus emerged quickly on the issue of free trade among the political parties in Quebec. For the Quebec Liberal Party under Robert Bourassa, free trade with the United States would provide the advantage, it was believed, of reducing the intervention capacity of the government of Canada and its national economic policies (which were seen as detrimental to Quebec interests). For the Parti Québécois, free trade with the United States would promote North–South rather than East–West trade, which would make Quebec less dependent on the Canadian domestic market, in addition to substantially reducing the costs of independence if it comes to that.

Nowadays, Quebec is part of a small, select group of non-sovereign federated states very active on the international stage (Criekemans 2010, pp. 37–64). In 2013–2014, the Ministère des Relations internationales, de la Francophonie et du Commerce extérieur (MRIFCE) had a budget of close to CAD 151.2 million and employed 638 civil servants, with some 232 posted abroad. An accurate count would also include employees of other ministries who work on such international matters as international trade negotiation, border security (growing in importance since 11 September 2001), immigration policy, environmental issues, education and culture. The government of Quebec estimates total Quebec government expenditures on international affairs at more than CAD 350 million yearly. This is the highest figure of any federated state in the world (Criekemans 2010). In 2013–2014, Quebec had 28 offices in 16 foreign countries, plus two representations in multilateral affairs, including a Paris office whose status approaches that of an embassy. In 2011–2012, the Quebec government carried out 54 international missions, an average of 4.5 per month, compared with 45 in 2010–2011 and 64 in 2009–2010.

Since 1965 Quebec has signed some 719 international agreements or 'ententes' with sovereign or federated states in close to 80 different countries. Over 369 of these agreements remain in force today.[4] Most involve sovereign countries such as France or the United States. The most important of these concern labour force mobility, education, social security, telecommunications and the environment. Quebec is also part of the Canadian delegation in many international negotiations. The most obvious recent case is its participation in the free trade negotiations between Canada and the European Union (Paquin 2013).

NEOCORPORATISM AND THE QUEBEC MODEL

The Quiet Revolution was essentially a 'top-down' approach where the state of Quebec remained the main player. This approach slowly changed in the 1970s after the election of the Parti Québécois and the holding of a series of summits with different socio-economic partners. This new approach is known in Quebec as the 'modèle québécois' (Gagnon and Latouche 1991; Rigaud et al. 2008). This Quebec model has some elements of neocorporatism, although it is not a fully institutionalized coordinated market economy as in Sweden for example.

Since the 1970s, in part because of the 'modèle québécois', Quebec has become even more than before a 'global society' within Canada. Quebec civil society is based on a very important associative pluralism, a strong network of businesses and an intense economic life that contribute to community-building. Civic life is anchored in a specific territory, that of Quebec, which favours the institutionalization of democratic space. Quebec has woven an extensive network of institutions and non-governmental organizations whose primary reference point is Quebec.

This network includes business associations such as the Conseil du patronat (business association), the Association des manufacturiers et exportateurs du Quebec (manufacturer and exporter association), Chambers of Commerce, associative organizations such as the Mouvement Desjardins (cooperative financial group) and a structured European-style union movement which includes among others the FTQ (Federation of Quebec Workers), the CSN (Confederation of National Trade Unions) and the CSQ (Congress of Democratic Trade Unions). Quebec has the highest union density rate in North America. The rate is around 40 per cent for Quebec compared to 30 per cent for Canada as a whole, while it is 11 per cent for the United States, and about 17 per cent for the average of OECD countries in 2011.[5]

Quebec public space is also occupied by political parties that limit their activities to the territory of Quebec. The Parti Québécois, the Liberal Party of Quebec, the Coalition Avenir Québec and Québec Solidaire may seek to influence policy at the federal political level, but their priority is in Quebec. These parties do not have institutional links with federal political parties even though in the case of the Liberal Party many members also have ties to the federal Liberals; the same is true with the provincial Parti Québécois and the federal Bloc Québécois.

One of the key features of the Quebec model is the mega-summits organized by the Quebec government. For example, a very important socio-economic summit on the future of Quebec was held in 1996, just after the referendum. The Parti Québécois government was able to obtain from all partners an agreement on guidelines to be adopted to bring Quebec's finances back into balance. Another important summit was the Youth Summit of 2000. Despite student demonstrations during the summit, the outcome was more positive than at the 1996 event, with the signing of a joint statement by several of the actors concerned. In 2005, the government of Quebec also held the 'Summit of Generations'. The summit was preceded by a tour of all the regions of Quebec to consult, in the same room, interest group representatives and the public at large. Following the crisis of the student strike in 2011–2012, a Summit on Higher Education was held to address the problems.

There are also many examples in Quebec of shared governance between the state of Quebec, state-owned society and civil society. According to Rigaud et al. (2010), the Caisse de dépôt et placement du Québec is an example of shared governance, since trade union representatives used to have a reserved seat on the board. Many other institutions, such as the Quebec Pension Board, the Board of Health and Safety and the Commission of Labour Market Partners, have representatives from civil society on their boards.

Other events are part of the Quebec model. Noteworthy among these is the Employment Forum 1988, which was organized by different actors from civil society, without direct government assistance. This forum was inspired by the Scandinavian development model according to Bourque and Lévesque (1999). In the late 1980s, the Quebec government promoted the 'industrial cluster', or *grappes industrielles*, strategy, which promoted more cooperation in the economic field to create a cluster of industry in a specific sector.

QUEBEC EXCEPTIONALISM IN NORTH AMERICA

Since 1965, the road travelled by Quebecers is probably unique in the western world. According to economist Pierre Fortin, in 1960 the standards of living in Quebec were 40 per cent lower than in Ontario. Nowadays, the standard of living in Quebec is comparable to Ontario.[6] That is a very big achievement. According to François Vaillancourt and Luc Vaillancourt (2005), francophone Quebecers have regained control of their economy. In 1961, the Quebec economy was only 47 per cent owned by French-speaking Quebecers (who represented over 80 per cent of the population), against 39 per cent for English-speaking Canadians and 14 per cent for foreigners, mainly Americans. In 2003, French Quebecers held 67 per cent of their businesses, a spectacular growth in a context of globalization and trade liberalization. These results are not explained by protectionism, since Quebec is open to foreign direct investments and also pro-free trade, but by the strategies of the government of Quebec to build national champions like SNC-Lavalin, Quebecor or Bombardier. The Quebec concertation model between key economic actors also protects Quebec businesses from hostile takeovers. In the financial sector, for example, many financial tools exist to protect the 'economic decision centres' of Quebec. The Caisse de dépôt et placement du Québec, the SGF (Société Générale de Financement), the Desjardins Group and the FTQ and CSN funds are key players. Respectively, they are state enterprises (Caisse de dépôt et placement and SGF), a cooperative (Desjardins Group), or trade union funds (FTQ and CSN). These institutions work together in concerted action to ensure the development of Quebec's economy and the protection of its 'decision centres'.

It is inevitable, and probably in many cases a good thing for investment, technology transfer and employment, that some major Quebec companies are bought by foreign firms. However, since the Caisse de dépôt et placement, the SGF and union funds are important shareholders and often controlling (that is to say, they have representatives on the company boards in which they invest), they have in the past, as in the case of Videotron, worked together to ensure that the decision centre remains in Quebec.

Quebec also has the most generous welfare state in North America. The impact of that is that Quebec has less income inequality than the rest of Canada and the United States as measured by the Gini index. The coefficient after taxes and transfers is 0.303 for Quebec and 0.324 for Canada as a whole. The average of OECD countries is 0.314. Quebec is thus less unequal than the average of OECD countries, while Canada as a whole is more unequal. In addition, since the mid-1990s, the growth of social inequality of income after taxes and transfers is less in the case of Quebec than in Sweden, Denmark and Finland.

Poverty rates in Quebec are also exceptional. The poverty rate for two-parent families in Quebec, after taxes and transfers, is comparable to that of Sweden, Denmark and Finland. That is a huge achievement in the North American context. With a rate of 2.4 per cent, Quebec is even better rated than Denmark and Finland, with a rate very similar to Sweden's. In the case of single-parent families, Quebec does not perform as well. This rate is at 24.6 per cent in Quebec compared to 9.1 in Sweden, 10.4 in Finland and 7.2 in Denmark. Still, Quebec performs much better than the United States, which has a rate of 39.5 per cent, and the rate for Canada as a whole is 36.6 per cent.

The most spectacular achievement is in education. The Ministry of Education was created in 1965 along with many colleges and universities. As we saw, prior to the 1960s, Quebec had one of the lowest rates of schooling in the western world. This has completely changed. If you were a male born in Quebec in 1966 you had, on average, 14 years of schooling compared to 13.9 for Ontarians, 12.9 for white Americans and 12.7 for African Americans (see Table 8.1).

CONCLUSION

As we noted, Quebec is not a sovereign country, so does not have access to all the public policy tools that sovereign states enjoy, such as monetary policy or control over foreign affairs. Because Quebec is a nation within a nation, and a francophone minority in North America, it faces a multitude of vulnerabilities. In order to cope with them, the government and civil society in Quebec have developed strategies and practices to create room for manoeuvre and an internal buffer in the Canadian federal system. The first strategy was to build the 'national state' of Quebec and to use it as a tool to reinforce the nation of Quebec. The second strategy was to develop an international strategy distinct to the foreign policy order of Canada to reinforce the Quebec nation. Quebec became in the 1980s a strong supporter of free trade with the United States because it was in its interest to do so but also because it limited the capacity of intervention of the Canadian government in the Quebec economy. The last strategy was to develop neocorporatist-like concerted action mechanisms to protect Quebec economic centres of decision and to create the most progressive welfare regime in North America. As we saw, the road travelled by Quebecers probably has few parallels in the western world.

It is hard to predict what the future holds for Quebec. Its population is highly educated; income inequality is fairly low, as is the poverty rate. Quebec's economy did not suffer too much because of the recession, but the recovery is very slow. Unemployment at 7.5 per cent in 2015 is lower than in some European countries but higher than in Canada as a whole.

One clear and present danger comes from the fact that Quebec's population is ageing faster than in the rest of Canada. This situation already means higher costs for healthcare and social services and less income for the government, since the employment rate is in decline. Quebec public debt is also a big problem. Quebec has the biggest public debt of any province in Canada. If we add Quebec's share of the federal government debt to the Quebec government debt, we have a debt-to-GDP ratio of about 94 per cent, which is comparable to that of France. This crisis of public finance has led to a series of state reforms since the mid-1990s. These reforms have weakened the state of Quebec and its ability to develop public policy. On top of that, the Liberal Party that was elected in 2014 does not seem to believe in the 'concerted action model' and prefers to adopt a top-down approach to government. In the last ten years, many corruption scandals at the federal and provincial level have also created widespread disillusionment, especially among the young generation. Trust in politicians, trade unions and the government of Quebec has reached a record low. Political trust in Quebec is clearly not what it was in the past. It is always hard to predict what the future holds, since the Liberal government has not been in office for a long time, but it does seem that the Quebec model is in decline.

NOTES

1. http://www.budget.finances.gouv.qc.ca/budget/2014-2015a/fr/documents/Graphiques_Budget1415.pdf.

2. http://cerberus.enap.ca/Observatoire/docs/Etat_quebecois/a-effectif-public-total.pdf.
3. http://www.budget.finances.gouv.qc.ca/budget/2014-2015a/fr/documents/Defi_Finances.pdf.
4. http://www.mrifce.gouv.qc.ca/fr/Ententes-et-Engagements/Ententes-internationales.
5. http://stats.oecd.org/Index.aspx?DataSetCode=UN_DEN&Lang=fr.
6. http://www.lactualite.com/opinions/chronique-de-pierre-fortin/recette-pour-un-quebec-prospere/   http://www.lactualite.com/lactualite-affaires/mise-a-jour-comment-se-comparent-le-quebec-et-lontario-en-niveau-de-vie/.

9.   Scotland as a potential small state
Malcolm Harvey

The inclusion of Scotland in a compendium on small states might come as a surprise to global observers who witnessed Scotland – by a margin of 55 per cent to 45 per cent – vote against the proposal to become an independent country in September 2014. Nevertheless, the process by which Scotland reached this decision, and the subsequent constitutional journey the UK itself embarked upon, provides a fascinating insight into how small would-be states think, plan and operate. The referendum campaign and, particularly, the Scottish National Party (SNP)'s proposals for independence were framed not, as one might expect, in terms of national identity and nationalism, but in terms of public policy outcomes and democratic accountability. From those proposals, it is clear to see the type of state that the SNP envisioned Scotland becoming.

This chapter, through analysis of the Scottish Government's (2013) White Paper on independence, *Scotland's Future*, as well as close consideration of the referendum campaign, contributes to the small-state literature by examining the prospective features of an independent Scottish state. Of particular interest here is the influence of the so-called 'Nordic model' on the Scottish Government's thinking – the proposals, specifically, to develop a social investment model, albeit with lower levels of taxation than most social investment states. It assesses the scope for changes to the institutional setting that would have been required to deliver such a model in Scotland.

TWO MODELS OF WELFARE

Keating and Harvey (2014) identify two distinct models – Weberian ideal-types – around which states can organize their political economies (see Chapter 1). These are the market liberal model and the social investment model. In the context of Scotland, they provide two very different directions for public policy, which could be achieved even without the full fiscal powers that independence would (theoretically) have delivered.

The market liberal model accepts the logic of global competition, attempting to compete in global markets by keeping production costs low and incentivizing foreign investment. It seeks to promote business by allowing flexibility in internal markets, limiting regulation and costs, and ensuring that wages remain low. The outcome for public policy is low taxes on business and, given low wages, on income. The public sector is seen as expensive, a drain on the productive economy, and therefore market liberals look to keep it small. High wage differentials are common in order to incentivize promotion, and often flat-rate (rather than progressive) taxation systems are pursued. This model has been pursued in the Baltic states of Estonia, Latvia and Lithuania, and was seen internally as a logical extension of their transition from Soviet communism to market economies. Rapid privatization of formerly nationalized industries, removal of barriers to foreign direct investment, fixed currency pegs and low, flat-rate taxation were quickly introduced in all three states as a means of declaring economic independence alongside political independence. This was a double transition of simultaneous radical constitutional and economic reform (Vilpišauskas 2014). Each was concerned that Russia remained the largest threat to its security, and that moving swiftly from a Soviet model to a Western, neo-liberal model would help to solidify national independence and provide a departure from the Soviet history. In this respect, socio-economic policies and the emergence of liberal market states in the Baltics were tied specifically to nation-state building (Bohle and Greskovits 2012) and the desire to seek political, economic and military shelter from Russia (see Chapter 3 for further consideration of this concept). This is of note because it suggests that neo-liberal economic models were not selected necessarily for economic or normative reasons, but as part of a new identity for the independent Baltic states. Thus, some of the reasons for adopting a liberal market model, such as global competitiveness, incentives for investment to encourage economic growth, and a small public sector to limit the drain on productivity, were not among the primary considerations for Baltic nation builders as they moved from centralized to deregulated economies (see Chapter 11). As a result of Scotland's welfare history and social democratic leanings (as well as the apparent rejection of centre-right politics) it appears that the prospects for pursuing this model are rather limited, even more so since, in rejecting independence, Scotland has no requirement to establish a new identity independent of the UK.

By contrast, the social investment model sees public expenditure as a productive part of the economy. Chapter 1 outlines the social investment model in detail, and, without repeating the argument here, two points are worth mentioning again. First, government spending (on education, research, healthcare, childcare and so on) is framed in terms of investment in measures that will ultimately help improve economic and social conditions. Second, this redefinition of spending emphasizes the priority on efficiency, with active labour market policies attempting to realign training with benefits and focus on preparation for employment. In so doing, social investment states can attempt to balance economic competitiveness with improvements to social conditions.

The social democratic social investment states of Denmark, Norway and Sweden have, for several decades, provided something of a benchmark for proponents of a high-tax, high-spend model. Indeed, the 'Nordic model' has been celebrated by social democrats – in Scotland as much as anywhere else – as a successful means of combining economic growth with social assistance programmes. The ideal-typical Nordic model was most closely followed by Norway. It combines a comprehensive social security system with institutionalized social rights, social solidarity, and a tripartite bargaining system that requires cooperation between employers' associations, employees (organized through widespread unionization) and the government (Brandal et al. 2013). It requires high levels of taxation to provide for generous active labour market policies such as universal unemployment and sickness insurance, and correspondingly high levels of employment to ensure that revenue from taxation exceeds spending on welfare payments. It also requires high levels of social solidarity, which is achieved through universal programmes, ensuring that the middle classes receive the benefits they pay for through taxation. Brandal and Bratberg, in Chapter 7, argue that there are overlaps between social democracy as a political philosophy which defines strategy in government and the social investment model as practised in the Nordic states, but, just as it is possible to have social democracy without a fully operationalized social investment model, so too can the model exist independently of a social democratic governing philosophy. This is an important distinction, for it emphasizes that Scotland's social democratic leanings (discussed below) may not require the whole development of a social investment system to be realized, though there are certainly other barriers to its delivery.

WHERE STANDS SCOTLAND?

The oft-stated starting point for political economy discussions in Scotland is indeed that of social democracy – that Scotland is an inherently centre-left polity, derived from the popular mythology surrounding 'Red Clydeside' and historic industrial towns and villages (Hutchison 2001). Certainly in the devolution period, this centre-left tendency has been manifest in political representation, with support for social democratic parties

Labour and, latterly, the SNP increasing substantially at the expense of conservatism. The (centre-right) Conservative Party lost all of its Westminster representation in Scotland in 1997, and remained an electoral force only because of the proportional element of voting in the Scottish Parliament in 1999. With support for the Conservatives declining to 14 per cent by the 2011 Scottish Parliament election, political debate gravitated towards the centre-left. Labour in Scotland has enjoyed substantial support and, between 1959 and 2010, never failed to return a majority of Scottish members of Parliament at Westminster. The Liberal Democrats – until entering into coalition government with the Conservatives after the 2010 UK election – had also been predominantly seen as a social democratic party, the party itself having been formed through the merger of the Liberal Party and the Social Democratic Party in the late 1980s. The electoral strength of the Liberal Democrats in Scotland varies geographically, with the rural areas attracted to the more liberal elements of economic policy, while urban (and, typically, student) areas were attracted to the more social democratic themes. Support for the SNP has fluctuated in strength in UK elections but, since the establishment of the Scottish Parliament, the party has found a considerable electoral advantage in a solely Scottish institution.

The electorate in Scotland has shown itself to be shrewd in its distinctions between voting at different electoral levels, calculating that Labour would provide more substantive numbers in competition with the Conservatives at the UK level, while entrusting the administration of devolved competences within the Scottish Parliament to the SNP, at least until the 2015 UK General Election. This was demonstrated most clearly with the UK election in 2010 (where Labour returned 41 seats to the SNP's 6), contrasting with the Scottish Parliament election in 2011, which delivered an SNP majority government with 69 of the 129 seats, while Labour returned 35. Indeed, the 2011 contest provides an interesting side-note to this point. The manifestos of the SNP and Labour included many of the same policies, with only the constitutional question dividing the two parties. This is a theme which has been consistent over the past four decades in Scotland, with the SNP and Labour subscribing to very similar political-economic philosophies, but fundamentally differing over how those could best be achieved: the SNP supporting the creation of an independent Scottish state, and Labour believing the cause of social justice could best be delivered within the UK. With the independence question settled – at least in the short term – an interesting dynamic to observe in Scottish politics will be how well these two large parties might be able to work together to deliver upon some of their shared social democratic ideals.

However, political representation notwithstanding, the Scottish electorate is not – at least according to social attitude surveys – substantially different from that of the rest of the UK. There is a slight tendency to be more left-wing than England on matters of welfare, but on the whole those differences are not pronounced (Curtice and Ormiston 2011). What distinguishes Scotland from the rest of the UK is the tendency to *vote* more consistently for social democratic parties. This is particularly true of the middle class – a reflection, partly, of the moves made by both the Labour–Liberal Democrat coalition (1999–2007) and by the SNP (2007 onwards) to make distinctive public policy universal in nature. Examples of this include free personal care for the elderly, introduced by Henry McLeish's administration in the early 2000s, and the abolition of university tuition fees and prescription charges for healthcare services, adopted by the SNP government as a minority administration. These policies were aimed at widening the availability of services in both healthcare and education to ensure that cost was not a determinant factor in uptake. Universality, while ensuring that low-income households were not excluded from affording services, also had a by-product: it provided services free of charge to the middle classes. In turn, this bound the middle class into the system and provided a clear feeling of reciprocity – that what was received out of the system (free services) was at least an equivalent to what was contributed through (higher levels of) taxation. And so social democratic voting patterns in Scotland became less about delivering on a perceived more egalitarian sense of society but about entitlement – getting out of the system what was put into it.

While social democracy in the Nordic states developed in concert with trade union activism, social partnership and tripartite negotiations, the infrastructures within which these discussions might have taken place in Scotland were dismantled or disempowered, or never existed in the first place. The United Kingdom toyed with corporatism in the 1960s and 1970s, and, though it played a successful role in limiting wage and price increases during periods of inflation, the system broke down in the early 1980s, amid hostility from the Thatcher government and soured relations with trade unions. Weakness on all three sides (militant grass-roots trade unions; weak organization on the part of business; and a government disinclined to compromise in the wake of strikes) led to the failure of corporatism in the UK (Keating and Harvey 2014). In the 30 years since, there has been limited formal space where relations between business, trade unions and government could be resurrected, and agreements have been limited.

Scotland finds itself in a position where it actively supports social democratic parties and the principles underpinning this political philosophy. However, it does so without the institutional capacity to build the kinds of business–union–government relations required to deliver substantive policy change and a social investment model in the mould of the Nordic states. Irrespective of the powers available to the Scottish Parliament, it appears that the institutional setting – and the unwillingness of actors to engage in formal decision-making processes on a national level – contributes to an inability to deliver upon social investment structures. As a result, wage bargaining, a key component of the social investment model, is difficult to deliver. In turn, this hampers further progress towards social investment outcomes.

THE CRASH, AUSTERITY AND DIVERGING ECONOMIC ATTITUDES

The global financial crisis, beginning in 2008, provided a challenging economic situation for small independent states. The countries around Scotland – Norway, Iceland and the Republic of Ireland, previously dubbed by Scotland's first minister the 'arc of prosperity' – were hit hard. Banks collapsed and required bail-outs, economies contracted significantly and entered recessions, and public spending was significantly scaled back. Many European governments embarked upon austerity policies, and the UK was no exception. After the UK General Election in 2010, when a Conservative–Liberal Democrat (centre-right) coalition replaced a social democratic Labour government, austerity policies were amplified in an attempt to recover the UK's economic position and deal with the burgeoning deficit. The change in government brought a change in economic philosophy, away from the Keynesian stimulus programmes instituted in the immediate aftermath of the 2008 financial crisis, to a much more conservative fiscal programme, which was replicated across the EU. In the UK, this took the form of a freeze on public sector pay and child benefits, a 2.5 per cent rise in VAT, and substantive spending cuts across several departments. More controversially, the UK Government instituted an end to what it called the 'spare-room subsidy' and which opponents dubbed the 'bedroom tax': a reduction in housing benefits to those claimants who had an 'extra' room in their home. In addition, and in sharp contrast to election pledges made by the Liberal Democrats, the government increased the cap on university tuition fees, allowing institutions in England to charge up to £9000 per year.

Against the backdrop of a centre-right UK Government, the SNP won a majority in the 2011 Scottish election, which appeared to underline the political differences between Scotland and the rest of the UK. Measures adopted in Scotland – including the abolition of tuition fees, in sharp contrast to the increases elsewhere in the UK, and the mitigation of the effect of the 'bedroom tax' in Scotland through the provision of government grants to cover the benefit cuts – portrayed the Scottish Government as more compassionate than its UK counterpart. Of course, much of the background to this was entirely political: the issue of the Scottish referendum on independence in 2014 played a significant role in public policy and perception of governance, and indeed the Scottish Government took any opportunity it could to demonstrate divergence from the prevailing political attitudes at Westminster. Nevertheless, the perception played out that not only was the Scottish Government leaning much more towards a social investment model than the rest of the UK, but this was a more acceptable public policy direction to the Scottish electorate. This principle was seized upon by the Scottish Government in the publication of its White Paper on independence, optimistically titled *Scotland's Future*.

SCOTLAND'S FUTURE – A BLUEPRINT FOR INDEPENDENCE?

The Scottish Government's (2013) White Paper on independence was clearly inspired by the social investment perspective – and, in particular, the Nordic model of adaptation, with its strong social democratic undertones. References to small, independent states were widespread, including the way that small states concentrate their ambitions on niche areas, the internal political structures, and an emphasis on science, research and development, human capital and infrastructure. There was an explicit argument made that small states are, given their stature, better equipped to deliver the infrastructure and societal attitudes required for a social investment approach. Indeed, the focus of *Scotland's Future* more broadly was on a 'social investment approach' to 'develop more targeted labour market policies' (Scottish Government 2013). The social investment model was seen as a means to foster 'a culture in society that is more inclusive, more respectful and more equal. It also places the cash transfers that people traditionally think of as welfare – such as out of work benefits and tax credits – in a wider, more cost-effective and socially beneficial context when viewed over the longer-term' (Scottish Government 2013).

Evidently, this took a wide-angle view of welfare, attempting to combine economic growth and social cohesion in one move, requiring increased levels of societal trust and a wider use of the benefit system in order to reduce inequality across the board. The social investment approach, it was argued, would provide an 'opportunity to invest in the supply of services, rather than subsidising demand', a change in focus which moved the

Table 9.1   Nordic mentions in Scotland's Future

Norway	42
Sweden	32
Denmark	31
Finland	24
Iceland	12
Nordic	5

Source: Scottish Government (2013).

emphasis from outputs to inputs (Scottish Government 2013). The Nordic states were referenced extensively as examples of best practice as to how the social investment model could operate in Scotland (see Table 9.1).

This was no more evident than in the section on childcare provision. The Scottish Government proposed a substantial increase in childcare facilities and services in the event of independence. This included increasing the provision of hours of childcare available over the lifespan of the next two Scottish Parliaments, initially allocating 600 hours of childcare per year for up to 50 per cent of Scotland's two-year-olds for the 2016–2020 parliamentary session, and then not only increasing the time to 1140 hours of childcare but also extending this provision to three- and four-year-olds, as well as vulnerable two-year-olds by 2024. In addition, there was a commitment to provide capital investment in facilities, with the establishment of 35000 new jobs in childcare services and the opportunity to help 100000 parents (predominantly mothers) back into the workforce. That the Scottish Government was criticized on several counts here – that the policy was uncosted, that there were not 100000 mothers who wanted to return to the workforce (nor 100000 jobs for them to take) and that the Scottish Parliament already had the power to deliver such a policy and that not doing so was simply a bribe to attract more 'Yes' votes in the referendum – was not a surprise (Andrews 2014). Nevertheless, the explicit argument that 'childcare has important benefits for children and it also provides a key support to participation in the labour market, particularly for women' saw the Scottish Government clearly endorse a move towards a Nordic-style social investment model in Scotland (Scottish Government 2013). Certainly, the line taken by the Scottish Government in promoting the policy was redolent of Nordic states' provision, arguing that enabling more women to return to the workforce would mean the policy would pay for itself. However, in the Nordic states, the provision of childcare services is not taken in isolation, but is part of a broader package of policies around employment, welfare and economic growth.

The Scottish Government is not the only proponent of the social investment model in Scotland. Despite the economic challenge that faced the Nordic states in the 1990s, and again after the global economic crash in the 2000s, there has been no shortage of admirers of the model in Scotland. The Common Weal programme emerged during the referendum campaign to promote social democratic principles and, in particular, the social investment model. Influences from the Nordic model include: a balanced and creative economy, with emphasis on cooperatives and social enterprises; a more progressive taxation system, including a welfare system based on active labour market policies; nationalization of industry, in particular public transport services; and a revitalization of democracy through more local government (Jimmy Reid Foundation 2013). The principle of universalism, long a staple of the Nordic model which helps to foster social solidarity and tie the middle classes into the high-tax, high-spend system, is seen by the Common Weal as a key factor in building such a social investment model in Scotland. Universal free childcare is also promoted heavily as a means of allowing mothers to return to the labour market. In theory, this should increase tax and national insurance revenues, decrease the amount government has to pay out in unemployment and other benefits, and allow wages to be spent on other areas – thereby, the argument goes, helping to grow the economy. The Common Weal programme has focused predominantly on importing the social democratic principles of the Nordic model. In particular, there is a concern with equality – both in economic terms, considering how wealth can be more equitably distributed within Scotland, and in more social terms, with regard to gender equality.

The Electoral Reform Society's Democracy Max programme also heavily featured ideas drawn from the Nordic states, though this is less focused on the political and economic outcomes of the system and more on the institutional setting within which the discussions take place. The organization here was focused on considering what Scotland's democracy would look like in 2030. Three examples in particular are worth mentioning. First, the gender balance of public institutions in the Nordic states, and the prevalence of female representatives, both as individual MPs and, in several cases, as party leaders, was noted as a clear objective for Scotland and an indication that gender balance is achievable. Second, a comparison was made between local democracy in Norway (with a turnout of 63 per cent in 2011) and Scotland (where the local election turnout in 2012 was closer to 40 per cent). A discussion at one of the round-table events focused on the contrast between the respective numbers of councillors in Scotland (1223) and Norway (10 781, plus 787 county councillors), with an argument made that, given the 1:10 ratio of councillors between the two, which have similar population levels, political power in Scotland remained centralized and local democracy under-utilized. Third, the openness of data in the Nordic states was also appreciated as a major aid to social solidarity. In particular, in Finland, Norway and Sweden, tax data are available online, allowing greater transparency about individual interests (Electoral Reform Society 2013). On all three counts, there was an ambition to mimic Nordic ideas, replicating the institutions and style of democracy which inform the political economy of these states. Clearly, were some of these ideas about the nature of democracy transferred to Scotland, they would fundamentally alter the nature of how Scotland, as a small European state, might operate.

SQUARING A CIRCLE

The Scottish Government's childcare policy, and attraction to Nordic levels of social spending, is consistent with a social investment strategy and a social democratic tilt to policy. However, it coexists within *Scotland's Future* with something akin to a market liberal approach focused on low corporate and personal taxation. Proposals for substantive capital outlay on childcare facilities sat alongside proposals not to increase taxation but to actively *reduce* it, with a commitment to cut corporation tax by 3 percentage points below the level set in the rest of the UK as a means of encouraging inward investment. There was also a proposal to cut, and then abolish entirely, air passenger duty as a means of encouraging business to Scotland, although this would have a limited but noticeable effect on total tax take, as well as a knock-on effect on efforts to meet climate change targets.

The White Paper also recognized that, while future Scottish governments might want to vary tax rates, they believed there would be 'no necessity to do so to pay for current spending' (Scottish Government 2013). Indeed, the proposals in *Scotland's Future* regarding taxation outlined changes only to how tax would be collected with independence, and not to the rates, with the exception of corporation tax. These proposals did nothing to quell criticism that the SNP wanted to have their cake and eat it too: that they wanted Nordic levels of public services without Nordic levels of taxation. While the Nordic states invariably have high levels of income tax, they also have rather broad tax bases, with tax on consumption important here. While not considered progressive, value added taxes have the benefit of applying across the board and, crucially, are not susceptible to avoidance schemes. Taxing the rich, while attractive to more left-wing types, is not a solution in isolation, since in Scotland in particular there are not nearly enough who pay tax in the higher bracket, and were those taxes increased substantially such taxpayers might simply move elsewhere (Bell and Eiser 2014). Additionally, taxation of land and property is important for this reason. It is difficult to avoid, is largely progressive, and encourages economic efficiency by dis-incentivizing large-scale land ownership. However, even on this latter point, the Scottish Government has been reluctant to act, freezing the local government council tax on its election to government in 2007 and continuing the freeze after its re-election in 2011.

Herein lies the fundamental issue with the proposals for instituting a social investment model in Scotland: the cost, both financial and political. The Scottish Parliament was established in 1999 with a single tax power, the ability to vary the basic rate of income tax by up to 3 pence in the pound. This was voted for as a second question in the referendum that overwhelmingly supported the creation of the legislature, and also received widespread support. Nevertheless, the power has never been used; indeed, the Scottish Government under the SNP allowed the register upon which the levy would be based to lapse, rendering the government unable to utilize the power even if it was its desire to do so.

The latter point, though, is perhaps more relevant: the desire to vary the tax rate in Scotland has never enjoyed wide public support. Only one party – the SNP itself – has ever campaigned with a pledge to use the policy (in 1999), and even in that instance the intention was not to raise the level of taxation but simply not to implement the 1 penny cut in income tax that the UK Government was introducing. The net impact of this would have been an increase in revenue available to the Scottish Parliament of approximately £230 million, representing just 1.5 per cent of the then-total £15.5 billion budget. The SNP announced in 2002 that it would discontinue the policy, and utilizing the tax-varying power has rarely been discussed since.

There appears little demand in Scotland for an increase in taxation, or indeed any variation in taxation between what is paid in Scotland and what is paid in the rest of the UK (Scottish Attitudes Survey 2012). While Scots are happy to see their taxes used to fund (universal) public services in the form of health and education – and, indeed, would be happy to see further funding in these areas if it improved the services available – they are reluctant to see taxation increased in order to fund higher spending. In addition, especially since the MPs' expenses scandal in 2009, trust in politicians has fallen. In the Nordic social investment states, the consensus model of politics plays a considerable role in delivering public policy, and, within that consensus, trust in political actors and institutions, as well as a considerable level of social solidarity, trust and empathy for fellow citizens, is an important contributory factor. The absence of that trust in politicians in Scotland, in addition to the lack of institutional structures within which wage bargaining and wider discussions around tax might be discussed, limits the ability to deliver substantial change to the tax arrangements, irrespective of the levers available to the Scottish Parliament.

WHAT WOULD INDEPENDENCE LOOK LIKE?

Taking these elements together – the emphasis within the referendum campaign upon issues related to political economy; the groups advocating the adoption of the social investment model; and the Scottish Government's prospectus for independence – the question of what independence would look like remains. One rather widespread criticism of the 'Yes Scotland' campaign in the referendum was that it offered a view of independence which was too non-specific. In many ways, this was by design. The Yes campaign had to build a broad base of support across various sectors; thus it could not afford to alienate any particular sector of society. This meant that more radical policies, such as republican proposals to abolish the monarchy, were not focused upon in any depth during the campaign.

Indeed, one of the paradoxes of the latter stages of the campaign was the Scottish Government's insistence that, even with independence, much would remain the same. Their intention was to retain the monarchical, monetary and social unions with the rest of the UK, defence union in NATO and membership of the European Union. The Better Together campaign emphasized a promise of further devolved powers should Scotland vote No. In one sense, this was an obvious strategy for the Yes campaign: the decision to secede is a radical one, and many questions with unknown answers are raised. By emphasizing the consistency of certain policies and institutions, this was an attempt to assuage the fears of the unknown and to appeal to the constitutional small-c conservatism apparent in Scotland's electorate.

While, to a point, this was a successful strategy, it also made the picture of what Scottish independence would look like that bit more vague. Of course, this was also because there were competing impressions of Scotland's future within the Yes campaign itself. The (SNP) Scottish Government's prospectus was laid out clearly in *Scotland's Future*, but there were elements there, such as the focus on oil and certain elements of energy policy, as well as the abolition of air passenger duty, which did not sit well with Yes campaign colleagues in the Scottish Green Party. The Scottish Socialist Party too were disappointed with the Scottish Government's proposal to cut corporation tax by 3 pence, while Business for Scotland welcomed it. While this was evidence that there was a wide base for a Yes vote, with support on both the left and the right of the political spectrum, it did rather confuse the picture of what an independent

Scotland would look like. The point they all agreed on, however, was that decisions which affected Scotland should be taken by those who cared most about Scotland, those who lived and worked there, a democratic appeal on the referendum question, rather than a political and economic one. In many ways, the question of what form Scottish independence would take was one which was never intended to be resolved prior to the referendum, and one which would have provoked much discussion over the political economy of Scotland had there been a Yes vote. Nevertheless, the Scottish Government's proposals, as well as those of various campaign groups, looked towards the small Nordic states as the blueprint for independence.

CONSTITUTIONAL ELASTICITY

While the Scottish independence referendum provided a dichotomous choice, a straightforward question of whether Scotland should be independent or remain a component nation within the UK, the reality of Scotland's position in the UK is much more complicated. With the promise of further powers for the Scottish Parliament to be delivered by the incoming government, the Scottish Parliament is – according to politicians negotiating the legislation – set to become one of the most powerful sub-state legislatures in the world. While this claim should be taken with a pinch of salt, it emphasizes that independence is not necessarily, as the SNP would perhaps argue, the 'Holy Grail', and that much can be achieved without the powers which 'full' independence might have delivered. Indeed, the SNP's proposals for independence were somewhat limited in what they desired to alter in the event of independence, effectively ceding sovereignty over currency and defence to larger neighbours and articulating a position which came to be described as 'independence-lite'.

While, as discussed above, this was a strategy aimed at securing a wider base of support for independence, it also bore some similarities to 'devolution-max', a constitutional option which (despite not appearing on the ballot paper) became the preference of the majority of Scotland's electorate. This was commonly understood to mean Scotland remaining inside the UK with control over all domestic policy within its borders except for foreign affairs, defence and monetary policy. It was never likely that the UK Government would cede quite so much power to the Scottish Parliament, but these concepts demonstrate that the dichotomy of independence or not is somewhat false, and that there is a range of constitutional options within which sub-state entities can exist.

Chapter 8 provides further evidence, in the context of Quebec, that independence is not required to deliver public policy which is markedly different from that of neighbouring territories. In this regard it appears that, if we view states on a spectrum from centralized polity through devolution to independence, there is a range of powers sub-state entities can obtain, develop and utilize in different ways to deliver different policy outcomes. In that regard, while the powers of independence and 'full sovereignty' are not forthcoming for Scotland, the Scottish Parliament does have some powers at its disposal to develop policies that would, theoretically, move it closer towards the Nordic idea of social investment. However, having the constitutional power to alter policy direction within a devolved legislature and actually having the ability to do so (given certain political and economic constraints placed upon actors) are, as we have seen, two separate issues.

EXPECTATIONS VERSUS REALITY

Expression of a vague desire for something resembling a Nordic system of social investment characterized the constitutional debate – at least, from the perspective of those supporting an independent Scotland. Two points are worth noting about the appearance of the Nordics in the debate. Firstly, there was a lack of clear articulation as to what a Nordic system of social democracy actually entailed, how it operated and how relative success had been achieved. Proponents lauded the Nordics (and, indeed, Ireland) as the 'arc of prosperity' prior to the global financial crisis. In its aftermath, critics derided these states as the 'arc of insolvency'. Neither position provided sophisticated analysis of the policies leading to these outcomes, preferring instead to caricature the cases in order to further its own constitutional preferences. So the Nordic states in particular were portrayed rather unrealistically. On the one hand, they were argued to be a social democratic nirvana, with high levels of equality and social solidar-ity, brought about through high levels of government spending on social protection. On the other, they were argued to be highly taxed, highly regu-lated anti-business states, with a lack of enterprise and the cost of a pint of beer – a cost which resonated with much of the Scottish population – claimed to be in the region of £10. On neither side was what was claimed the whole story. Equality was built in the Nordics through social solidarity forged in the inter-war and post-war periods, and relationships between business, trade unions and governments were fostered to provide an insti-tutional setting which would allow negotiations over wages, taxation and social spending.

There have been challenges to the social investment models in each of the Nordic states – in the early 1990s, and again after the global financial crisis in 2008 – after which adjustments to how they operated were made. They continue to follow the social investment approach, funding high levels of social spending through high levels of personal taxation (which, in turn, is funded by high wage levels), negotiated through frequent tripartite bargaining meetings, comprising government, business and unions. These elements are key to how the social investment system operates, and, in particular, the social democratic variant which exists in the Nordic states. The Scottish population are generally amenable to the idea of generous and universal public services (as the abolition of university tuition fees and prescription charges has shown). However, the lack of discussion about the revenue side of the ledger – the requirement for higher levels of individual taxation in order to fund more generous welfare spending, as well as higher wages and a structured wage-bargaining system – means that public support for such a tax increase is limited.

The second point is that, aside from the Scottish Government's White Paper expressly discussing spending plans consistent with a social investment model (albeit without the taxation levels to support it), promotion of the Nordic social investment model has not come from mainstream political parties. Campaign groups like the Jimmy Reid Foundation and the Electoral Reform Society have, for several years, played a role in civic society in Scotland, contributing to the broader political campaign environment. However, their views on reform of the political and institutional setting remain on the margins of political debate in Scotland, and radical solutions to social and economic issues are not the mainstay of political parties, which prefer to tinker around the edges of the current system than institute substantive changes.

CONCLUSION

With the independence referendum providing an apparently decisive 10-percentage-point margin of victory for the No campaign, the prospects of Scottish independence, at least in the short term, appear rather small. However, there are several caveats to note with regard to that statement. The first is that constitutional change is coming to Scotland and, indeed, the UK as a whole. In the final weeks of the campaign – as well as in televised addresses in the wake of the referendum outcome becoming known – prime minister David Cameron and leader of the opposition Labour Party Ed Miliband recommitted themselves to delivering 'substantial' more powers to the Scottish Parliament. At the time of writing, these powers include proposals to devolve a proportion of income tax, as well as some powers over welfare policy in Scotland. So the Scottish Parliament will be a more powerful institution as a result of the referendum, and this will give it the opportunity for further divergence of policy from the UK.

The second issue of note is the size of the minority which voted in favour of independence. Six weeks prior to the referendum it appeared likely that the outcome would be even more decisive – some Unionist politicians were talking of a margin of around 70 per cent to 30 per cent in favour of a No vote. Given that 45 per cent voted for independence – 1.6 million Scots – there is clearly a substantial (minority) demand for independence. 'The 45 per cent', as they have taken to calling themselves on social media, will not remain silent going forward, with several campaigns rising in order to continue to fight for independence. Membership of parties which supported independence increased substantially in the weeks following the vote. By mid-October 2014, the SNP had over 80000 members, trebling its membership and comfortably becoming the third-largest party in the UK (after Labour and the Conservatives, overtaking the Liberal Democrats and the United Kingdom Independence Party).

While there is not (yet) any academic research into the demographics of this new membership, it is likely – given the profile of those who voted Yes in the referendum – that many of these new members are considerably to the left of the political spectrum (much more so than the SNP itself defines) as well as more fundamentalist (in constitutional terms, desiring rapid delivery of independence) as opposed to gradualist. This will undoubtedly be a challenge to the new leadership of the party – how to maintain the support of party activists who might become disillusioned by gradualist, moderate progress on the constitutional question. The Scottish Greens also trebled in size, to around 6000 members, while the Scottish Socialist Party overtook the Scottish Liberal Democrats, announcing membership of 3500 one month after the referendum. Going forward, Scotland will have a more powerful parliament with new powers, as well as political parties which are much larger in terms of active membership than at any time in the past four decades. The referendum has breathed new life into political engagement in Scotland, and in particular among the supporters of independence. The constitutional question has an apparently decisive short-term answer, but the vote itself will continue to have implications for politics in Scotland for a much longer period.

Scotland is not (yet) a small state, and in September 2014 the Scottish electorate rejected this constitutional option – at least for the foreseeable future. However, Scotland provides a fascinating case study of just how small nations deal with the question of constitutional change and state design, as well as the viability of small states in the twenty-first century. The long referendum campaign in Scotland allowed consideration of the constitution, as well as wider issues in Scottish society, by politicians, academics and the (incredibly politically engaged) electorate more broadly. The referendum itself had one question, but the campaign went far beyond that narrow constitutional focus. Issues were raised about currency, collective defence mechanisms, the political economy, membership of international institutions and the shape of future Scottish society. The way in which these issues were dealt with gives an insight into what kind of state Scotland might be if it did become independent.

The political economy of Scotland played a central role in the constitutional debate. This was largely at the expense of issues surrounding identity, suggesting small-state nationalism has become largely pragmatic in nature. 'Independence in Europe', the centrepiece of the SNP's rhetoric in the 1990s, has developed from a campaign focusing on sovereignty, external independence and national symbols to one which considers how society might be shaped in an alternative manner. In the SNP's case, defining national identity in broad, civic terms defused claims that its nationalism was 'anti-English' and reduced identity to a minor role in the referendum campaign. Instead, the Scottish Government's White Paper on independence focused on potential public policy divergence from the UK towards a social investment model. However, while there were examples of a shift in policy towards a social investment approach, the reality is that they did not really form a cohesive strategy for an independent state.

The Nordic model, a social democratic, social investment system, comes as a package. It is impossible to 'pick and mix' elements from the social investment model with that of a Baltic-style market liberal approach without sustaining incredibly large public debt. The high-wage economy of the Nordic states is a result of decades of tripartite bargaining, with trade unions accepting wage restraint in periods of economic decline as a trade-off for high levels of unemployment benefits. The social solidarity of the Nordic states, forged in the inter-war period and exploited to deliver universalism in the post-war period, continues to develop as a result of the same universalism that it helped to create. The principles and the outcomes are delivered as a package. And this contrasts sharply with some of the contributions of the social investment model to the constitutional debate in Scotland. Scotland has a great history of trade unions, with the movement heavily aligned to the Labour Party throughout the twentieth century. However, the trade unions have not been involved in wage negotiations in the same manner as in the Nordic states – tripartite bargaining is non-existent. And, while the Scottish Parliament was established as a Scandinavian-type assembly, with attempts made to deliver consensus politics, the reality has been a return to Westminster-style conflict. Further powers will be devolved to the Scottish Parliament, allowing the parliament, for the first time, to control some of the revenue it raises – which, in turn, will have an impact upon what it can spend. This means there is scope for wider application of social investment strategies within the Scottish political sphere.

The lack of university tuition fees or prescription charges for medication shows that there is an appetite for universalism within public services in Scotland. However, any expansion of universalism into other fields would carry a cost burden, and there is little evidence that politicians want to deliver tax increases or that the public would accept them. And therein lies the fundamental problem for Scottish politicians learning from the Nordic states. The Scottish public want to have their cake and eat it. They like the idea of generous universal services, but would resist any increase in taxation to fund such an expansion. While there is the potential for policy learning on an area-by-area basis, and indeed some empathy with the principles of the social investment strategy, the potential to adopt the model outright is slim.

Indeed, it might be that further autonomy for Scotland does not result in substantial alteration to public policy in Scotland, with parties afraid that the cost – both political and economic – is too much to bear to attempt to deliver upon a social investment model. Further devolution to the Scottish Parliament might make the institution a more powerful body, to be sure, and Scotland will be able to replicate some of the features of small states which are evident in Quebec. However, actually utilizing the powers at its disposal to effect substantive social and economic changes is probably some way from delivery. The barriers to adoption of a social investment model in Scotland are not related to size or institutional capacity, given the likelihood of further devolved powers at the disposal of the parliament. Rather, the political culture and social attitudes towards taxation are more influential in limiting the scope for developing a social investment model.

PART V

The adaptability of small states – shock
therapy or concerted elites?

10. The state that reinvented itself: New Zealand's transition to the market competition state

Jeffrey McNeill

THE REINVENTED SMALL STATE

New Zealand is a geographically isolated small state that has reinvented itself several times in its short history as it responded to changing wider geopolitical and economic conditions. Because of its geography and history, New Zealand faces some very different conditions compared to other advanced economy small states. Its remoteness from its overseas markets makes the friction of distance very real, while its colonial history set it on a trajectory that makes it vulnerable to other countries' economic and geopolitical decisions. Its transition in the 1980s from a corporatist to a market competition state and its rejection of the social investment model are remarkable for their comprehensiveness and rapidity. Accordingly, New Zealand's experiences provide a laboratory for testing Keating's model of transition (Chapter 1).

This chapter describes New Zealand's challenges as a small state, particularly from the late 1970s to post-global financial crisis (GFC), as it reinvented itself to adapt to changing global conditions. It then explores attempts to modify exogenous forces, as well as the internal changes to enable the country to respond to these forces. It explores the institutional arrangements that enabled change and rate of change in order to consider opportunities for further adaptation to continuing globalization.

VULNERABILITY FROM SIZE AND ISOLATION

New Zealand is a remote small state in the South Pacific Ocean, first inhabited only 800 years ago by humans. Colonized by the United Kingdom in the early nineteenth century, it shares similarities with European small states. Its population of 4.5 million inhabitants and population density are comparable to those of the Nordic countries. Its people have strong European cultural ties and identity and strong democratic traditions and institutions, with a unitary parliamentary government operating under the Westminster system. Its citizens enjoy a comparable standard of living to Europeans, and it has a strong social welfare tradition. This standard of living is, however, vulnerable owing to an economy shaped by its geography and history, and trading conditions set by its trading partners, mediated by its own responses to these vulnerabilities.

Like other small states, its internal economy is too small to be self-supporting and is dependent on exports to support its way in the world. However, New Zealand's remoteness makes it unlike European small states. A circle drawn on a map with a radius of around 2000 kilometres centred on Dublin or Helsinki encompasses most of the European Union with its 500 million people. The same radius circle centred on New Zealand's capital, Wellington, almost reaches the Australian coast. A wider radius that includes the Australian eastern states, where most Australians live, contains a population of less than 25 million.

Its vulnerability is also structural. Its economy is in many ways post-industrial while still largely reliant on agriculture. New Zealand's temperate climate is ideal for European-model agricultural production, so New Zealand, like other British colonies, developed primarily as a commodity producer, the 'farm of Britain', lacking a strongly developed manufacturing sector. The types of produce exported have changed over time, but continue to be exported mostly as commodities, with relatively little value-added processing and with prices set by international markets (Nixon and Yeabsley 2002). This can work to its advantage; in the late 1940s and 1950s, high international demand for primary produce enabled New Zealanders to enjoy one of the highest standards of living world-wide. And increasing demand by China for milk has been critical for economic growth over the last 15 years.

However, reliance on exporting a few commodity products to a few countries also makes it vulnerable to exogenous forces. From the 1870s until the 1950s most New Zealand exports were to Britain (over 80 per cent by 1920). Even in 1970 the UK took over 90 per cent of New Zealand's butter exports, 75 per cent of cheese exports and nearly half of sheep meat exports. Today, this reliance on a narrow sector exporting to a dominant market for economic prosperity continues, so that a quarter of exports are now milk products to China. Major changes in trading partners' conditions have had major impacts, most notably the UK joining the then European Economic Community (EEC) in 1973. This led to a loss of a major market; the 1971 Luxembourg agreement reduced the butter quota by about 17 per cent and cheese quota by 68 per cent in five years, then reducing by about a further half again after 1977. The collapse of the USSR in the 1990s similarly led to significant market disruption (the Russians reportedly sought to barter butter imports for a nuclear submarine!).

New Zealand's isolation is double-edged, challenging economic development, but also limiting possibilities of direct aggression, so it has never been attacked. However, its reliance on shipping to get goods to market and across borders has always been to the front of foreign policy. Membership of and support for the British Empire was in part reliance on the British navy to protect vital sea routes. The fall of Singapore in the Second World War shattered belief in the UK to uphold trade route security, leading to post-war defence treaties, notably the 1951 ANZUS (Australia, New Zealand and United States of America) Treaty. More subtly, trade access has been used by larger powers for achieving geopolitical ends. For example, New Zealand's export access to the USA in the 1960s reportedly was contingent on support for and participation in the Vietnam War (James 1987). Similarly, New Zealand's decision to support the EU trade embargo on Russia in 2014 immediately preceded the opening of negotiations for a long-sought-after free trade agreement with the EU.

Although New Zealand is sheltered from the consequences of direct geopolitical conflict, the geological forces that created its islands remain active but unpredictable, with sometimes catastrophic consequences. Several towns have suffered catastrophic damage over the last century from earthquakes. Recovery from and reconstruction after these events, for example, distort the domestic economy through diversion of government money needed for recovery and a massive inflow of overseas funds from reinsurance payments, quite apart from the personal costs they wreak. And its reliance on the primary sector exposes the economy to production losses from periodic severe floods and droughts.

In summary, New Zealand's vulnerability stems largely from relying on production and export of low-value primary produce to relatively few countries. It is also challenged by its physical isolation from the rest of the world. These make it different to many other small states within economic unions with large internal markets and collective defence umbrellas.

NEW ZEALAND'S SEARCH FOR SECURITY

In response to this vulnerability, New Zealand's history can be seen as an ongoing quest for economic and social security (Sutch 1966). Successive governments have sought to modify exogenous conditions to reduce challenges by increasing its resource base and increasing its economic size. Secondly, and to a large extent separately, policies have been implemented to realign internal arrangements to adapt to prevailing exogenous conditions.

New Zealand has explored different ways to reduce the impacts resulting from its small size. Perhaps the most obvious way to solve the challenges of being a small state is to become a bigger one. It has sought to do so by increasing both its physical and its economic size to increase its resource base. It has also sought to seek security from big friends.

Colonization has historically been a favoured means to expand a state's resource base, adopted by small states such as Belgium and the Netherlands. New Zealand's Pacific sub-imperialist ambitions in the late nineteenth century resulted in colonization of the Cook Islands and Niue (Brooking 2014), and the 1914 conquest of German Samoa in the First World War. Such initiatives have not been successful economically. However, modern-day colonization of a sort by the private sector is now apparent. For example, the dominant New Zealand primary sector company Fonterra has sought to overcome internal domestic resource and seasonal limits to dairying by establishing New Zealand model farms and processing plants in China and South America, essentially appropriating others' resources.

More recently, changes to international marine law prescribed by the United Nations Convention on the Law of the Sea 1982 has afforded growth through geographic expansion. Because of its outlying islands, New Zealand now has the world's fourth-largest exclusive economic zone (EEZ), some 20 times its land area, giving it rights over exploration and use of marine resources. The EEZ vastly expands New Zealand's natural resource base of fisheries, seabed minerals, gas and oil. These resources are relatively under-exploited, but promise increased wealth. New Zealand could simply join with a larger state to gain critical mass. Intermittent discussion continues about whether New Zealand should join the Commonwealth of Australia, and in fact a 1900 provision in the Australian Constitution allows this. However, this option has never been politically attractive, seen rather as being colonized by Australia, although closer economic ties are realistic (see below).

An alternative way to achieve economic mass is to increase its population to create a sustainable internal economy. Calls for a larger population are not new and resurface regularly; for example, a report (NZIER 2012) recommends a population of some 15 million by 2050. Under current conditions, 6 million is seen as more likely, noting that this growth rate is double that of the Nordic countries. New Zealand has also had a long tradition of increasing its population by immigration, predominantly from Europe and particularly the United Kingdom, since colonization in the 1830s, with assisted immigration in the 1890s and again after the

Second World War. More recently, successive governments have loosened immigration requirements, encouraging high-net-worth immigrants, many from China. However, immigration is politically controversial and so has not been promoted explicitly as a strategy.

A second way to increase its size has been to break down export barriers for New Zealand produce in order to create larger and more efficient markets through and beyond its political borders. The preference has been to work under the umbrella of supranational organizations, notably GATT and subsequently the World Trade Organization (WTO), particularly through the Doha Round. However, the protracted nature of these negotiations underlines the need to seek simultaneously bilateral and multilateral free trade agreements (FTAs). So far, some nine FTAs have been made, with another ten under negotiation, including the Trans-Pacific Partnership involving 12 Asia Pacific countries. These have potentially large impacts; the ASEAN–Australia–New Zealand FTA that came into force for all parties in 2012, covering all sectors, goods, services, investment and intellectual property, encompasses over 620 million people, comparable to the EU, with a combined GDP of US$2.3 trillion. This FTA is seen as a key building block in New Zealand's developing relationship with South-east Asia and commitment to greater regional integration.

However, the most significant effort that has been made to expand virtual size is economic and trade relationships with Australia, building on Australia's proximity and size, as well as historical and cultural connections. This relationship is based on a comprehensive set of agreements deepening economic integration, collectively known as closer economic relations (CER), built on successive agreements initiated with the 1966 New Zealand Australia Free Trade Agreement. Economic integration through free trade and services was achieved by 1990, and subsequent efforts have sought deeper integration through harmonization, coordination and mutual recognition of policies, laws and regulatory regimes. The countries eliminated most tariff and quantitative restrictions on each other's imports by the early 1990s and opened their labour markets to each other. Since then, policy coordination has extended to liberalization of services, opening of government procurement, a mutual recognition scheme for goods and professional qualifications, elimination of anti-dumping and countervailing measures, and harmonization of business and tax laws. The 2013 Investment Protocol establishes the most comprehensive bilateral free trade agreement in the world (Leslie and Elijah 2012).

New Zealand has taken a dual approach to international relations, seeking security from supranational associations and organizations, but also seeking to promote international economic conditions compatible with its own open economy. Its stance, again, has been to increase its virtual size: seeking protection from aligning interests with international bodies, especially the United Nations, and through open access to other markets. The two interests are not always exclusive, with some overlapping.

New Zealand has been acutely aware of its vulnerability as a small state and has sought umbrella protection. It was part of the British Empire, but after the Second World War it looked increasingly wider, to the United States and Australia, for defence. It was and remains a strong supporter of and participant within multi-national organizations, especially within the auspices of the United Nations institutional framework. It was, up until the Second World War, one of the few supporters of the League of Nations and in 1945 took a strong founding position for the United Nations. It has also taken a seat on the Security Council four times, most recently in October 2014, following a ten-year campaign.

It has championed an independent foreign policy, including a long-standing campaign beginning in the 1970s against nuclear bomb testing in the Pacific that pitted it directly against France. The 1980s Labour government that introduced neoliberal reform (see below) also ran a very independent foreign policy, refusing to allow American nuclear-powered or nuclear-armed boats into New Zealand, which effectively ended the ANZUS Treaty, souring relations between the two countries for two decades.

Foreign security policy, while seeking distinct diplomatic goals, has also been co-opted for economic purposes. Britain's announcement that it was seeking to join the EEC in 1961 was greeted with dismay in New Zealand, given that the EEC's common agricultural policy effectively excluded outside markets. It led to a decade of lobbying the United Kingdom and EEC, leading to the 1971 Luxembourg agreement to stage agricultural tariff exemptions on New Zealand's butter, cheese and lamb trades into the EEC as part of the UK membership agreement. The negotiations gained New Zealand the most agricultural tariff concessions of any country exporting into the EU. Even New Zealand's 2014 election to the UN Security Council shows overlapping interests: the prime minister, John Key, stated:

> from a more selfish point of view, sitting on the council has you sitting at the big table with the big players. It does give you a chance to advance your interests, talk to countries about relationships in the trade and economic area and so on, but we also think we can help New Zealand's interests as well. (Young and Trevett 2014)

ADAPTATION STRATEGIES

While seeking to modify exogenous forces acting on New Zealand, successive governments have sought to modify domestic conditions to adapt to these forces. New Zealand has been described as having had three policy revolutions over the last 150 years, each redefining the role of the state (Bollard et al. 1996). The first, dating to the 1890s, can be seen to set the groundwork for state involvement in the economy and leads through to the second policy revolution, the formation of the welfare state in 1938, which survived until the market competition revolution in the 1980s. It is this third revolution, from corporatist to market competition economy, that provides insights into Keating's hypothesis for how small states strategize to reduce their vulnerabilities in a global economy.

The Corporatist State 1938–1984

New Zealand from 1938 to 1984 was marked by the consolidation and expansion of the welfare state within a mixed economy and was consistent with Katzenstein's (1985) corporatist model. State intervention was predicated on public acceptance of large-scale government participation in the economy to deliver social goals in an egalitarian society and to buffer the economy from exogenous shocks. Policies evolved over time, but by the 1970s privileged the pastoral sector as the dominant foreign exchange earner, while protecting local industry producing import substitutes through high import tariffs and licensing. Policies also promoted full employment and a social wage, negotiated between the government, and employer and union peak bodies. Union membership was compulsory, and there was a strong reliance within government on bureaucratic procedures to avoid politicization of the public sector, as had happened in earlier times. The state invested heavily in road construction and energy infrastructure, as well as providing most services. Until the mid-1960s, this economic approach seemed highly successful; New Zealanders enjoyed one of the highest standards of living in the world, underpinned by strong international demand for post-war food and fibre.

A few calls made to broaden the economy and promote industrialization in the 1950s and 1960s (e.g. Sutch 1966) were ignored. Rather, successive governments were conservative within the welfare state framework, favouring gradualist rather than step changes, so that by the 1970s New Zealand had 'a market economy where markets are seldom permitted to operate efficiently, together with a centrally-planned economy without a central plan. The allocation of resources is to a large extent determined neither by market mechanisms nor government decision, but by historical patterns fossilised in institutional procedures' (McLean 1978, pp. 14–15). However, the economy was increasingly pressured by changing international conditions. By the late 1960s demand for primary produce had dropped, and in the 1970s the country was hit by the oil shocks, and then reduced exports to the UK when the latter joined the EEC, leading to even more intervention in response.

The corporatist model reached its nadir with Prime Minister Muldoon's 1975–1984 National government's increasingly desperate measures to bulwark the status quo. It increased the scope and size of agricultural subsidies to pastoral farming and export meat processors to buffer market volatility. The underlying assumption, or hope, was that commodity prices would rebound, rather than continue to slump as a result of changing consumption patterns and increasing production. The government also embarked on major industrial development with its 'Think Big' energy and petroleum conversion projects, seeking to industrialize the country and reduce dependency on overseas oil. Finally, in desperation, the government imposed a three-year wage and price freeze, and sought to regulate bank interest rates. The result was a foreign exchange crisis and the near bankruptcy of the country. In a snap election in 1984, the nominally conservative National government was replaced in a landslide election by the traditionally social-democratic Labour Party. The corporatist experiment had run its course and collapsed.

The Market Competition Revolution 1984–1993

The third revolution was the market-liberal revolution that sought to roll back the state between 1984 and 1993 (Chapman and Duncan 2007). This period was remarkable for the scope and extent of changes imposed by successive centre-left and centre-right parties that liberalized the economy. The period ended with the general referendum supporting changing the parliamentary electoral system, which sent a strong message from the electorate saying it had had enough radical change by either political party.

This revolution can be seen to have had two phases, each drawing on different theories, both implemented in response to a crisis. The first part of the revolution was triggered by a foreign exchange crisis necessitating a sudden devaluation of the New Zealand dollar as soon as the 1984 Labour government was elected. But underlying this was long-term failure to address structural problems, viewed by the Treasury as the unwillingness to adjust to changing external conditions, which would require real relative income loss and a dramatic increase in unemployment (Treasury [New Zealand] 1984, p. 104).

In the first phase, the incoming 1984 government's first action, within days of coming into power, was to devalue the New Zealand dollar by 20 per cent, followed by free-floating the currency to stop further currency speculation. Other reforms then quickly followed, largely informed by New Institutional Economics theory (Scott et al. 1990; Boston 1991;

Scott 2001), which sought to open the state sector to market competition and reduce its role within the economy. The changes were many and comprehensive. All agricultural subsidies were removed, and state-owned industries were moved to arm's-length distance from political control, operating as profit-seeking state-owned enterprises (SOEs). The Bank of New Zealand, nationalized in 1944, was partially privatized (the government retaining a 51 per cent shareholding), along with the national airline, Air New Zealand. The public sector was reformed and local government radically reorganized, informed by New Public Management (NPM) theory, of a particularly purist and coherent ilk (Hood 1991), and the taxation system was simplified and broadened. Economic institutions were depoliticized and economic information made publicly available. For example, the Reserve Bank moved to an arm's-length distance, with a statutory responsibility to maintain stability in the general level of prices, while the Fiscal Responsibility Act (now part of the Public Finance Act) required the Treasury to disclose the fiscal risks facing an incoming government prior to every election.

While there was a recognition that many of the changes were necessary, the costs were felt by many to be too high, resulting in increasing public and political resistance to further change; efforts by the minister of finance to introduce a flat tax regime precipitated his dismissal. Dissent within the Labour Party and the government, and public opposition to change, finally led to the Labour government losing in a landslide victory to the centre-right National Party in the 1990 elections. A Royal Commission on Social Policy (Royal Commission on Social Policy and Ivor Richardson 1988) was established to address these concerns in 1986, partly to address the Labour Party left wing. The controversial findings were buried within four large volumes with little cogency, enabling it to be easily criticized or dismissed (one minister used his copy as a door-stop). As a result, the comprehensive and integrated market approach remained intellectually little challenged.

The second wave of reforms introduced by the incoming 1990 National government were more ideologically driven, informed by von Hayekian neoliberalism, and they cut deeper into the welfare state. The minister of finance from 1990 to 1993 who drove them explained her reasoning: '[f]or me [reform] was a matter of conviction; for [the prime minister] a matter of necessity [that drew on a] conviction of the benefits of liberty in all its forms; personal, economic, social and political' (Richardson 2008, p. 142).

They, too, were triggered by crisis. The incoming government had campaigned on 'a fairer society', promising to soften the impacts of the Labour government. But, in coming into office, it had immediately to bail out the Bank of New Zealand, which serviced some 40 per cent of

New Zealand businesses, with NZ$380 million to avoid collapse, while the Treasury predicted a ballooning public deficit. As with the previous Labour government, market-liberal Cabinet ministers, informed by Treasury officials, promised solutions to their colleagues to the crisis that committed them to further reform. Accordingly, the finance minister in her 1991 'Mother of all Budgets' was able to set in motion a programme to privatize monopoly services, including the railways, Air New Zealand, the Bank of New Zealand, the major telecommunications network operator and part of the electricity generation infrastructure. Public hospitals, the bastion of the welfare state with their free medical treatment, were redefined as Crown health enterprises and expected to make a profit. Welfare benefits were slashed. Organized labour was directly targeted with legislation that abolished the special legal status and monopoly representation rights of unions, and facilitated worksite rather than national industry sector collective bargaining.

These reforms, too, were seen as a bridge too far, with hospitals being expected to return profits regarded as particularly offensive by a public that still valued the welfare state. The 1993 election book-ends the revolution. The National government returned with a single-seat majority, while a national referendum on the electoral system supported a change from the Westminster first-past-the-post system. As a consequence, the prime minister replaced his libertarian minister of finance with a moderate, while the next year New Zealand adopted a new electoral system, the German-style mixed member (MMP) representation.

From 1993 to the Present

The new electoral system, first used in the 1996 elections, together with an enlarged Parliament, has delivered coalition governments ever since, succeeding the former two-party winner-take-all government. Since 1993, centre-left and centre-right coalition governments have all been pragmatic and increasingly opinion-poll-driven in their policy. They have focused on providing stability and staying in power, with subsequent Labour and National governments both enjoying three-term offices. Significantly, even the 1999–2008 Labour coalition government did not seek to challenge fundamentally the market competition model that is now entrenched within the economy and public thinking. Rather it sought to mitigate the excesses of the labour market legislation, while partially or fully renationalizing failing former state-owned enterprises – Air New Zealand and the railways (2008) – and establishing a new state-owned bank (2002) to try to break the Australian banking cartel (the government took up 80 per cent ownership of Air New Zealand in 2001, but subsequently sold down its share to 53 per cent in 2013). The government also supported a mega-merger of the remaining dairy cooperative companies to create 'New Zealand's Nokia', Fonterra, to drive economic growth. Fonterra is now the world's sixth-largest global dairy firm (the next largest, Arla Foods, is a joint Danish–Swedish cooperative company).

They also have sought to mitigate the more extreme elements of the public sector reforms, catalysed by a guest review (Schick 1996) that was highly critical of many NPM innovations. It recommended tightening up and focusing the public sector, as well as promoting collective employment agreements, and state assistance to encourage innovation and regional development, albeit in small amounts. It also called for more central direction and collaborative capacity. Successive governments also sought answers to how to make the economy more successful – for example, Michael E. Porter was invited to develop a national strategy (Crocombe et al. 1991) – but these were never implemented with any great enthusiasm.

A change to a centre-right government coincided with the 2008 global financial crisis. As a consequence of these policies and general fiscal prudence, the government was able to generate a trade surplus before the crisis that enabled it to buffer the immediate impacts of the GFC, while a tightly managed banking sector minimized the impact of the toxic loans that bedevilled other countries. The smaller and less regulated secondary finance companies did however collapse, taking with them private wealth and government bail-outs. The centre-right coalition, re-elected in 2011 and again in 2014, has sought in part to roll the state back through further privatizations of electricity generating companies, but has also provided finance to the private sector for major infrastructure. It has also sought to further redefine the welfare state within a neoliberal framework, for example by redefining welfare beneficiaries as 'clients' and encouraging service provision by the private and voluntary sectors.

The different governments' policies post-revolution are, however, more a matter of degree than substantive change. As Chapman and Duncan (2007) argue, even the Clark Labour-led government showed itself as fiscally conservative and unwilling to dismantle monetary and other NPM/neoliberal reforms, rather softening the impact through introducing socially progressive, centre-left policy initiatives. This government was seen to adopt elements of the Third Way politics of Tony Blair's British Labour government, which ameliorated the excesses of neoliberalism while retaining the overarching neoliberal framework, albeit laced with political pragmatism. A notable example was attempts to address child poverty. The Clark Labour-led government introduced an in-work tax credit package, 'Working for Families' (St John and Dale 2012). This redefined social benefits to assist low-income earners with families, and incentivize the unemployed to work. That government then expanded the scheme to cover many middle-class working families. In the 2008 election campaign, the National Party 'swallowed the dead rat', promising no change to the policy in order to remove it expeditiously from election policy debate – political pragmatism over ideology.

Accordingly, government strategy now lacks theoretical coherence, with both Labour and National governments adopting expediency without abandoning core market competition principles. Subsequent government has reverted to gradualist change, with a roll-back of what were widely seen as some of the more extreme positions adopted during the market-liberal revolution.

Force majeure also helped maintain the status quo. The 2010 and 2011 Canterbury earthquakes devastated the centre of Christchurch, a 450 000 population city. Nearly half of all central business district buildings and some 10 000 homes were destroyed or required demolition, with over 100 000 homes, and university and school buildings damaged. The total rebuild cost, assessed at NZ$40 billion (€25 billion) or 17 per cent of GDP, is injecting overseas reinsurance money and forcing the government to commit about NZ$15 billion to the domestic economy. The consequence is that, quite apart from any government strategy, the economy has been driven during and since the global financial crisis by high dairy export prices driven by the Chinese market, and the Canterbury rebuild. The resulting robust economy, with low unemployment and about 3 per cent annual growth, makes it quite different compared to other small states' responses to the GFC. Certainly, there is an underlying recognition that strong institutions prevented wholesale disaster from the GFC, but that current economic health relies on a Keynesian-style recovery from a major natural disaster and, continuing in a historical style, a narrow-based commodity export economy. Both elements make the economy vulnerable: the Christchurch rebuild is projected to peak in 2016, while the Chinese-driven price for milk solids halved in 2014.

CONSEQUENCES AND OPPORTUNITIES

The New Zealand experience provides an almost textbook example of the transition from Katzenstein's (1985) corporatist model to Keating's market competition model. Ironically, Katzenstein's model was being comprehensively demolished in New Zealand just as his book describing it was published. New Zealand's isolation means that change has been less mediated by other states and associations. However, the experience is perhaps more nuanced than Keating's model suggests. It suggests small states do have the ability to modify, at least at the margins, some of the exogenous forces that drive change in small states and that different trajectories are possible within a strategy.

The Treasury's advice promoting a market competition model to successive governments was clearly framed within the context of managing a small state economy. For example, the Treasury (1990) in its advice to the incoming 1990 government explicitly ruled out a return to protectionism or government financing a programme of heavy industrialization, while noting that traditional agricultural commodities trade was unlikely to provide any catalyst for growth. Rather it advised the government to remove barriers to growth and international competitiveness, opening the whole economy to competition to provide the necessary incentives to improve productivity, invest in new techniques and upgrade skills and quality. New Zealand's living standards should be judged, the Treasury advised, by the country's 'ability to compete internationally and respond rapidly and efficiently to changes in the world environment' (Treasury [New Zealand] 1990, p. 38). It nowhere advanced an alternative social investment strategy.

The transition from corporatist to market competition economy was rapid and comprehensive. It was perhaps also inevitable. As James (1987) notes, pressure was mounting within the previous 1975–1984 Muldoon government for change, albeit gradual rather than revolutionary change. In addition, 1984 marked a changing of the guard: previous governments had consisted largely of politicians who had experienced the 1930s Great Depression and the Second World War. They were necessarily cautious. The Labour and succeeding National governments consisted of politicians born after the war, who were part of the 'Vietnam generation', and impatient with and intolerant of existing conditions (James 1987). Chapman and Duncan (Chapman and Duncan 2007; Duncan and Chapman 2010) similarly observe that there was general acceptance among political and career civil-service decision-makers that the reforms were necessary at the time. Their memories of the Muldoon government's failed corporatist experiment must also have made them chary of interventionist governments. However, Boston and Eichbaum (2014) argue that the neoliberal revolution was only half-complete, as is the constitutional counter-push against it, left unfinished as intellectual projects. They note that neoliberalism still enjoys a degree of currency within political and intellectual discourse, with a robust epistemic community and policy community continuing to support it. The reform agenda had multiple aims; while some were to deliver better economic outcomes, another was much more ideological – to establish a neoliberal orthodoxy. Thus the reforms were only partly about addressing small state vulnerability through structural change. They were also about seeking a shift in the national psyche.

The move from mixed economy administered by fiat to market competition economy had a major impact on structural conditions, and the short-term costs were high and the impacts deep. Deregulation led to loss in the import substitute manufacturing sector, primarily owing to uncompetitive practices developed behind import restrictions, and the outsourcing of unskilled and semi-skilled work to Asia. Agriculture had been supported through increasing government subsidies throughout the 1970s and early 1980s to guarantee minimum prices for sheep. The 1984 Labour government's removal of all subsidies caused massive rural dislocation. However, the sector subsequently responded to clear market signals, significantly altering the landscape as well as economy. In the 20 years between 1992 and 2012, the national sheep flock decreased by 41 per cent (53 million to 31 million), replaced largely by dairy cattle, which increased by 86 per cent (3.5 million to 6.4 million), and grapes for the maturing wine industry (6000–36 000 hectares in productive vines). Entire Marlborough valleys where sheep had grazed for over a century are now completely converted to vineyards as part of a wine-making industry that had hardly existed. The dry South Island plains, home of Canterbury lamb, have largely been converted to irrigated dairy farms. The primary sectors' peak organizations are now adamant that they do not want a return to subsidies and join government officials promoting agricultural subsidy removal in international trade negotiation. Nevertheless, there has largely been a substitute of one commodity product by another; fundamental structural change has not happened.

The market competition strategy completely overturned the labour market. The unemployment rate rose from 4 per cent in the early 1980s to over 10 per cent in the early 1990s, before returning to around 4 per cent for most of the last decade. It now stands above 6 per cent. Organized labour was also impacted. Some 54 per cent of wage and salary earners belonged to unions in 1986, dropping to 24 per cent by 1995. Today union membership represents 17 per cent of the total employed force. Only a few sectors remain unionized, and these all are in the public sector.

Under the previous regime, industrial stoppage rates were persistently high compared to those of other OECD countries. Since the 1990s stoppages have been infrequent, from over 200 stoppages a year in the 1980s to fewer than 20 a year in recent times. The reduction in strikes matches reduction in union membership and density, resulting from employment legislation, but also mirroring the decline in the manufacturing and processing sectors, which traditionally have had the highest level of disputes (Thickett 2002).

The reforms introduced by successive governments were seen to erode the welfare state foundations. Nevertheless, underlying welfare state expectations remain, for free public health care, unemployment and social welfare assistance, and a state superannuation for the elderly. There has also been the rise of a dual economy, with large growth in the largest city, Auckland, but relatively static populations and economic conditions for the rest of the country. This has led to housing shortages and escalating living costs in Auckland, where a quarter of the population now live. Most other regions' economies are static.

It can be argued that adopting the market competition strategy was successful or, at least, not unsuccessful. As early as 1990 the Treasury (1990) estimated that economic reforms throughout the 1980s had contributed to labour productivity growing in the preceding five years by as much as it had in the previous 20 years. And certainly the GFC had very little substantive impact on the national economy compared to other countries, continuing to grow about 3–4 per cent annually, with around 6 per cent unemployment. Critics of its performance, however, would point to an element of serendipity; economic growth is driven largely by the Christchurch earthquake rebuild and a strong Chinese demand for dairy products, neither sustainable. They would also point to its slip from a top ten OECD economic ranking until 1975 to around 20 in the 1980s, a ranking that persists until today, and less than spectacular growth over that period. Indeed, the 2003 OECD economic survey identified the New Zealand paradox that still remains: '[T]he mystery is why a country that seems close to best practice in most of the policies that are regarded as the key drivers of growth is nevertheless just an average performer' (OECD 2003).

The social costs and wisdom of radically adopting this model have long been questioned (e.g. Kelsey 1995, 2002), but more recently the social costs have begun to be more publicly questioned, highlighted in the 2014 general election as 'child poverty'. These concerns have started to gain political salience that even the returning centre-right coalition government has had to acknowledge.

Perhaps more critically, the economy is still largely reliant on a narrow-structured commodity base. This has increased the country's vulnerability to future shocks, whether a slowing or collapse of the Chinese economy, or increased supply of milk on to the world market. Already European producers are increasing dairy production and are intending to expand further (e.g. National Dairy Council [Ireland] 2013). Further, the future of the sector within New Zealand is dominated by one firm, Fonterra, making it indeed 'New Zealand's Nokia'. The call to diversify the economy to produce more than a narrow portfolio of primary commodity products is not new and has been made since at least the 1950s. Attempts have been made, such as the government-sponsored 'Porter Project' (Crocombe et al. 1991), drawing on Michael E. Porter's notion of competitive advantage.

This was in fact little different in its analysis from that made some 30 years previously by Bill Sutch (1966). But there has been little serious long-term commitment to or implementation of any such strategic thinking. Even the market-liberal think tank the New Zealand Institute has identified the lack of commitment to implementing strategy (Boven et al. 2010).

Commentators such as McCann and Skilling, who both spent time in New Zealand, suggest that New Zealand has become policy moribund, or at least reactive, failing to recognize and respond to changes in the nature of globalization over the last 20 years. They and other commentators argue that the reforms undertaken in the 1980s and 1990s are now no longer sufficient for the twenty-first-century globalized economy. McCann (2009) suggests that new globalization prioritizes information, and this has changed the economic order, re-establishing the criticality of distance, and places New Zealand at the periphery, marginalized by its distance and lack of critical mass. For him, solutions are less about increasing actual size, and more about seeking a networked and linked internal market and society so that New Zealand performs as a single city-state. He argues that, linked, the country would then gain a critical mass that reduces the friction of distance within it. This view is consistent with OECD regional development research (OECD 2012) that argues for greater investment in regions to grow national wealth. This requires a more hands-on approach to strategically planning within the country. Skilling (2012b) simply argues that there is no such thing as domestic policy anymore; everything is global. These views suggest that New Zealand's options for reducing its vulnerability are indeed limited.

SMALL STATES IN A BIG WORLD

New Zealand's experience suggests that small states do not adopt any single strategy, but rather a suite of strategies with overlapping interests and drivers that collectively situate them to survive in a larger hostile world and indeed among internal challenges. In New Zealand's case, successive centre-left and centre-right governments have adopted broadly similar policy suites of ensuring fiscal prudence and internationally competitive economies on the one hand and big friends internationally on the other. The differences are more of degree than direction. New Zealand's experience over the last 30 years is consistent with Keating's proposition for transition from corporatist to market competition state. It recognized that, in the post-war period, security came from size or in the shelter of a large state for security from aggressors, and security for continued trade with protecting states. The welfare state (which in New Zealand preceded this epoch, reaching back to the nineteenth century) established the state itself as the means for providing security, and it sought its own version of the EU with closer economic relations with Australia.

It is more nuanced, however, as New Zealand adopted dual and somewhat independent strategies, seeking to moderate exogenous forces through international institutions while adapting internally to these conditions. Other small states have also adopted dual strategies, and New Zealand is not alone in expanding its sphere of control under international law, such as the EEZ, to strengthen its resource base. Norway and Scotland both were able to increase their economic wealth from developing natural gas under their marine EEZs, while Denmark is now claiming Arctic seabed rights of some 900 000 square kilometres above Greenland up to the North Pole for its physical resources (see Government of Denmark et al. 2011).

The EEZ claim is only one example of a range of international institutions that small states rely on in the twenty-first century. They are also relying on others, such as the WTO for resolving trade disputes. There is an implicit expectation that large powers will accept and respect the legitimacy of these supranational organizations. But strong and active support for the United Nations, as well as other institutions such as the WTO, does not preclude bilateral actions, for example FTAs and regional defence, reflecting a wariness born of the historical experience of small states relying on any single large nation to support their interests. And, like European small states, New Zealand seeks economic integration that may develop further. In particular CER, as Leslie and Elijah (2012) argue, provides trans-Tasman 'behind borders' integration comparable to European integration, 'deepening' regional integration. However, the institutions underpinning this relationship lack the visibility of the EU.

But the intersection of foreign and economic policy is not necessarily so straightforward. An underlying tension remains, as New Zealand's trade and security interests are not necessarily aligned, creating a new paradox. New Zealand is caught between two super-powers with potentially conflicting interests in the Pacific Ocean, relying on China for economic growth, but on the USA for security (Mapp 2014). At the same time, its experience is that its domestic arrangements must inevitably recognize the wider world order, though how it recognizes it is more open. The early 1980s provide compelling evidence of protectionism. Again, its realization is nuanced. The trajectory of the later 1980s, and its argument that its neoliberal turn was inevitable, seems less deterministic. Pressure for a freer market had been building over the previous decade, with proponents on both sides of Parliament, so that either political party could have introduced market reforms. The argument that economic circumstances in July 1984 were so dire that there was no alternative may have had some truth, but the different rationalities employed in 1984 and 1990 indicate flexibility in approach, so the policy was not entirely path dependent.

The ability to manage change may reflect individual countries' institutional arrangements. And there was wide public dissatisfaction with the former corporatist strategy that facilitated ongoing change – the Labour government was returned in 1987 after embarking on its first tranche of reform. However, the New Zealand experience runs counter to Keating's assertion that the market-liberal turn was successful in the Baltic states given their need to transition to market economies and the absence of strong unions, but difficult to replicate in mature European welfare states where public services are seen as a permanent social gain and where trade unions are part of national life (see Chapter 1). New Zealand had a very strong union membership, and the welfare state was strongly ingrained in the national psyche.

While the economic crises had catalysed rapid change, the speed and comprehensiveness were achieved where the institutional arrangements, the 'perfect Westminster majoritarian democracy' that Lijphart described in 1984 (pp. 16–19), provided a mechanism for railroading unpopular radical change, triggered by a crisis. The public rejection of this 'elected dictatorship' that the unicameral, two-party Westminster system produces subsequently led to a change of voting system that essentially hobbled further significant change. If, for example, Skilling is right and the market competition model is indeed inappropriate for a globalized world, New Zealand faces real problems. The mechanism that enabled change to a market competition model no longer exists to enable a change strategy. At present, an apparently successful economy brooks little domestic enthusiasm for significant change. Additionally, New Zealand's greater level of independence, compared to European small states that are largely integrated into a single large economy and defence pacts, means it has little direct external pressure for change. This reading suggests a strategy lock that will be hard to open. New Zealand's independence, isolation and geographic remoteness mean, metaphorically and literally, that New Zealand is a small state alone in a stormy sea.

11. Small states and national elites in a neoliberal era

Anton Steen

INTRODUCTION

Neoliberal economic reforms have rightly been seen as elite-driven and part of a broader internationalization process in which rapidly changing environments especially affected small countries with open economies. From the middle of the 1980s, neoliberal ideas profoundly affected established democracies where the traditional welfare state came under pressure, and from the early 1990s such ideas also became crucial for the transformations of post-communist states into market economies. It is well documented how post-communist governments adapted national policies to international recommendations for state deregulation and international competition despite economic hardship for the general population. However, there is little knowledge about to what extent the broader elite supported the reforms and how country context and external shocks influenced their attitudes. The focus here is on how various elite segments responded to neoliberal ideas in the small Baltic states of Estonia, Latvia and Lithuania, as well as in Norway, and why there are considerable differences in orientations among their elites.

The economic successes of small states have been explained by unitary national politics founded on elite consensus and formalized social partnership (Katzenstein 1985). In order to meet the challenges of insecure international environments and globalized markets, a certain level of national solidarity and harmony on basic policy issues has to be in place. National identity formation becomes vital to political compromise and collective action, and takes on many practices like formally organized venues, but also informal interaction among the elite and more diffuse configurations based on shared basic beliefs, which are the focal point here. Smaller countries more than larger countries are vulnerable to international pressure, both economically and militarily, and therefore exposed to considerable uncertainties. In order to cope with such uncertainties and strategically respond to changes in their environments, Katzenstein (1985) argues, their elites need to be more cohesive than those in larger countries, not only in population size, but also in the political context. As they are newly independent from the former Soviet Union and have large Russian minorities, the Baltic countries are different from Norway.[1] Coming after a long period of economic growth, the sudden financial crisis of 2008 hit the Baltic states harder than most countries, and one interesting question is if such a shock had any significance for the elites' beliefs in neoliberalism. Following Katzenstein, a national crisis will motivate converging orientations, especially in small nations. Do the different sizes, historical experiences and varying environments under which the elites operate have an impact on their belief patterns?

SMALL STATES AND ELITE ALIGNMENTS

Elite alignments may be ingrained in nationally embedded consensus-making institutions like corporatist arrangements or in less structured networks of political actors as an inter-subjective creation of meanings emerging from common experiences. In pluralist democracies, elites are competing for power while also sharing basic common values and respecting the rules of the political game. Historically, such 'consensually integrated elites' have been the source for change of the political and economic regime in East European countries (Higley and Lengyel 2000) and also a necessary condition for more gradual democratic and economic reforms in Western countries (Higley and Burton 2006).

Elite orientations emerge at two levels (Putnam 1973). The first level is associated with fundamental values in society such as 'justice', with an offshoot where a preference for an equal income distribution is characteristic. The other level concerns how such values condition political action or, in other words, policy implications for the functions of the state and which instruments are applied with respect to regulation, the achievement of social equality, and private property. Sabatier and Jenkins-Smith (1999) adopt the same view when they explain stability and change in specific policy areas. Their basic unit is the 'policy subsystem' comprising established elite networks which are united on the basis of fundamental values and interests. The values of a subsystem can come to completely dominate a policy sector, but different elite subsystems may also compete with each other for control.

The states studied here have in common that they are small, but they differ as to national circumstances like historical experiences, population size, demography and uncertainties related to national security. In the Baltic states, economic reforms became entangled with safeguarding independence after seceding from the USSR in 1991 (Bohle and Greskovits 2012), while in Norway neoliberalism was a question of making the welfare state more efficient, rather than of national security. Especially in newly independent countries like the Baltics with large minority groups, elites will try to reduce military insecurity by building a strong state for the titular nation and combining nation-state building with neoliberalist economic policies.

According to the small state thesis, a fairly high level of consensus is expected across elite groups, and the smaller the state and the greater the insecurity the more cohesive the elites; shocks in the international environment are particularly conducive to national elite cohesion. Three propositions follow from this argument. First, the Baltic elites are more united and pro-state than the Norwegian elites, and one may further expect that the Estonian and Latvian elites will express more robust and cohesive support for a strong state than the elites in Lithuania, where the issue of a large Russian minority is less salient. In the smallest country, Estonia, where there is a particularly tense nationality situation, elite unity will be most visible.

Critics have referred to the conception of 'the neoliberal Utopia', which, according to Bourdieu (1998), has a specific relation to individuals with power and influence. Bourdieu argues that the leaders of business organizations have a direct financial interest in a neoliberal economic programme. Therefore, the second proposition is that to the extent the elites are split in a given country the dominant divide is likely to be between the business leaders and the political-administrative segment, since the former are more likely to benefit from state deregulation. Leaders of business enterprises have often been mentioned as a key lobby group for market solutions, and one may expect that this group has both clearer neoliberal attitudes than other groups and similar orientations across national boundaries. The third proposition is that convergence across elite groups is strengthened after international shocks like the 2008 financial crisis, which was felt particularly intensely in the Baltics. One suggestion is that in these states scepticism towards neoliberal ideas will increase not only in the political and administrative sectors but also among business leaders.

THE CHALLENGE OF NEOLIBERALISM – WEST AND EAST

Neoliberalism can be defined in several ways. Initially, the ideal is seen as a displacement of the politico-economic centre of gravity from the state to the market. The core tenet of neoliberalism is that state functions should be restricted and subjected to the market mechanism to the greatest possible degree. Market transactions result in growth, and income differences stimulate competition and more favourable use of societal resources in the long run. One consequence is that the state boundaries might be too restricted so that the market may function optimally. Free movement of capital is a major factor in what is referred to as 'globalization'. The reform ideas originated in the research community in the United States, and the economic models based on these ideals were diffused to national political and economic elites by powerful organizations such as the IMF, the World Bank and OECD (D.S. Jones 2012).

NEOLIBERALISM UNDER POST-SOCIAL DEMOCRACY

From the end of the Second World War until the 1970s, Norway can be characterized as a social democratic state where the Labour Party formed the political fundament. Promotion of economic growth was exercised through a gradual liberalization of trade policy, but was balanced by a Keynesian budgetary policy, national financial control, equalization of incomes, a large public sector and universal welfare arrangements. During the 1970s, an economic backlash occurred, with excessive pressure on the public sector, which called for management reforms. The wealth arising from oil and gas enabled Norway to defer any reforms far longer than most other Western countries, and management by objectives in the public sector gradually transformed the character of the social democratic state. The social democratic Labour Party lost its hegemonic position and simultaneously changed its political profile away from traditional state regulation in order to appeal to a new and broader group of voters.

An important and characteristic change, executed by a non-socialist government in the mid-1980s, was the liberalization of capital movements across national boundaries, in keeping with an international trend headed by the more neoliberal governments in the UK and the United States. Neoliberal ideas were widely accepted by political and other elites, including among the leadership in the Scandinavian social democratic parties. Klitgaard (2007) argues that the paradoxical pro-market orientation of leading social democrats is explained by the universal welfare state as a means for political elites to stay in power – a relation that needed to be reshaped owing to changing economic conditions. In many countries this resulted in deregulation and privatization in a number of important areas, and the public administration apparatus became largely subject to business principles under the label of 'New Public Management'. In Scandinavia, however, despite management reforms, public services associated with welfare were largely protected.

The economic liberalization of the 1990s was succeeded in Norway by a number of reforms within the public sector. State property was partly or wholly privatized, public utilities were opened to competition, state corporations were reorganized as limited companies (with or without the state as a shareholder), and new management techniques were introduced into the public sector based on the principles applied in the private sector. The political argument was that the population – as consumers – would benefit from increased competition in the availability of services while at the same time a reduced state would be able to concentrate on superior welfare objectives, the general framework of capitalism and the instruments of control.

In Norway, some deregulation and privatization of state tasks have taken place, while the basic corporatist institutions and social partnership were mainly preserved. The elite's main context is an open economy and an ambitious welfare state with a rather homogeneous population. Also here the issue of national independence, and in particular relations with the EU, has been high on the political agenda, and a distrustful population rejected EU membership in two referenda, in sharp contrast to the predominantly positive elite. Consequently, here one would expect widespread neoliberal attitudes but also a more divided elite.

NEOLIBERALISM UNDER POST-SOCIALISM

The rapid termination of state planning and regulation of details, and the desire to emulate Western market economies were the foundation of the post-communist elites' programme for changing society. The cessation of state-controlled economies and the establishment of new democratic institutions were not merely an expression of political freedom, but equally linked to the hope of material growth and welfare. In many post-socialist countries, neoliberal Western advisers persuaded the core elite to accelerate the transformation process, fearing that repeated compromises would dilute the reforms (Gustafson 1999). Particularly in Russia, a closed network around the president came to operate as an exclusive 'clan'. Åslund and Dmitriev (1999) explain the lack of economic success in Russia by such 'rent-seekers' drawing the advantage from the fact that the market was not functioning and providing the opportunity for private monopolies.

In the Baltic countries, the situation was different in that from the mid-1990s the international community, including the EU, the Council of

Europe and NATO, was able to observe how the reforms had developed, both economically and politically. In the first period, however, technocratic 'change teams' were insulated from politics and able to carry out economic 'shock therapy'. But this group of Western-oriented technocratic liberals with direct access to the most central decision makers could not operate in a political vacuum over a long period. Soon, free political elections indicated that, if the reforms were to continue, they had to build upon broader elite coalitions (Nissinen 1999). The positive attitudes held by the elites in the early phase served to stimulate the economic reforms, but, because the social experiences associated with extreme market reforms and cuts in state expenditures had to be borne by large segments of the general population, particularly elderly people, the elites' initial beliefs in radical market solutions became less enthusiastic (Steen 2007). Moreover, large Russian minorities continued to challenge the new nation-states, which responded with a nationalist type of neoliberalist policies, implying considerable state control (Bohle and Greskovits 2012). These authors argue that, 'Due to shared beliefs in the urgency of (re)building their nations, Baltic elites were less constrained by the economic and social costs of radical transformation than was the case in other East Central European Countries' (Bohle and Greskovits 2012, p. 96). In the Baltic states, recently independent from Soviet occupation, the national elites were attracted by the neoliberal ideas of reducing state control and opening their economies mainly as a lever to become integrated into the Western security sphere.

THE DATA

The elite orientations studied here essentially comprise two data sets based on face-to-face questionnaire interviews. The first is a selection of questions posed in the Norwegian Power Elite Study conducted between 1998 and 2003. This survey included a comprehensive study of leadership based on systematic interviews of almost 2000 leaders at different levels in a number of spheres in society including politics, the business sector, defence, the bureaucracy, organizations, research and higher education, the church and cultural life (Gulbrandsen et al. 2002). The interviews were conducted by Statistics Norway in the winter of 2000–2001.

The second data set covers the three Baltic states and uses the same questions as in the Norwegian Power Elite Study, posed in surveys at two points in time. The first survey was in winter 2006–2007 (Estonia), spring 2007 (Latvia) and autumn 2007 (Lithuania), and it was repeated in autumn 2012 (Latvia) and autumn 2012/spring 2013 (Lithuania). The interviews were conducted by the following polling companies: Saar Poll in Estonia, the Baltic Institute of Social Sciences in Latvia, and Baltic Surveys Ltd in Lithuania.

The total number for each Baltic country is approximately 300, and includes the top leaders of eight elite groups, which constitute the major part of the country's institutional leaders, fairly similar to the Norwegian Power Elite Study. In addition to comparing the total elites between the countries, political, administrative and business elites were selected as particularly relevant to neoliberalism, and compared across and within the countries.

THE NATIONAL ELITES – HOW DIFFERENT?

In this section the total national elites are compared between the countries. According to Katzenstein (1985) and Bohle and Greskovits (2012), elites in small states who are exposed to economic uncertainties and threats will exhibit unified orientations. Further, one may expect that elites will generally be attracted by neoliberal ideas propagated by renowned international institutions. Is it possible to identify a transnational convergence of elite attitudes in these small nations traversing post-social democratic and post-communist contexts? Do differences in population size have any effect? And to what extent do external threats have an impact on elite consensus?

The survey questions, first posed to the Norwegian elites, are directly associated with essential features of the neoliberal ideal such as the size of the public sector, state regulation, internationalization and national self-determination. These questions were translated into the respective Baltic languages, and also into Russian where relevant, and in 2006 and 2012 they were included in a more comprehensive survey that the author has been conducting regularly in the Baltic states since 1993–1994 (see Table 11.1).

Concerning regulation of the market – the influence of the state in commercial activity – a majority in all countries consider that such influence should be reduced, but the proportion in Estonia is markedly below the level in the other countries. This is at first glance surprising, because in most areas Estonia is considered to be very neoliberal in its economic policy and leading by example in reforms. However, Estonia's economic 'shock therapy', which had considerable success for economic growth but also negative social consequences for major parts of the population, may have reduced opposition to state regulation. Probably more important is that with little state left there is little to reduce. The most critical attitudes to state regulation of business are found in Latvia and Lithuania, where economic reforms started later. Since the financial crisis, the elites' beliefs in reduced state influence over private business continue to be strong in

Table 11.1   The national elites (percentages agreeing with the statements)

Statements	Norway 2001	Estonia 2006	Latvia 2006 2012/2013	Lithuania 2006 2012
1. 'State influence over private business should be reduced'	65 (n=1520)	56 (n=258)	73 (n=277) 68 (n=228)	75 (n=301) 76 (n=279)
2. 'The state is too powerful'	52 (n=1522)	27 (n=258)	41 (n=271) 35 (n=234)	46 (n=298) 44 (n=278)
3. 'International financial markets are too influential'	61 (n=1501)	61 (n=256)	76 (n=266) 83 (n=229)	63 (n=276) 82 (n=266)
4. 'National self-determination is too weak'	27 (n=1521)	56 (n=261)	58 (n=274) 66 (n=228)	51 (n=298) 61 (n=270)

Notes:
Percentages are of those completely or partially in agreement with the statements.
The combined elite comprise in Norway the following institutions: parliament, administration, the legal professions, private business, state business sectors, NGOs, culture, the mass media and local government. Church leaders and leaders in the defence sector were included in the original Norwegian study but are for comparable purposes excluded here. In the Baltic countries, the elite come from the same institutions as mentioned above (also excluding church and defence).
'No reply' and 'don't know' responses are treated as missing values.
The response rates for the various questions were between 95 and 100 per cent.

Lithuania, while in Latvia they have become somewhat less critical to state influence. A clear majority of the Norwegian elite express beliefs in reducing the state's influence, and in fact express more neoliberal enthusiasm than Estonian leaders although less than those in Latvia and Lithuania.

These differences between the Baltic states are confirmed in the following statement: 'The state is too powerful.' Only 27 per cent of the Estonian elite agree; this is a sharp reduction compared to the previous question related to state regulation of business. Approximately the same reduction of about 30 per cent is found in Latvia and Lithuania. Norway stands out as having the elite most sceptical of the state, with 52 per cent agreeing that the state is too powerful. In summary, in all countries the elites are clearly more sceptical of reducing state power in general than of specifically abolishing regulation in business affairs. For the Baltic states, the dissimilar patterns on statements 1 and 2 may be due to the fact that a nationalist type of neoliberalism emerged in a context of redefining nationhood among the indigenous people, and therefore a majority of the elites support a strong nation-state but not a state involved in economic regulation. This pattern gives support to Bohle and Greskovits (2012) and Kattel and Raudla (2013), who argue that identity politics presupposes a viable and strong state for safeguarding new national political institutions. The attitudes are particularly clear in Estonia but also visible in Latvia, two 'newborn' states with large Russian-speaking minority groups. The Norwegian elite's considerably lower enthusiasm for a strong state and relative closeness to the Lithuanian pattern can be explained by the absence of similar challenges related to large minorities and the nationality issue. Although differences are small, as expected the 2008 economic meltdown resulted in increasing support for the state, especially in Latvia.

INTERNATIONAL MARKETS AND NATIONAL AUTONOMY

When it comes to the power of international financial institutions the majority of the elite in all four countries exhibit critical attitudes. This was the case especially for Latvia in 2006, where 76 per cent said financial markets were too influential, but also in the other countries more than 60 per cent of the elite agreed. A few years later the financial crisis had incited scepticism in more than 80 per cent of respondents in Latvia and Lithuania. A widespread distrust in the financial markets seems to join national elite majorities across borders and is in sharp contrast to one fundamental aspect of neoliberal ideology, the internationalization of the capital market.

The widespread negative attitudes towards the international finance system in the Baltic countries find resonance in the next statement about national self-determination. Here more than 50 per cent consider that national autonomy is too limited, and the percentage increases distinctly after 2008. The Baltic pattern is in sharp contrast with Norway, where only 27 per cent of respondents share this view. One explanation may be the different relationships to the EU. EU membership for the Baltic countries from 2004 implied a significant transfer of authority to international bodies, and can be assumed to have influenced the elites' view of national self-determination. The view that Norway has considerable national self-determination may also be interpreted as an indication that the pro-EU elite regard this as a problem for Norwegian EU membership.

To sum up, support for neoliberal policies of reducing state control is less widespread than expected. While a majority in all countries support economic deregulation, in the Baltic states only a minority want to reduce the power of the state. The Baltic elites tend to be more in favour of a strong state than the Norwegians are. This accentuates the argument of Bohle and Greskovits (2012), who claim that securing national independence with a large Russian minority was feasible only with nationalist policies encouraged by an active state. The issue of international markets and national autonomy rather clearly shows, as argued by Katzenstein (1984), that insecure economic environments necessitate cohesive small state elites and that delegating state power to supranational institutions has consequences for elite concern for national self-determination, as shown in statement 4. The economic meltdown in the Baltic states evidently intensified such concerns.

THE NATIONAL ELITE GROUPS – HOW COHESIVE?

A main feature of a democratic society is pluralist elites who compete for popular support (Dahl 1982). 'Strategic elites' (Keller 1991), however, can establish a 'tight community' where special interests are maintained and encouraged through institutionalized subsystems, for example arrangements of organized sector representation, or, possibly of equal importance, through loose groups consisting of elites in several institutions sharing the same basic orientations (Sabatier and Jenkins-Smith 1999). The focus here is on similarities among the subgroups. Katzenstein (1985, p. 32) sees elite consensus on economic and social policies in established democracies like Norway as 'an ideology of social partnership' not emanating from the country's smallness per se but as a result of corporatist arrangements and bargaining institutions. In new democracies lacking corporate traditions, elite groups are not joined by sector representation and formalized meeting places but by shared national issue-framings, and they meet only ad hoc in loose networks where attitudes and the issues on the agenda draw the actors together into a potentially significant unit.

Of similar importance to resemblances between the national elites in different countries is convergence of orientations among groups in the separate nations. Homogeneous attitudes indicate that the elites may have a particular common focal interest, in contrast to heterogeneous attitudes, which may serve to split them. The same applies to elite groups in the individual nations. The opinions of the three subgroups – parliament deputies, administrative leaders and business leaders – are compared in Table 11.2.

The statement goes to the core idea of neoliberalism, advocating less state regulation over private business activities. In all the countries the leaders of private business companies overwhelmingly agree that state influence should be reduced (80–96 per cent). Among top state bureaucrats

*Table 11.2   Elite attitudes to the state and the business sector, statement 1:
'State influence over private business should be reduced'
(percentages who agree)*

	Year	Politicians	State administration	Business sector
Norway	2001	51 (n=137)	65 (n=101)	94 (n=145)
Estonia	2006	52 (n=27)	56 (n=25)	82 (n=34)
Latvia	2006	69 (n=67)	70 (n=30)	87 (n=30)
	2013	64 (n=56)	83 (n=23)	80 (n=25)
Lithuania	2006	76 (n=93)	70 (n=30)	91 (n=34)
	2013	70 (n=81)	69 (n=29)	96 (n=28)

*Table 11.3   Elite attitudes to state power, statement 2: 'The state is too
powerful' (percentages who agree)*

	Year	Politicians	State administration	Business sector
Norway	2001	47 (n=135)	27 (n=101)	86 (n=145)
Estonia	2006	8 (n=26)	8 (n=25)	44 (n=34)
Latvia	2006	41 (n=67)	35 (n=29)	59 (n=29)
	2013	24 (n=58)	25 (n=24)	60 (n=25)
Lithuania	2006	46 (n=90)	20 (n=30)	79 (n=33)
	2013	43 (n=82)	25 (n=28)	68 (n=25)

a majority agree, but support is less substantial than in the private sector.
The politicians in Norway and Estonia are split down the middle and
clearly the least enthusiastic about decreasing state influence over business.
The financial crisis seems to have made politicians somewhat more sceptical of reducing state power, while there is no clear tendency for reduced
distrust among the bureaucrats and in the business sector in these two
countries.

The picture is quite different with the statement concerning state power
in general (see Table 11.3). In the Norwegian business sector a large
majority agree that the state has too much power, while in the Baltic countries remarkably fewer of these leaders are in agreement. Estonian business
leaders especially have modest critical attitudes to a powerful state. The
same trend is found among Latvian and Lithuanian business elites but is
not so prominent. As expected, a minority of state administrators share
the view that the state is too powerful; this is a substantial reduction compared to the previous statement about state influence on private business.
Estonia stands out with only 8 per cent of bureaucrats agreeing that the

state is too dominant. A majority of the politicians in all four countries support a strong state in general. This also applies to Norway but is especially notable in the three Baltic states and in particular in Estonia. As for the effects of the financial crisis, the ensuing economic decay seems to have intensified the beliefs in more state power especially among politicians and the state administration in Latvia, although it did not affect the Lithuanian elites the same way, with the exception of business.

Summarizing the orientations towards market regulation and state power, it is obvious that politicians' and state administrators' support for deregulating state influence over business (statement 1) is not associated with the same level of support for reducing state power in general (statement 2). This tendency is also clear for the business community, especially in the Baltic states. Among the business leaders in Estonia and Latvia it seems easier to accept a powerful state than among their Lithuanian colleagues. The Norwegian business elite stand out as the most forthright supporters of both further marketization and a generally weaker state.

INTERNATIONAL MARKETS AND NATIONAL AUTONOMY

As shown, about 60 per cent of the total elite in Norway, Estonia and Lithuania and about 75 per cent in Latvia consider the international financial markets too influential (Table 11.1). Asked about national self-determination, a majority of the Baltic elite answer that it is too weak, and increasing to more than 60 per cent after the financial crisis. An astonishingly low 27 per cent of the overall Norwegian elites agree on this issue. To what extent are the orientations of the three subgroups in accordance about the role of the financial markets and the nation-state?

A majority of the politicians are worried in all four countries, and after the financial crisis scepticism in international financial actors soared in Latvia and Lithuania. The Norwegian business elite has the lowest disbelief (32 per cent), compared to considerably more concerned colleagues in the other countries (see Table 11.4). After the 2008 economic collapse the Baltic business leaders' substantial initial worry increased sharply to a level with, and sometimes higher than, that of politicians and state administrators.

Statement 4 goes to the core of the nation-state and the problem of national autonomy. It should be noted that statement 4 does not specifically refer to transnational economic relationships but focuses on national self-determination in general.

The responses to statement 4 illustrate how the elite reflect on national

Table 11.4 *Elite attitudes to international finance markets, statement 3:*
'International financial markets are too influential'
(percentages who agree)

	Year	Politicians	State administration	Business sector
Norway	2001	79 (n=135)	62 (n=101)	32 (n=145)
Estonia	2006	70 (n=27)	36 (n=25)	68 (n=34)
Latvia	2006	73 (n=70)	79 (n=28)	55 (n=29)
	2013	81 (n=58)	76 (n=25)	79 (n=24)
Lithuania	2006	52 (n=79)	50 (n=28)	74 (n=31)
	2013	89 (n=73)	67 (n=27)	89 (n=27)

Table 11.5 *Elite attitudes to national self-determination, statement 4:*
'National self-determination is too weak' (percentages who
agree)

	Year	Politicians	State administration	Business sector
Norway	2001	37 (n=135)	21 (n=101)	12 (n=145)
Estonia	2006	52 (n=27)	44 (n=25)	53 (n=34)
Latvia	2006	54 (n=69)	43 (n=30)	55 (n=29)
	2013	56 (n=55)	48 (n=23)	72 (n=25)
Lithuania	2006	46 (n=92)	42 (n=31)	53 (n=32)
	2013	65 (n=71)	59 (n=29)	74 (n=30)

autonomy and may indicate the extent of their nationalist orientations (see Table 11.5). First, only a minority of the Norwegian elite group think national self-determination is too weak, and especially among business leaders very few are concerned. The overall Norwegian pattern is in sharp contrast to the Baltic elites' much higher apprehensions about national sovereignty. For these states it is unexpected to observe that the business elites actually are more alarmed than politicians and state chief officers about fragile national self-determination. The concerns increased sharply after the financial crisis, especially among Latvian and Lithuanian business leaders.

Statements 3 and 4 evidently indicate that the general effect of global markets on national sovereignty is a case for concern among political and bureaucratic elites in all four countries and particularly among the business elites in the Baltic states. A possible explanation for the anomalous state-embracing reactions of the Baltic business leaders may be that more than others they experienced the harsh consequences of 'wild capitalism'.

The Norwegian business leaders are strikingly more liberal in their views on financial markets, and this tendency is even more noticeable concerning the discounting of national self-determination.

For the Baltic countries the pressure from international markets and the historical trauma of Russian domination seem to activate nationalist affinities and harmonize such views across elite groups. This is in sharp contrast to Norway, where the question of international competition splits the elites and national autonomy is of considerably less importance.

NEOLIBERALISM – EMBEDDED IN NATIONALISM

The neoliberal ideas of Friedrich von Hayek and Milton Friedman were widely disseminated at the beginning of the 1980s by neo-conservative Western think tanks which questioned the efficiency of the modern welfare state and the international trade system and called for massive deregulation and open borders (D.S. Jones 2012). The Baltic states, more than other post-communist countries, embraced these ideas and are thus regarded as the prototype model of neoliberal capitalism. Bohle and Greskovits (2012, p.97) argue, however, that reforms were heavily influenced by nationalist politics 'to reverse the effects of the massive influx of Russian speakers in Soviet times', and maintain that Estonia and Latvia typify a specific neoliberalism based on a nationalist social contract in contrast to the 'welfarist social contracts' found in the Visegrad countries. The Baltic radical economic reforms became intrinsically tied to nationalist ideology. Elites justifying market reforms with the purpose of safeguarding nation-state building was reflected in what has been named 'national neoliberalism' (Kattel and Raudla 2013). However, as Zake (2002) argues, some Latvian political elites used market reforms and international integration for the opposite purpose, namely reducing ethnic confrontation and promoting more class-based politics and a common Latvian identity. The People's Party was quite successful with this strategy in the 1998 parliamentary election, which indicates that ethnic-centred nationalism was contested and not the only means of political mobilization.

Owing to differences in national, political and economic circumstances, varieties of neoliberal processes appeared across Western and Eastern Europe (Birch and Mykhnenko 2009). The carrying out of WTO rules became more a matter of how actors framed the issue in national discourses than implementation of a fixed formal design (De Ville 2012). In the early Polish transition phase, the loss of Solidarity's influence, and thereby the possibility of a Scandinavian negotiated economy model, is an interesting example of how a social bottom-up approach to economic reforms was overruled by the influence of neoliberal technocrats in the absence of a nationalist type of neoliberalism (Zeniewski 2011).

The Baltic states' radical economic reforms became a catalyst for cutting bonds with the Russian economy and protecting national interests. Therefore, international integration and entry into the EU and NATO became closely embedded in a nationalist type of economic reform (Kattel and Raudla 2013, p.443). At the end of the 1990s, following international pressure from the EU and the Council of Europe, the citizenship laws in Estonia and Latvia were to some extent liberalized to include more segments of the Russian-speaking population. The requirement for democratization was a precondition to attaining membership in the EU and NATO, but, as shown in Steen (2010), amending the citizenship laws and gaining full membership in these organizations did not make the elite's attitudes more positive to including the Russophone populations. Obviously, attaining security in international organizations was the overarching goal, but it had its costs for national sovereignty, as reflected in the grudging passing of more liberal citizenship laws and in the Baltic elites' perception of weak national self-determination identified here. The nation-building processes in these 'newborn' states became entangled in neoliberal reform ideas and international commitments that have favoured fundamental changes of formal institutions in tandem with a nationalizing project. In Estonia and Latvia the elite ambition to build nation-states for the indigenous populations could not be fulfilled while at the same time becoming members of Europe. However, an exclusionist and nationalist elite culture still remains following a change of formal institutions.

Bohle and Greskovits (2012) argue that, owing to different national circumstances in Central and Eastern Europe (CEE), various types of capitalism emerged after the fall of communism. Early on, the three Baltic countries adopted a neoliberal regime, with the most radical economic transformations in close cooperation with Western advisers and combined neoliberal economic policies with nationalist politics and elements of exclusionary democracy found in Estonia and Latvia. The gloomy legacy of the Soviet period is crucial to understanding the neoliberal reforms as an instrument for preserving newly attained national independence. It explains why the high transformation costs the general population had to bear were less politicized compared to the case in other CEE countries. The elite's engagement in rebuilding their nation-states was founded on a shared belief that high social costs were a necessary investment in future integration into the Western sphere; this became the major rationale for draconian economic measures.

The aim of protecting the culture of the indigenous population from the previous hegemony of a large Russian minority and their bordering

national 'homeland' is attained by 'struggles of institutionally consti-
tuted national elites' (Brubaker 1996, p. 25) and stimulated by building a
'nationalizing state'. However, the strategic power elites could not promote
such a project without dedicated support from the broader elites in politics,
the state administration and business. Neoliberalism as part of a nation-
state project necessitated 'specific elite building with a discernible *esprit
de corps*, visible in perhaps its purest form again in Estonia because of
stable governments' (Kattel and Raudla 2013, p. 443). This observation of
the Estonian elite as particularly integrated, disciplined and nationalistic
coincides with other observations describing it as more ethnically homogeneous and with a clearer anti-Soviet front during the occupation period
compared to Latvia and Lithuania (Misiunas and Taagepera 1993; Lieven
1994; Steen 1997). Estonia was a forerunner of reform and is occasionally
called the most dynamic 'Baltic economic tiger'.[2] Support for a strong
state, as expressed by the elite, was necessary in order to implement reform
while safeguarding the nationalist 'contract' (Bohle and Greskovits 2012)
between the elite and the people in this particularly small and vulnerable
nation-state.

CONCLUSION: NEOLIBERALISM, ELITE CONVERGENCE AND POWER

The comparison of Norway and the Baltic countries illustrates that elite
convergence around a neoliberal programme is not a general trend. The
orientations investigated across these four countries challenge the notion
of neoliberalism as a cohesive reform ideal with extensive elite support.
Further, there are manifest differences between the elite groups, especially
in Norway. The conspicuous neoliberal view of Norwegian business entrepreneurs stands out both nationally and internationally. As the data presented here show, the Norwegian elite in general, and the business sector
in particular, are markedly less engaged with national self-determination
compared to the Baltic elites.

Obviously, circumstances related to basic national security issues have
an impact on the elites' beliefs in neoliberalism. Returning to Katzenstein's
(1985) basic thesis arguing that a high level of consensus is expected
among elites in small states, I claimed, first, that the smaller the state
and the greater the insecurity the more cohesive the elites. Elite support
for deregulation and marketization to some extent goes in tandem with
nationalist orientations like support for a strong state and protection from
external competition. This nationalist type of neoliberalism is most visible
in Estonia and also detectable in Latvia; it may be explained by harsh

historical experiences with Soviet occupation and fears concerning the loyalty of large Russian minorities to the new nation-states. This interpretation is in accordance with Bohle and Greskovits (2012), who argue that Baltic elites, in particular Estonian and Latvian leaders, saw radical economic transformation as a strategy for building national identities aimed at a radical departure from the past.

The second proposition was that the dominant elite divide is likely to be observed between the business leaders and the political-administrative segment, since the former are more likely to have a direct interest in neoliberal reforms and benefit from state deregulation. In Norway the traditional societal corporatist model came under pressure from neoliberal reform ideas, including scepticism from leading social democrats and especially from an international-oriented business sector with less concern for national self-determination. The surveys exhibit the Norwegian business elite expressing more purely liberal views than their Baltic counterparts. There are also noticeable differences among the Baltic countries. One possible explanation for the overall pattern – with business neoliberalism more outspoken in Norway – is that the Norwegian business community is ideologically more disconnected from the framework of the nation-state, while recent national struggles for independence weigh on the Baltic consciousness even among the entrepreneurial class.

Third, it was suggested that shocks in the international environment are particularly conducive to national elite cohesion. The interviews repeated in Latvia and Lithuania several years after the 2008 financial crisis show that the economic repercussions spurred even more united opinions, scepticism towards international markets, and support for national self-determination. Since the financial meltdown the Baltic elites strikingly have become more negative towards international financial institutions and more supportive of state self-determination, while the crisis has had little effect on attitudes towards internal state–market relations. The elite still support deregulation of state control over business but have become far more sceptical towards the reduction of national autonomy. The business sector in Latvia and Lithuania was especially affected by the economic meltdown, and quite unexpectedly (from the perspective of neoliberal ideology) their leaders are at the forefront of efforts to protect the national economy against turbulent international environments.

Why do Norwegian leaders of business enterprises distinguish themselves from other elite groups with energetic neoliberal orientations, while their Baltic counterparts do not? National and international circumstances can be influential in a variety of ways. One probable explanation, following the argument of Bohle and Greskovits (2012), is that business elites and others must work together more closely during a period of establishing a new nation-state. In traditional nation-states such as Norway, business leaders regard the state more as a 'company' and less as a nation-state, while elites in politics and administration have the nation-state as the most important frame of reference. Neoliberal solutions would serve the economic interests of the business community, and therefore that is what their orientations most probably express. Because the business community in Norway is ideologically more disconnected from the framework of national autonomy, belief in neoliberalism has become more prevalent; in the Baltic states, in contrast, recent national independence is part of the national consciousness even among the business leaders, which probably explains their unexpected propensity for nationalist orientations. The contrasting orientations of the Baltic and Norwegian business elites raise the question of whether neoliberal ideas serve more as an instrument for control than an ideology uniting elites across sectors and countries.

Neoliberalism may be regarded as an ideology to be realized, or as a package of instruments strategic actors may make use of for purposes of political and economic control and not mainly related to putting a neoliberal programme per se into effect, as several research contributions indicate is the case for the 'nationalist neoliberalism' of the Baltics (Bohle and Greskovits 2012; Kattel and Raudla 2013). The same can be maintained about welfare reforms in Scandinavia when the Social Democrats introduced some deregulation and privatization to safeguard the welfare state and accordingly their own power (Klitgaard 2007). In Klitgaard's view, neoliberalism is a matter of institutional design and power, more essential than welfare and economic changes as such, where reforms imply how political control is to be distributed among strategic actors. The Social Democrats are not studied specifically here, but the rather widespread neoliberal orientations among Norwegian politicians and administrative leaders who mostly vote with the Social Democratic Party are more fruitfully understood as adjusting the boundaries of the welfare state. Thereby they are supporting their power basis rather than abolishing it by introducing a neoliberal regime. The same argument can be made for the Norwegian business leaders; more than acting as neoliberal crusaders, they can be understood to be increasing their power basis through their affirmative orientations by advocating even better economic circumstances for their enterprises.

In the Baltic states, the nationalist approach to neoliberal reforms explains why their elites are sympathetic to national independence and sceptical of international finance. Neoliberal policy, however, with all its social costs, was implemented to the satisfaction of the international community and paradoxically became a strategic means for indigenous control in order to accomplish the paramount goal of safeguarding the reborn small nation-states against internal and external threats.

ACKNOWLEDGEMENT

I am grateful to the Department of Political Science, University of Oslo, for providing research grants making data collection in the Baltic states possible, and to the NSD for access to the Norwegian Power Elite Study. Parts of this chapter have benefited from Steen and Østerud (2007).

NOTES

1. In the early 2000s the number of inhabitants in Estonia was approximately 1.4 million (26 per cent Russians), Latvia 2.4 million (30 per cent Russians), Lithuania 3.5 million (6 per cent Russians) and Norway 4.5 million.
2. Ironically, in 1999 Estonia had some difficulties in joining the World Trade Organization (WTO) because it had no tariffs, and was requested to implement a tariff system in order to take part in negotiations of tariff reductions (Hoen 2011, p. 36).

12. Small state, huge assets: the problem of fiscal discipline in an oil-rich country – the case of Norway

Harald Baldersheim

> The larger the visible fortune becomes, the larger the risk that principles of sound management recede into the background.
> (Qvigstad 2012)

WAGGING THE DOG – THE OIL FUND AS A SOURCE OF VULNERABILITY

Over the last decade and a half the State of Norway has accumulated one of the world's largest sovereign funds based on oil revenues from the North Sea. The fund is invested in government bonds and equities in markets worldwide. By spring 2015 the combined market value of the fund equalled more than two years of the Norwegian GDP or more than five times the annual state budget, and the fund is still growing. The state is increasingly dependent upon income from the fund to balance the budget and in consequence subjected to the vicissitudes of international markets. The fund, which was intended as a buffer against the volatility of markets, increasingly looks like a source of vulnerability. What kind of vulnerability the fund entails has changed over time, however. One type of vulnerability springs from uncertainty about oil revenues; the second type is related to the spending of the oil dividend. This chapter deals mainly with the second type, but the first type sometimes impacts on the second.

The situation of the Norwegian state and also that of Norwegian politics more and more resembles the proverbial tail wagging the dog: a small state with a large fortune, the management of which puts national politics into a conundrum. This chapter makes no attempt to review the whole series of strategies put in place to dampen the effect of the wagging. I focus on one particular challenge that stems from the growth of the fund: that of maintaining fiscal discipline in public budgeting against the background of an apparently ever-richer state. The problem of fiscal discipline, however, opens up a window for studying the political consequences of oil riches in a small state, consequences that may amount to a transformation of the traditional political landscape.

As suggested by Katzenstein (1985), small states in world markets have to learn to adapt quickly to changes in market conditions. The adaptability of the small states he investigated in the 1980s, including Norway, hinged on cooperation among elites through corporatist arrangements that facilitated the emergence of concerted opinions on policy choices. In Katzenstein's analysis, however, the emergence of elite consensus across traditional political divides was driven by fear – the perception of threats emanating from a hostile environment. Consequently, small countries could be expected to be more financially responsible than larger countries for fear of exposing themselves to great dangers (I shall call this 'the Katzenstein hypothesis').

But what happens to consensus and adaptation when the perception of threat recedes into the background and that of abundance and unlimited opportunities becomes dominant? Such a situation may take governance into new waters that are unfamiliar to the political actors as well as to political analysts. In 'normal' democratic politics a central mechanism of accountability is the need to impose (unpopular) taxes in order to spend. In Norwegian politics, the growth of the oil fund may have reduced the effect of this basic law. As Francis Fukuyama points out, accountability is one of the mainstays of democracy, along with a state apparatus and the rule of law; it is the balance between the three components that constitutes a *sound* democracy (Fukuyama 2014, pp. 37, 519ff.), of which Denmark is held out as a prime example. If accountability is weakened, the balance may be weakened. If accountability is weakened, decision makers may be less hesitant about taking risks with public money, including the oil fund, which may lead to fiscally irresponsible behaviour (I shall call this 'the Fukuyama hypothesis'). A small country with a large fortune could be more prone to this type of behaviour compared to a large country with a similar fortune and end up in a place much like that of Greece[1] (or like Iceland in the wake of the financial crisis of 2008; see Chapter 3).

The maintenance of fiscal discipline in public budgeting – house-keeping within available means – is a virtue that few politicians would disagree with. Adhering to such an ideal in practice is a wholly different matter. In countries around the world a variety of strategies have been devised to promote fiscal discipline – ranging from constitutionally required balanced budgets to independent audits, from tax ceilings to spending caps. The list of back doors invented by politicians to get around such requirements is equally long. Politicians in national office find themselves permanently under electoral expectations that exceed available resources as long as

Small states in the modern world

spending is financed through a common pool resource such as the state budget. The political pressure is understandably larger the faster the common pool resource increases. This is where Norway is now, with no state debt and a growing oil fund that has turned the Norwegian state into one of the largest investors in the world. How much should the state spend from its oil revenues on worthy purposes over current budgets each year? This has become a central issue in Norwegian politics and public discourse.

Until the mid-1990s the answer was to use almost all oil-related income on current spending in annual budgets. The State Oil Fund (since 2006 known as the Government Pension Fund Global) was in fact established in 1990, but little money was actually put into the fund before 2000. However, owing to rising oil prices the fund grew rapidly after the turn of the millennium (see Figure 12.1). Along with the growth of the fund the fear of a potential 'resource curse' was also spreading. In public discourse, the so-called Dutch disease, named after the gas-related incomes which drove inflated public spending in the Netherlands in the 1980s, was compared to the impact on Spain of gold from the New World. A classic analysis

Billion kroner

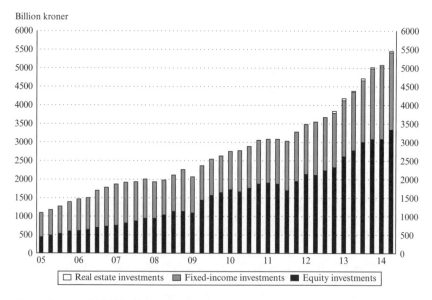

Note: 1 euro = 8.7 NOK, February 2015.

Source: http://www.nbim.no/fondet/markedsverdi/.

Figure 12.1   Development of the Government Pension Fund Global 2005–2014

of resource-rich countries summarized the experience of these states with the expression 'the paradox of plenty' (Karl 1997), which meant that a resource-based boom often was followed by a long period of stagnation. A more recent study has presented a more nuanced picture and shown that the developments may vary also among resource-rich countries; outcomes depend to a significant extent on the quality of public institutions (Torvik 2009).

What also needs to be nuanced, however, is the picture of Norway as a country that has fully managed to escape the resource curse. Back in 1974 when the Norwegian oil era was in its infancy, a government white paper outlined the challenges associated with an oil and gas economy. The main challenges were to protect the land-based economy from competition from off-shore activities for scarce labour, since oil companies would be able to outbid any wages that land-based industries could offer and, furthermore, to avoid capture of the regulatory agencies by the oil industry. To achieve the first goal, oil exploration and extraction should proceed at a moderate pace, which was stipulated at a production of 90 million tonnes of oil equivalents a year. To reach the second goal Parliament wanted to make sure that a plurality of national oil companies would come into being, not just one big state company, as originally suggested by the government of the day (St. meld. nr. 25 1974). What happened? By 2004, when oil and gas production peaked, production had reached 264 million tonnes a year (Ryggvik 2014), and labour costs had soared so that Norwegian industrial wages were 30 per cent higher on average than those of Norway's main trading partners (Olsen 2015). Of the three national oil companies that were established during the 1970s only one remained by 2010; the other two were merged with the state company.

THE SPENDING RULE

'The Spending Rule' (SR) was formulated in 2001 as a response to the welfare paradox. It sets an upper limit to how much money could be taken from the oil fund annually for spending over current state budgets. The limit was set at 4 per cent of the fund's capital at any given time. The limit of 4 per cent was supposed to correspond to the long-term return on invested capital. If the SR is adhered to, and if investments are wise, the fund is expected to be a lasting source for public spending even when the oil age is over and no oil revenues are available anymore.

The SR was adopted in order to achieve control over public spending of oil revenues, since politicians when they felt the pinch had hitherto succumbed too easily to the temptation of balancing the budget with oil incomes. A further aim was better management of the overall impacts of the oil activities on the national economy at large. Consequently, a strategy had to be devised to protect the fund's capital from depletion. The relabelling of the fund as the Government Pension Fund Global was part of such a strategy. Other aims supposedly served by the SR were also outlined (St. meld. nr. 29 2000–2001).

The SR and other strategies for the management of the fund won broad support among national politicians with the exception of the Progress Party, which agitated in favour of a more liberal spending of the fund's resources. The party saw the 4 per cent SR as a 'straitjacket' preventing 'sensible' use of resources and long-term state spending. Views such as these were not without echoes in public opinion. Over time other parties have also become more ambiguous in their attitudes to the SR. These developments will be analysed in more detail in the section 'The SR as a political cleavage'.

Figures 12.2a and 12.2b illustrate the financial challenges of the Norwegian state. Figure 12.2a shows that the deficit of the state budget in monetary terms has been steadily growing since 2000 and especially in the

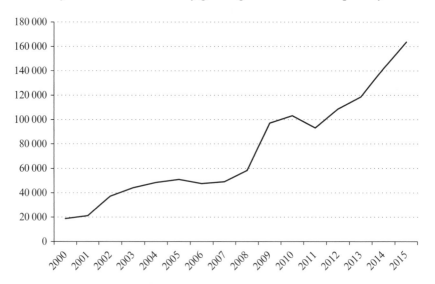

Note: In million NOK.

Source: St. meld. nr. 2 (2013–2014, Table 1.1: Det strukturelle, oljekorrigerte budsjettoverskuddet).

Figure 12.2a   State budget deficit 2000–2015, corresponding to actual use of the oil dividend in the state budget

last part of the period. The deficit has been covered by the oil dividend, so the use of the dividend is largely reflected in the size of the deficit. The deficit is driven by an underlying annual budget expansion, not a loss of ordinary state revenues. Figure 12.2b shows, first, the budget deficit as a percentage of the gross domestic product (dotted line). The deficit is increasing faster than the GDP (which has also been increasing in this period, which again underlines the growth of the state budget). The second line in the figure (solid line) represents the potential yield of the 4 per cent oil dividend over the same period in time, also measured as a percentage of the GDP. The two curves follow each other fairly closely, rising with the same slope. At the beginning, the deficit was larger than the dividend; towards the end, the dividend was larger. The latter fact again could be taken to demonstrate that the decision makers have shown some restraint with regard to spending the oil money. However, 4 per cent dividend from an increasing capital stock will of course yield an increasing dividend. So far, the deficit and the dividend have been increasing at approximately

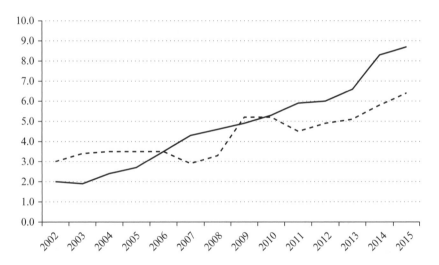

Notes: Dotted line: state budget deficit as a percentage of on-shore GDP; solid line: yield of 4 per cent oil dividend as a percentage of GDP.

Sources: State budget deficit as a percentage of on-shore GDP: St. meld. nr. 2 (2013–2014, Table 1.28); yield of 4 per cent oil dividend as a percentage of GDP: Olsen (2015, Figure 15 numbers).

Figure 12.2b   State budget deficit as a percentage of on-shore GDP and the yield of 4 per cent oil dividend as a percentage of GDP 2002–2015

the same rate annually. In other words, there is an underlying pressure on politicians to increase spending; in recent years, they have been able to cover the spending well within the 4 per cent rule, but the expenditure growth seems relentless, thus challenging the long-term sustainability of state finances.

The main issue of this chapter is how politically sustainable the SR is. What are the features of public discourse regarding the SR? What are the arguments fronted by political actors in favour of the SR, and what are the arguments fielded against the rule? Who are the actors engaged in the discourse on the SR? Do they have an alternative to the SR? To what extent are the actors actually concerned with fiscal discipline at all?

THEORIES ON FISCAL DISCIPLINE

The SR is a strategy for fiscal discipline, limiting how much money the state may withdraw from the fund at any given time. The rule amounts formally to a cap on the revenue side of the budget, since the rule sets a limit to the sum that can be transferred from the fund and added to state incomes. The intention is of course that the limit on state incomes is to result in corresponding limits on state spending, so the rule is in practice also a cap on spending, since the state is subject to a norm of balanced budgets. The SR is not legally based; it is a political contract between the main political actors (parties), with the exception of the Progress Party. It may perhaps 'seem surprising that [the SR] is not legally binding. The duration and implementation is fully left to political life' (E. Smith 2012). The actors are tied to the mast for as long as they want to be. Can we be confident that the ties will last? What does budget theory say on this issue?

One of the pioneers of analysis of public budgeting, Aaron Wildavsky, saw the process of budgeting as a game between advocates and guardians (Wildavsky 1975). The advocates were champions of various worthy purposes that should benefit from public resources, while the guardians sought to restrain spending; the latter often portrayed themselves as protectors of the large group of unorganized taxpayers. An additional role – the gatherers – was identified by the Swedes Nils Brunsson and Björn Rombach in their studies of budget games in Swedish municipalities. The gatherers emphasized amassing financial reserves for a rainy day (Brunsson and Rombach 1982). They wanted to restrict spending even more than the guardians: while the guardians were satisfied with a balanced budget (spending equal to revenues), the gatherers favoured a solid budget surplus, preferably hidden away in a separate fund that could not be so easily accessed by the politicians.

It is not difficult to locate the actors in the Norwegian budget game in such a tripartite drama: the minister of finance is usually the guardian of the public purse, the various other ministers represent the advocates (often backed by representatives from the corresponding parliamentary committees), and the Central Bank functions as the gatherer, especially as it is also the responsible manager for the Government Pension Fund Global. In this latter capacity it was only natural that the head of the Central Bank recently advocated reducing the SR from 4 to 3 per cent; if the rule had been revised accordingly, more reserves would of course have been left in the fund for a rainy day.

According to Wildavsky (1975), budgeting is mostly an incremental activity, with only marginal changes from year to year in the volume of resources allocated to various activities. The budgetary process retains the balance between actors and budgetary items. Outcomes are largely path dependent. Dramatic changes are unlikely. The level of fiscal discipline that can be achieved depends on the institutional balance between advocates and guardians. The former are always more numerous than the latter (and also more numerous than the gatherers). The advocates are often well organized and supported by public opinion; they fight for worthy purposes – more for the old, the young, the sick and so on. The guardians may at best claim to be standing up for the cause of amorphous groups of taxpayers or future generations. None of these groups enters the game as a well-organized pressure group, and the gatherers can easily be portrayed as unfeeling money grubbers. A rational budgetary process is therefore in need of special institutional protection of guardians and gatherers. In Norway, is the institutional protection sufficient for the sustainability of the SR? The issue will be further discussed in the next section.

Wildavsky later added a cultural dimension to his budgetary theory. Budgetary behaviour is affected by the cultural features of the societies in which the budgeting games take place. Societal culture shapes the ways in which political decisions are made. Inspired by the anthropologist Mary Douglas, Wildavsky identified four types of culture: egalitarian, collectivistic, fatalistic and individualistic (Wildavsky 1987). Norwegian culture is often claimed to be strongly egalitarian (Graubard 1986). According to Wildavsky an egalitarian culture makes for consensual decision making. This may fit well with major political decisions in Norwegian politics over the last few decades, broad compacts between political parties and interest groups. Consensual politics does not create clear winners and losers but rather package solutions with something for (almost) everyone. The SR fits this pattern. But how deeply anchored is the compact on the SR? Will it survive also in economic downturns accompanied by budgetary cutbacks?

Budgeting may, furthermore, be influenced by the electoral cycle, as highlighted by MacRae (1975) and Golden and Poterba (1985). In a democracy, actors are legitimized through regular, recurring elections. This fact shapes the behaviour of actors, including budgetary behaviour. Politicians behave differently in election years; they are more sensitive to electoral expectations. The theory of the political business cycle states that budgets expand extraordinarily in election years as politicians outbid each other, which may be good for certain groups of voters but bad for fiscal discipline. The theory leads to rather pessimistic hypotheses regarding fiscal discipline. The more intense the political competition is, the more politicians will seek to outbid each other, and the worse is the outlook for fiscal discipline.

Analyses of budgetary behaviour have often been conducted in situations characterized by scarce resources, mostly situations in which the agenda has been set by the need to negotiate the distribution of budget cuts. A budgetary game against a background of increasing financial surpluses, a game in which actors are faced with a problem of abundance, is rarely encountered in the literature on public budgeting. The Norwegian budgetary processes may thus have unusual features and actor constellations. The theory on organizational slack may offer an analytical take on understanding budgetary behaviour in a situation of abundance. The theory postulates that actors at all levels in an organization seek to create a resource buffer that may protect performance and collaborative relations if a sudden drop in resources were to happen (Cyert and March 1963). A resource buffer makes it easier to maintain an even level of performance and also to maintain a collaborative climate in the organization and avoid conflicts. The prospect of extraordinary resources creates a motive to exaggerate actual resource needs ('dishonest' reporting) in order to obtain access to new resources. In consequence, fiscal pressure increases and so does the cost of public operations. If the growing oil fund motivates dishonest reporting in this manner, then the prospects of fiscal discipline are rather bleak, at least for as long as the fund keeps on growing.

The potential impact of dishonest reporting may be balanced by the institutionalization of fiscal discipline. How strongly is fiscal discipline institutionalized in Norway? Ways and means of institutionalization – and budgetary regulations to this end – are reviewed in the next section.

INSTITUTIONALIZATION OF FISCAL DISCIPLINE – HOW STRONG IN NORWAY?

In many countries fiscal discipline is sought through legal regulations; one of the most widespread legal requirements is that of budgetary balance,

Table 12.1   Strategies of fiscal discipline and their adoption in Norway

Strategies	Adoption in Norway
Regulations requiring balanced budget:	
In constitution	No
In ordinary legislation	No
Customary stipulation	Yes
At start of year (1) or at end of year (2)	1
Procedural stipulations:	
Regarding preparation of budget	Yes
Regarding voting on budget	Yes
Regarding spending of budget/accounting (e.g. carry-over)	Yes, partly
Transparency requirements:	
Based on quality standard	Yes, partly
Based on independent quality checks	No nationally, yes locally
Legal/judicial control	No
Results specifications	Yes
Quantitative regulations (e.g. Golden Rule)	Only the SR
Citizen power:	
Referenda required for tax increases, borrowing, etc.	No

Sources: Bohn and Inman (1996); Alesina and Perotti (1999); OECD (2004); own assessment of Norway's adoption of strategies.

so that expenditures cannot exceed revenues (e.g. in France or Sweden), including the specification of sources of revenue. Requirements such as these may even be backed by constitutional clauses (in the USA and most of continental Europe). However, Norway, like Denmark, has no specific budgetary legislation or constitutional requirements regarding the state budget (see Table 12.1) except that the government is obliged to present a budget at the beginning of every parliamentary session (the first Tuesday of October). The budgetary process is further regulated through decrees and the Parliamentary Code.[2] It is nevertheless an established custom to present a balanced budget.

The balance requirement normally applies to the budget as presented to and/or passed by Parliament. An even more stringent requirement is the stipulation that the budget, or rather the accounts, should be balanced at the end of the fiscal year, which means that administrative agencies are duty-bound not only to keep spending within specified levels but also to spend the whole budget by the year end.

Alesina and Perotti (1999) claim that norms that stipulate budget balance in numerical terms do not necessarily lead to more fiscal discipline. They argue that good procedural stipulations give more flexibility and will reduce public deficits more efficiently. Procedural stipulations may apply to control over budget preparation as well as rules regarding parliamentary decision making. Most countries have a ministry of finance with the task of coordinating the preparation of the budget, but the power of the ministry of finance relative to that of the line ministries may vary from country to country. In most systems of government its role is to act as a brake on new expenditure proposals coming from other ministries. Nevertheless, the authority of this role varies from that of real screening to being just a mailbox for proposals from other ministries. In the Norwegian case, the function of the ministry of finance is more that of a screen than a mailbox.

Many national assemblies, like the Norwegian Parliament, have specific regulations regarding budgetary procedures. Some countries have adopted procedures akin to those of Norway, which require that the total volume of the budget is decided first, including allocations for the respective sub-fields. After that, members of the respective parliamentary committees decide on priorities for their fields inside the known allocation. Other countries maintain a practice that was also the case in Norway until 2001, whereby the committees first set the budgetary priorities for their fields and then the total of the budget is enacted in a final round of negotiations.

Procedural stipulations may also regulate situations of under- or over-spending at the year end, for example whether unspent resources may be carried over to the next year. The rationale of allowing carry-over of unspent means is to prevent irrational shopping sprees towards the end of the year out of fear that underspending might result in smaller appropriations the following year. The companion regulation of carry-over is that overspending must be covered by savings in the following year's budget. The basic idea of carry-over and savings regulation is that of providing incentives for enhancing efficiency in public operations.

Alesina and Perotti (1999) distinguish between a hierarchical and a collegial model in their analyses of the allocations of power and authority in budgetary processes. The hierarchical model is top-down, with most authority concentrated in the prime minister and/or the ministry of finance and may even reach into decision making in Parliament. The collegial model is more open to initiatives from actors at several stages of the process, from various ministries as well as from parliamentary committees. The authors find that the hierarchical model may result in more fiscal discipline, while the collegial model may be seen as more democratic. Norwegian budgetary procedures are, overall, closer to the hierarchical than to the collegial model.[3] However, the parliamentary situations may influence how the Norwegian procedures work: coalition governments may lead to processes closer to the collegial model and so may governments without a clear parliamentary majority, of which Norway has had a series in recent decades (Rommetvedt 2011).

In fiscally tight circumstances politicians may be tempted to resort to unrealistic transactions to fulfil the balanced-budget requirement, such as unrealistic revenue estimates, excessive borrowing or keeping certain expenditures off the formal state budget. Greece has provided a series of examples in this regard. Consequently, budgetary transparency is often recommended as a means to fiscal discipline. The test is whether procedures exist that will make it possible to reveal budgetary obfuscation and hold the responsible politicians to account. Transparency may be served by analysing the budget against recognized standards for public budgeting, such as those of the OECD (2002, 2004), by independent experts or through court reviews. Furthermore, a budget with clearly specified objectives and performance stipulations will also enhance transparency compared to one limited to overall appropriations. The idea is that, by clearly specifying how the administration is to be held accountable, the more responsible spending will be.

Transparency may also be served by quantitative restrictions regarding spending or revenues, such as limiting the overall budget to a certain proportion of GNP, or by setting a limit to budget deficits relative to the GDP (such as the regulations which apply to members of the Eurozone). The German constitution states that total state borrowing must not exceed total public investments in the same year. According to regulations, the UK cannot finance current expenditures through borrowing, and until a few years ago total public debt could not exceed 40 per cent of GDP (OECD 2004, pp. 89–90).

The SR is a regulation in this category specifying a quantitative limit to transfers from the oil fund, which again limits the overall budget as long as the norm of a balanced budget is respected.

Finally, fiscal discipline may be achieved through citizen empowerment and self-interest. The US offers many examples in this regard. In many cities, tax increases and borrowing are subject to approval by citizen referendum. The movement in this direction started with the famous Proposition 13 in California in 1976 and has since then spread to many other states. It is a strategy for limiting public expenditures that may have proved to have been too effective given the state of public infrastructure and quality of public education in some states. Citizen's dividend is a further example of disciplining strategies of this type. Citizen's dividends are cash payments to individual citizens from incomes from the exploitation of natural resources. The state of Alaska, for example, pays most of the returns from the Alaska Permanent Fund directly to its citizens. The idea is that this practice gives citizens an interest in the sound, long-term management of the fund.[4] The fund is still expanding and has yielded fairly good returns. The Alberta Heritage Fund is based on similar ideas; it was established at the same time as the Alaska Fund, but with much weaker institutional protection, and has had a much poorer performance.[5] Similar ideas for the Norwegian oil fund have been aired by the Progress Party but have not been seriously considered by other parties so far (see below).

In summary, in Norway the institutional mechanisms for fiscal discipline are, overall, moderately strong. There are no legal or constitutional brakes regarding state budgets. In practice, however, budgeting procedures are of a rather hierarchical nature, offering guardians a reasonable degree of control. The budget structure is fairly transparent. So far, however, fiscal discipline through citizen empowerment has not been seriously considered.

Theories of budgetary behaviour discussed above lead mostly to rather pessimistic hypotheses regarding the maintenance of fiscal discipline in the long run. Furthermore, the institutional setting of state budgeting does not contain any really strong brakes on expenditures. As mentioned above, in 'normal' politics the main disciplinary mechanism is the need to impose (unpopular) taxes in order to spend. The growth of the oil fund has weakened this basic law in Norwegian politics. The disciplinary mechanism that remains is a self-imposed political norm of restraint such as the SR. Will the mechanism hold? The issue is addressed through analyses of the support of the SR in public debate, among voters, and in the respective political parties.

THE SR IN PUBLIC OPINION

How much interest is there in the media regarding the SR? Figure 12.3 shows how often the SR was mentioned in the most important national and provincial newspapers between 2000 and 2013. Any mention of the SR is counted. In 2001, the first year after its adoption, the SR was mentioned 100 times. The next year, the score is 500 but drops again in 2003. Media interest increases steadily from 2005 more or less in proportion to the growth of the fund itself. There is a conspicuous jump in interest in 2012 and further in 2013 when the SR became a central topic of the election campaigns even though only one party (the Progress Party) campaigned for the abolition of the rule.

A further analysis of the content of media coverage of the SR has been carried out based on a smaller number of newspapers, national as well as

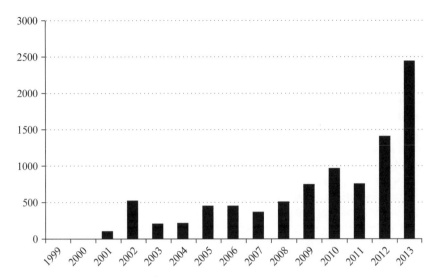

Source: A-tekst data base (data base of major daily newspapers).

Figure 12.3 Frequency of newspaper coverage of SR, 1999 to September 2013

Table 12.2 Attitudes to the SR in newspaper articles or reports

	2004/2005	2008/2009	2012/2013	Total
Keep SR	6	3	55	64
Abolish SR	1	0	1	2
Change spending pattern	7	10	76	93
Lower SR	0	1	19	20
Higher SR	0	2	2	4
Undefined adjustment of SR	0	0	3	3
Other statements on SR	102	119	184	405
Total	116	135	340	591

Note: Absolute numbers.

Source: A-tekst data base (data base of major daily newspapers). Coding by own research team.

provincial (Table 12.2). One-year periods have been selected leading up to the parliamentary elections of 2005, 2009 and 2013. For this analysis only articles that deal with the SR as a major subject (but not necessarily the only subject) have been included. In the 2004/2005 and 2008/2009 periods the SR was the subject of 116 and 135 articles respectively, while coverage intensified substantially in 2012/2013 with 340 articles in all.

The interest in the SR in the first two periods is mostly in the form of news items or neutral reporting. Only a few of the writers express an attitude for or against the SR or suggest any adjustments. This has changed substantially in the last period. Now there is clearly a debate taking place, with strong opinions on the SR. Twelve per cent of authors state explicitly that they want to keep the SR. Only one single article argues for the complete abolition of the SR, but 22 per cent argue for some kind of adjustment. The bulk of adjustments being advocated are about the pattern of spending of the oil dividend: more should be spent on infrastructure and 'growth-enhancing' purposes, not on general-purpose items. Many of the authors of this group belong to the Progress Party, and many of the articles bear the signs of a coordinated press campaign.

Is interest in the SR reflected in the electorate at large? Or is it just a debate taking place among the political elites? Voter surveys have repeatedly asked voters about their perceptions of political issues in the months leading up to national elections. Asked what they thought were the most important issues of the 2001 election campaign, no voters mentioned the SR or other issues related to the management of the oil fund. In 2005, 1.3 per cent of respondents mentioned the oil fund as an important issue. When the question was repeated in 2013 less than 1 per cent identified the SR or related issues as important ones.[6] Other surveys have asked more precise questions about the oil dividend, such as the voters' preferred level of spending from the fund. In 2009, 85 per cent of the respondents actually had an opinion on this issue. The majority of those holding an opinion were in favour of keeping spending at the existing level, while 33 per cent would have liked to spend more. The proportions in favour of stable as against higher levels of spending were the same in 2013. Opinions on spending levels may not of course reflect a deep knowledge of the SR among voters. A survey conducted by Toril Aalberg and others showed that, in 2010, 38 per cent of voters could explain correctly what the SR was about.[7]

The overall impression is that, to voters in general, spending of the oil fund was of much less concern than it was to the political elites, and that the majority of voters with an opinion on the matter would like to keep spending at existing levels. Nevertheless, the influx of oil revenues could be feeding a 'revolution of rising expectations'. A study based on 2001 survey data demonstrated that voters who would like to spend more of the oil money had less trust in politicians and were less satisfied with the way Norwegian democracy worked (Listhaug 2007, p. 145). It could be sentiments such as these that some of the political parties were beginning to pick up.

Table 12.3   Parliamentary submissions (innst. St.) and speeches of members of Parliament dealing with the SR

Parliamentary session	Frequency
2001 (s/a)	49
2004/2005 (a/s)	69
2008/2009 (a/s)	95
2012/2013 (a/s)	184
Total	397

Notes:
Absolute numbers.
a = autumn; s = spring.

Source: Parliamentary data base of documents and debates.

THE SR AS A POLITICAL CLEAVAGE

From 2001, political parties began to mention the SR in their electoral manifestos, although with varying detail and clarity. The attitudes of the respective parties were also expressed in parliamentary debates on finance policy and sometimes also in debates in other policy fields. Just as in public debates, increasing interest in and attention to the SR could be registered in parliamentary debates. Table 12.3 reflects the frequency with which the SR was mentioned in documents and by parliamentary speakers in one-year periods leading up to elections from 2001 to 2013. Again, the frequency of attention was growing along with the fund itself, from 49 registrations in 2001 (spring and autumn) to 184 registrations in 2012/2013 (autumn and spring).

The more precise attitudes to SR and the use of the oil dividend expressed by members of Parliament over this period of time (2001–2013) are brought out in Table 12.4.

The largest number of speeches on the SR are given by members of the Labour Party, and then by members from the Progress Party and the Conservative Party. When variation in number of seats is taken into account, the Progress Party appears to be the party most concerned with the SR. As expected, Labour members are almost unanimously in favour of keeping the rule as it is and also for maintaining existing guidelines on spending. The Progress Party represents the opposing view, its members wanting to abolish the SR and provide new guidelines on spending. The Conservatives occupy a middle ground – to keep the rule but develop new guidelines. The parties of the centre and the Left Socialist Party also want

Table 12.4   Attitudes to the SR by speakers in parliamentary debates 2001–2012/2013

Party	Keep SR	Abolish SR	New spending pattern	Higher or lower SR	No clear opinion	Total
Labour	83	0	3	0	28	114
Progress	1	20	14	1	32	68
Conservative	14	0	32	0	15	61
Christian	6	0	9	0	2	17
Centre	5	0	3	0	7	15
Left Socialist	5	0	4	0	8	17
Liberals	5	0	4	1	5	15
						307

Note: Absolute numbers.

Source: Parliamentary data base of documents and debates. Coding by own research team.

to keep the rule but share the attitude of changing guidelines, only they have different ideas as to how the spending should change (see below).

POLICY ARGUMENTS AND DISCURSIVE FRAMES: THE SHADOW OF THE FUTURE, POOR RELATIVES AND A WASTEFUL STATE

Policy arguments have three main components: observations, recommendations and framing (Dunn 2008, ch. 8). Framing helps bridge the gap between factual observations and policy choices or recommendations. Frames provide a value-laden background to policy choices. In parliamentary debates on the SR as well as in public opinion and party programmes, three sets of discursive frames can be discerned: the shadow of the future, the poor relatives and the wasteful state.[8]

'The shadow of the future' is a line of reasoning much favoured by the advocates of the SR. The future will bring challenges that we had better prepare to meet here and now while we can. The state has, for example, incurred vast obligations in the form of pension entitlements that the oil fund will help meet; otherwise, taxes will have to be increased enormously to be paid by ever fewer of the younger generations. Therefore, setting aside money for future pensions is also an expression of solidarity among the generations. Spending it all now would put an intolerable burden on future generations. The other aspect of the shadow of the future is consideration of the land-based economy. Spending too much of the oil dividend would drive up the prices of labour and goods, make the rest of the economy uncompetitive in world markets and thus lead to the loss of jobs in industry by driving industry to invest more abroad. These lines of reasoning echo concerns voiced in policy documents almost since oil extraction started in the North Sea.

'The poor relatives' are a mixed bag of concerns that would-be policy makers would like to address with extra resources from the oil fund. These may be national concerns, especially infrastructure, as well as unfilled needs in foreign lands that the policy maker thinks should benefit from Norwegian resources, for example start-up companies in developing countries that suffer from a lack of venture capital. Closely related to 'the poor relatives' frame is that of 'the rich uncle' argument. Norway, with its oil riches, is in a lucky position; riches bring obligations, and Norway should spend its riches to the benefit of those less fortunate.

The third frame, 'the wasteful state', often goes hand in hand with the 'poor relatives' frame. The oil revenues represent capital that should be used for productive investments, not current state expenditures. Therefore, oil revenues should primarily be used for investments that will yield a future return, not be wasted on unproductive general state expenditures. It is not always clear if the champions of such ideas have the uses of the 4 per cent dividend or the more general management and investment portfolio of the oil fund in mind. However, some of them do argue in favour of setting up parallel funds dedicated to specific types of investments, for example an infrastructure fund, or a fund for green technologies. Sometimes the idea of 'productive investments' is stretched well beyond normal usage, for example spending more on education and research or highways. Critics of this line of reasoning claim that the ideas weaken the defences of the SR and just open a back door for more state spending.

The Labour Party, as the architect of the SR, delivers unwavering support for it in its electoral manifestos as well as in parliamentary debates. The SR as a means to intergenerational solidarity is especially emphasized in the 2009 manifesto. A recurrent theme is that of economic stability and full employment which a moderate use of the oil dividend will help to achieve. In 2013, the international financial crisis of 2007–2009 was invoked as a demonstration of the importance of 'keeping an orderly house'.

At the other end of the political spectrum the Progress Party appears in constant opposition to the SR and the guidelines for the oil fund. Oil revenues should be spent on investments, especially on infrastructure. Roads in particular are favourite items but also railways. The manifestos of 2001 and 2005 also argue in favour of transfers directly to the citizens – 'the real owners' of the oil fortune. The 2013 manifesto emphasizes the distinction between current spending and investments; the latter type of appropriations from the oil fund should not be covered by the SR but should be seen as redeployment of assets. Examples of productive redeployment include appropriations for roads, railways, police, health and ICT. The party has argued again and again in Parliament that more of the oil dividend could be spent without hurting the national economy.

The Conservative manifestos did not focus explicitly on the SR before 2013 but have consistently argued in favour of moderation with regard to the spending of the oil dividend. In 2013 the SR is mentioned as a safeguard for pensions and protection against industrial flight as a result of pressure from high wages and prices. In 2013 'the wasteful state' frame also appears: the Conservatives are critical with regard to the use of the returns from the fund and would like to see more spending on communications, R&D, green technologies and 'growth-promoting tax relief'.

The parties of the centre, the Liberals, the Christians and the Centre Party, have all become more in favour of a stringent rule for spending the oil dividend over the years. They all, however, have 'poor relatives' they would like to favour with appropriations, but differ somewhat as to who these are. The Liberals have a list fairly close to that of the Conservatives, while the Christians would also like to support 'sustainable companies in the Third World' and emphasize ethically responsible management of the oil fund. The Christians also think that the fund should divest its portfolio of government bonds and go more heavily into real estate.

The Left Socialist Party would, on the one hand, in pursuit of the party's green policies, like to reduce the volume of oil exploitation, and it has also been critical of the oil fund's involvement in international equity markets. On the other hand, the party has a series of causes it would like to promote with the oil dividend, such as more aid to developing countries and various green policies. The establishment of a separate fund for relief in connection with international catastrophes is another favourite.

In summary, the attitudes to the SR and the management of the oil fund vary across parties. All parties are aware of the shadow of the future but draw different conclusions regarding responses to the challenges. Most of them have poor relatives they would like to help; however, the means for helping might amount to restructuring the fund, not just different priorities for spending. The argument of the wasteful state might point to new strategies for the management of the fund. What would happen if the most critical of the parties, the Progress Party, came into office and got a hand on the wheel?

THE OUTLOOK FOR FISCAL DISCIPLINE – TOWARDS DENMARK OR GREECE?

Will fiscal discipline survive? What outcome is most likely to prevail: the one predicted by the Katzenstein hypothesis (fear-driven restraint) or the one predicted by the Fukuyama hypothesis (non-accountable risk taking)? The theories of budgetary behaviour outlined above lean towards the Fukuyama outcome. The theory of incremental budgeting leads to expectations of steady budgetary growth; cutbacks only happen in situations of grave crisis. Egalitarian political culture reinforces the trend of incremental growth; package solutions are favoured rather than clear priorities with winners and losers; thus the underlying budgetary pressure will continue to grow as long as there are available resources. The theory of organizational slack highlights another source of budgetary expansion – the bureaucratic apparatus of the state itself, combined with the growth of the oil fund, is the engine of slack-driven pressure.

The fairly hierarchical nature of budgeting procedures in Norway may provide some institutional protection for the forces of moderation with regard to the spending of oil revenues in the state budget, as long as the guardians remain at the top of the pyramid. The task of the guardians is aided by one of the dominant frames of policy arguments in this field, the shadow of the future, a frame that should help the Katzenstein outcome. However, this frame is challenged by two other frames – those of the poor relatives and the wasteful state.

By the end of 2014 the political and economic setting in which the SR was to be practised had changed dramatically. After the parliamentary elections of 2013 a new right-wing government took office, composed of the Conservative Party and the Progress Party, the very party that for years had proclaimed its disdain for the SR. The Conservatives were the senior government partner, however, and ensured that the government's political platform contained clauses that bound the government to respect the SR. The government's budget for 2015 was considered by many commentators to be the test of its capability to adhere to the SR, which it did with a substantial margin, despite grumblings from the rank and file of the Progress Party. According to one survey, almost 40 per cent of the party's local leaders would have preferred spending of the oil dividend to have reached at least the 4 per cent mark.

The growth of the oil fund, however, has been such that the SR is in the eyes of many financial experts becoming obsolete as a mechanism for fiscal discipline. Spending a 4 per cent dividend from the fund would by now mean a far too expansionary budget. In response to this view, the government in October 2014 appointed a group of experts to suggest revisions to the SR. Interestingly, the second clause of the group's mandate was to identify ways of spending the dividend that would 'promote growth and enhance competitiveness' in the on-shore part of the economy.[9] The latter part of the mandate could be read as a concession to the junior partner of the government and could open up a Pandora's box of poor relatives and creative investment programmes.[10]

However, a stark reminder of the vulnerability of the small state in world markets came in the shape of a sudden drop in oil prices from over 100 USD a barrel in June 2014 to less than 50 USD a barrel six months later. At the lower price, several prospective oil fields were no longer considered viable and, furthermore, the contribution of oil revenues to the oil fund could be expected to drop sharply. On 12 February 2015, the head of the Central Bank tried to drive home the implications of the latter point in his annual speech to the combined Norwegian political and industrial establishment when he presented a graph showing that already in 2015 the deficit of the state budget will equal the oil revenues put into the fund (Olsen 2015). Time will show whether this demonstration sufficed to put the required fear back into the elites. The Katzenstein outcome may still prevail, but it should not be forgotten that the last part of Fukuyama's magnum opus is dedicated to the subject of political decay. Norway could still lose its way to Denmark and end up in a place like Greece.

ACKNOWLEDGEMENTS

I am thankful for comments on drafts from Øyvind Bratberg, Detlef Sprinz and Øyvind Østerud and from participants in the Democracy Programme at the University of Oslo; I acknowledge, furthermore, financial assistance from the Programme for data collection. I also wish to thank the organizers of the WIPCAD seminar at the University of Potsdam for the opportunity to present an early draft of the chapter in December 2013.

NOTES

1. New studies of and comments on the Greek debt crisis appear almost daily. I have found the following reviews particularly helpful: Pettifer (2012); and Pryce (2012). See Knight (2013) for a bottom-up view of the crisis: how it affects people's daily lives and their attribution of responsibility for the crisis.
2. The Parliamentary Code (Stortingets forretningsorden) regulates the parliamentary budget process:

- Stortingets forretningsorden §43 has rules regarding the national budget, the state budget and the pension budget.
- Stortingets forretningsorden §14 states that the government's budget bill is to be divided among the respective parliamentary committees according to the committees' fields of responsibility.
- Stortingets forretningsorden §27 has rules on hearings regarding the budget and other issues.

The Code on Appropriations (Bevilgningsreglementet) regulates the details of the state budget.

3. See Budsjettkalender [Budgetary Calendar] regarding the administrative and political preparation of the state budget: http://www.regjeringen.no/nb/dep/fin/tema/Statsbudsjettet/Budsjettkalender.html?id=439273 (accessed 23 October 2013).
4. The fund was established in 1976 by an amendment to the state constitution and is protected by specific constitutional rules.
5. 'From 1976 to 1982, 30 per cent of all oil and gas royalties were invested in the [Alberta] Heritage Fund, as well as all financial investment yields. From 1982 to 1987 these royalty deposits had decreased by half, and no financial yields were retained. Since 1987 there have been no royalty deposits or retained financial yields. This iconic fund has been essentially moribund for more than 20 years, steadily decreasing in relative value due to population growth and inflation. According to Warrack, the fund and its lost legacy has become a source of "continuous embarrassment to the government"' (http://thetyee.ca/Opinion/2011/04/13/HarpersBigQuestion/).
6. Private communication from the Election Project 2013 by Stine Hesstvedt, 21 November 2014.
7. Private communication from T. Aalberg to the author; see also Curran et al. (2012).
8. The material presented in this section is based on analyses of the electoral manifestos of the political parties for the parliamentary elections of 2001, 2005, 2009 and 2013. Texts commenting on the SR have been coded according to the same coding scheme used for parliamentary debates and newspaper articles. For the purpose of this chapter, qualitative illustrations are used.
9. http://www.regjeringen.no/nb/dep/fin/pressesenter/pressemeldinger/2014/To-ekspertutv alg-om-praktisering-av-handlingsregelen-og-flerarige-budsjetter/Mandat-for-ekspertut valg-om-bruken-av-oljeinntekter.html?id=770979 (accessed 30 November 2014).
10. The group of experts presented its report on 18 June 2015. As regards the latter part of the mandate the group warned against earmarking the oil dividend for particular spending purposes, arguing that this would reduce the transparency of the budget and, besides, that identifying particularly growth-enhancing spending was not feasible (NOU 2015, p. 211). Whether this line of reasoning will shape future government policy remains to be seen.

13. Conclusions

Harald Baldersheim

Being a small state is a risky business, if we are to believe much of the small state literature. Nevertheless, small states multiply, and many prosper. We must assume, therefore, that in the modern world there are also opportunities for small states, not only risks. It is easier, however, to make a catalogue of the risks than of the opportunities. In this book we have tried to analyse both sides of the coin – risks and risk management as well as outlining how small states have responded to opportunities or created new opportunities. Indeed, sometimes the two sides are difficult to separate, as new opportunities grow out of crises and risk management.

The cases presented here are mostly success stories: first, a selection of small states with a long history as stable democracies that have successfully adapted to changing circumstances (the Nordic countries and New Zealand); second, states that are being observed in their formative stages as independent polities (the Baltic countries and Slovakia); and third, semi-sovereign polities that aspire to higher levels of independence, if not necessarily full independence (Scotland and Quebec). Analysis of the last two cases yields insights into perceptions of opportunities in the modern world – the visions of regional elites that motivate them to seek more independence for their regions, perhaps one day full independence. The Baltic countries are cases that present in particularly stark form the struggles of small states at a formative period of their history, while the Nordic countries and New Zealand are cases that highlight the adaptive capacity of small, mature democracies.

What are the yardsticks of a successful small state beyond its ability to survive for a period of time? In the *modern* state, according to Francis Fukuyama (2011, pp. 14, 431–434; 2014, p. 37), good governance is based on a balance between a strong state apparatus, the rule of law, and accountability. A strong state is needed to guarantee the security of citizens; a reign of law means that citizens are treated equally, impartially and predictably by the state, while accountability ensures that no group of citizens can be systematically neglected by the regime over long periods of time. It is the interaction and balance of these three elements that constitute the modern state and a sound democracy. Denmark is held out as an example of a country that got the balance right, and many small countries of the world would like to 'get to Denmark', in Fukuyama's phrase, but he also shows that the road is not an easy one. He reminds us that even stable democracies may decay; if one or more of the three mainstays of democracy are weakened, the balance may be disrupted and the country end up in a place perhaps somewhat like Greece. Such a process might even proceed faster in a small country, as suggested by the case of Iceland (see below).

A LESS DANGEROUS PLACE FOR SMALL STATES? SECURITY AND DIPLOMACY OPTIONS OF SMALL STATES

Alyson J.K. Bailes (Chapter 2) points out that national security has many aspects. Military threats from large neighbours represent important dimensions in an overall security calculus, but modern conceptions of security also include softer considerations such as supply of vital resources, preparedness for disasters and breakdowns, or control of immigration. Small states on their own will normally be disadvantaged in military confrontations but not necessarily so in other fields of security. The five small Nordic countries are interesting cases in this regard. Four of them experienced military confrontation or occupation by larger neighbours during the Second World War. Did these experiences lead to common solutions to problems of security and perhaps a key to small state approaches to peace? Reviewing the security options and choices of the five Nordic states, Bailes concludes that there is no such thing as a common Nordic security model, and therefore also no *sui generis* small state model. The five Nordics have chosen different solutions to their respective military predicaments: three are members of NATO, and two have opted for versions of armed neutrality; only two of them have joined the EU's military cooperation. Norway and Iceland are not even members of the EU, but nevertheless belong to Schengen. They also differ in their approaches to other aspects of social and economic security, largely because of different underlying economic structures. They do join forces, however, in building regional structures to draw in Russia in practical multilateral cooperation (the Barents Euro-Arctic Circle, the Council of Baltic Sea States). They have also acquired a reputation for efforts in peace-building or peace-keeping operations, but this has not kept them from joining US-led military operations when the call has come (Afghanistan, Iraq, Libya). The main point is that their security rests on several pillars, of which military alliance and alignment with the hegemon are but two. Involvement in multilateral security arrangements and soft policies enhance their ability to pursue their interests pro-actively internationally. An impressive achievement in this regard was Norway's acquisition of a vast economic zone in the northern waters through international negotiations under the UN system in the 1960s; the acquisition was later to lead to Norway's oil riches.

Baldur Thorhallsson's account of the case of Iceland (Chapter 3) demonstrates, however, how vulnerable small state actors can be when they try to punch above their weight without the protection of multilateral arrangements. When the financial gales hit Iceland in 2008 the country found itself alone far out to sea with no rescue team in sight. The predicament was, of course, largely of the country's own doing, as it had declined EU membership, shown little interest in heeding international advisory agencies such as the World Bank, and neglected to establish national regulatory capabilities. The end result was that Iceland's over-expansionary banks nearly pulled the state down when they hit the rocks. The example of Iceland shows that small states need shelters in tough times but also that they may need the protection of strong national institutions against their own elites, who can too easily become the victims of 'optimism bias' (Kahnemann 2011).

THE SMALL STATE IN MULTI-LEVEL GOVERNANCE – NEW OPPORTUNITIES?

The international state system has been transformed into a system of not only mutual dependencies but also to some extent multi-level governance. There are few regions where this is more evident than in the European Union. Precisely what kind of political system the EU is evolving into is still very much open to discussion, but the multi-level nature of decision making in the EU is evident, meaning that policy making not only takes place through intergovernmental negotiations but also opens up for input from myriad actors at other levels of government, including regions and municipalities. The characteristic feature is policy integration across levels of government. Perhaps it is this system more than anything else in the modern world that opens up opportunities for small states and levels the playing field in favour of small states, but it is of course not without costs.

According to Diana Panke (Chapter 4), when decisions are made in EU institutions small states may have disadvantages because they have fewer seats in the European Parliament and on various committees and weaker human resources in quantitative and qualitative terms; nevertheless, small states may deal with disadvantages by setting clear priorities and concentrating on influencing those issues that really count in terms of national interests. In this way they may sometimes punch above their weight. Sikk and Cianetti (Chapter 6) follow up on this analysis by showing that the small Baltic states more than larger states tend to elect nationally experienced politicians as European MPs, whereas, in larger states, elections to the European Parliament more often open up careers for politicians on the fringes of the political system. In small states both the pool of available candidates and the number of seats are more limited, which makes for more integration between national and European politics and also quicker adoption of EU regulations at the national level. Jozef Bátora (Chapter 5) shows how small states may deal with limitations regarding diplomatic coverage by entering into symbiotic relationships with the diplomatic network of the EU, thus overcoming gaps in resources and labour. The price to be paid, however, may be a blurring of the representation of the national interest as a consequence of coordination with the general EU position on particular issues. The difficult choice here is finding the balance between effective and extensive diplomatic representation.

THE SOCIAL INVESTMENT STATE – ON 'GETTING TO DENMARK'

As outlined by Michael Keating in Chapter 1, in many countries, from the early 1980s, the corporatist arrangements of the post-war period were being replaced by a neoliberal market state as the solution to effective public services and international competitiveness; a couple of decades later the 'social investment state' may be outperforming the neoliberal state. The Nordic states may be the closest real-life approximations to the social investment state as an ideal type. The type is characterized by high taxes and high social expenditure, especially in fields related to human resource development. Quite a few small countries have looked to this model in admiration. But can it be transposed to different socio-cultural environments outside the Nordic area? And how closely related is it to a social democratic type of regime, the central features of which are redistributory policies in the service of egalitarian political goals? Can the social investment model be married to other types of regime?

In the Nordic countries, social investment policies have long been a standard part of the repertoire for all governments, left and right. However, when the economy comes under stress and policy adjustments are needed one would think that expensive, universal social policies would be first abandoned by governments of the right, while left-wing governments would cling more tenaciously to these policies. The financial crisis, which also hit the Nordic countries around 2008, was a test situation for this hypothesis. Nik Brandal and Øivind Bratberg (Chapter 7) suggest that, 'By investigating how the three Scandinavian countries have responded to the recession, we address the dilemma between *competitiveness* (typically seen as resulting from social investment) and *solidarity* (seen as emblematic of social democracy).' As it turned out, according to Brandal and Bratberg, all three Scandinavian countries stuck to the basics of the Nordic model, without resorting to serious cutbacks of welfare programmes. This was also the case in the two countries that were at the time governed by liberal or centre-right coalitions, Denmark and Sweden. In other words, a commitment to social democratic political philosophy is not a precondition for the model to survive. This is not to say there were no adjustments of policies; to the contrary, adjustments did take place, for example a greater reliance on incentives to bring people back to work; however, these were adjustments largely accepted across the left–right divide with the help of the established concertation structures between labour and capital.

But can the model be transposed to societies imbued with different traditions and economic structures? This issue came to the forefront in the battles over Scottish independence. In Malcolm Harvey's account of the pro-independence campaign (Chapter 9), the Nordic model figured as an attractive end, which the pro-independence side claimed could be more easily reached by an independent Scotland. The campaign was not just about getting out of the United Kingdom but about realizing a different type of state – 'getting to Denmark' in the phrase coined by Francis Fukuyama (2011). Although full independence was not supported by the majority of the voters, further devolution of policy-making powers is probably on the way, so the book is by no means closed as regards the choice of future for Scotland. However, as Harvey also points out, in the Scottish case, barriers to installing the social investment model may not be primarily related to size or lack of independence but perhaps more to a political culture sceptical of the high taxes required by such a state. Building the required level of political trust will therefore be a long-term task for Scotland's political leaders.

Stéphane Paquin (Chapter 8) describes how the Canadian province of Quebec took steps towards more independence from the 1960s onwards by establishing a series of international representations and by constructing a specific Quebec model of economic development. The latter had many of the features of a social investment model as well as certain corporatist elements. It seemed that Quebec had found its own way to Denmark. However, the future of the model looks gloomy: on the one hand, fiscal challenges are mounting, driven by indebtedness and increasing welfare needs, such as pension obligations; on the other hand, the political trust needed to maintain spending is eroding. On top of that, the Liberal Party that was the architect of the Quebec model seems to have lost faith in it. Is Quebec steering a course away from 'Denmark'?

THE ADAPTABILITY OF SMALL STATES – SHOCK THERAPY OR CONCERTED ELITES?

Small states have to be good at changing with the times or at being ahead of the game. They cannot rely on being able to force the environment to change to suit their needs. But what are the mechanics of national adaptability and the drivers of adaptation? Are external shocks needed to bring about required change? Or are negotiated agreements between elites through channels of concertation the more typical way? Four cases give insights into the mechanics of adaptation. New Zealand acquired a reputation for radical reform during the 1980s. The Baltic countries went through fundamental transformations politically, socially and economically during the 1990s. Few countries were as hard hit by the international financial crisis as Iceland, and the country is still struggling with the aftermath. From the turn of the millennium, Norway faced the prospect of a resource curse derived from an oil-driven boom; managing a budgetary surplus turned out to be just as challenging as handling a deficit, but the former led into more uncharted waters.

New Zealand was a pioneer in installing elements of the neoliberal market model in response to the loss of British markets that resulted from Britain's Common Market membership. Jeffrey McNeill (Chapter 10) shows how the dismantling of agricultural subsidies led to a restructuring of the economy, while reforms of the workings of the state were inspired by the tenets of New Public Management. In consequence, would-be reformers flocked to New Zealand from abroad to learn from 'the country that reinvented itself'. How deeply the country was 'reinvented' is open to discussion. Agricultural production still forms the backbone of the economy and dominates exports; and export earnings still depend on relatively few markets, with concomitant vulnerability. New Zealanders still expect their welfare state to deliver the benefits they have been accustomed to throughout the post-war period. While the first period of reform was marked by a certain ideological zeal, successive governments have chosen to retain most of the basic elements while tinkering cautiously with elements that have become unpopular among voters, such as profit-driven hospitals. Two features stand out in the New Zealand reform saga: pragmatism and consensus. Governments retain that which has been found to work without worrying about strategy and the coherence of the wider picture; and changes in government do not lead to abrupt changes of policy or institutions – continuity is the name of the game.

Elite cohesion in small democracies is analysed by Anton Steen (Chapter 11), drawing on material from the Baltic states and Norway. The four countries pursued a neoliberal reform agenda during the 1990s and early 2000s, most radically in the Baltic countries as they strove to recover from a long period of Soviet dominance. Overall, fairly high levels of elite cohesion should be expected in all four countries, and, if there are variations across countries, cohesion should be higher in the Baltic states given their recent traumatic histories. An argument against higher cohesion in the Baltic states would be that it may take time to establish cohesion, and that in new states lessons have not yet been learnt. The overall impression of the data is that agreement among elites is moderately high in all the countries; a second impression is that in all four countries there are divides between business elites on the one hand and political and administrative elites on the other hand, especially as regards views on international financial markets and state control over business and industry. Furthermore, in the two Baltic countries where this question was posed in a second round of data collection the business elites had clearly been taught a lesson by the international financial crisis of 2008 – attitudes had come more into line with those of the political and administrative establishment. The Baltic countries demonstrate that in small, new democracies, because of less path dependency, the trajectories of adaptation may be somewhat more erratic than in mature democracies but also, for the same reason, faster (Baldersheim and Bátora 2012a).

Thorhallsson's study of Iceland and the financial crisis (Chapter 3) demonstrates that there was perhaps too much consensus in the boom years before the crisis, too much mutual trust and too little critical scrutiny – elite consensus degenerated into complacency and crony capitalism. Complacency led to insufficient attention to the need for buffering institutions at home and shelter in international frameworks. However, widespread narratives of historical dependence also shaped the Icelanders' perceptions of challenges and how they should be tackled. Perhaps a crisis of such proportions was needed to shake off some illusions.

In many ways Norway's situation was the opposite of that of Iceland. Harald Baldersheim (Chapter 12) argues that, paradoxically, Norway's predicament as a small state was heightened by the wealth earned from oil extraction in the North Sea. The core of the problem was how to deal with the vast assets that were accumulating in the national oil fund, assets that dwarfed the land-based economy. The more the fund grew, the more pressing the problem became. The growth of the fund strained the elite consensus that had led to the establishment of the fund in the first place.

The guideline for spending from the fund became a political cleavage in its own right. It dawned gradually on the political elite that the guideline that was supposed to bring about fiscal discipline had become a recipe for overspending. Arguments that suggest that Norway has managed to avoid the resource curse seem overstated. The sudden fall in oil prices during 2014 will provide the ultimate test in this regard. The jury is still out.

PULLING THE THREADS TOGETHER

We have noted that the number of small states is still growing, and there is probably no definitive end to the continuing emergence of new small states. It is not possible to predict how many member states the United Nations will have in 30 or 50 years. The history of the small states that have been analysed here demonstrates that there is nothing inevitable about this process. The emergence of these states owes a lot to accidents and circumstances that could have turned out differently. At the start of the nineteenth century, Denmark was a medium-sized European power and became a small state because of unfortunate alliances and lost wars: Norway was lost to Sweden at the end of the Napoleonic wars because of an alliance with France; the German-speaking parts were lost in wars with Prussia. Sweden lost Finland and other territories in wars with Russia. Norway broke out of union with Sweden in 1905 on a flimsy pretext; more flexibility on the Swedish side could have saved the union, or Sweden could have responded militarily and kept Norway in, at least for a time. Finland took the opportunity to declare independence when Russia was weakened by revolution in 1918; Stalin took back some parts of Finnish territory in the 1940s and seriously circumscribed Finnish sovereignty for a long time. The present-day Baltic states also made use of an opportunity that emerged as history took a turn foreseen by almost nobody – the collapse of the Soviet Union. Slovak independence came about through a negotiated break-up of a federation (Czechoslovakia) held together more by outside pressure than a common identity.

These small states seek their security through multilateral frameworks and alliances, but at the end of the day they are dependent upon a hegemon, the US – even the formally neutral states of Sweden and Finland. They have, as regards economic security and development, made clever use of international frameworks and vigorously pursued the games of multi-level governance. Norway in particular has managed to have its cake and eat it: first, by promoting and benefiting from international treaties on economic zones and thereby gaining control over enormous quantities of resources; and second, by staying formally outside the EU but enjoying full access to the inner market for most of its products. Slovakia extends its diplomatic reach in symbiosis with EU representations in capitals around the world. There is a price to pay, however. The price Norway pays is obligatory implementation of all EU directives, in which it had no say. Where Slovakia is represented through the EU delegations, Slovakia must subordinate its positions to those of the larger union.

Economic competitiveness is an imperative for small states but is pursued in different ways. The choice between the neoliberal market model and the social investment model is more path-dependent than ideologically driven. A tradition of concertation among the social partners seems to favour the adoption of the latter model, regardless of the ideology of the government of the day. Solidarity and equality – outcomes favoured especially by social democrats – are fortunate by-products of the model, while gains in competitiveness are the primary concern of liberal or right-wing governments. The model requires high levels of taxation and institutionalization of concertation as a precondition for making the model work. Quebec is an interesting case in this regard, since it appears to be in the process of abandoning its version of the social investment model through a combination of lack of fiscal discipline and political corruption.

The adaptability of small states is promoted partly top down, as highlighted by Katzenstein (1985) – through elite consensus driven by the common perception of external threats. There is also, however, an important bottom-up element to adaptability, especially to 'the road to Denmark', which should be emphasized: trust between citizens and elites. Without trust, collaboration at the top is not likely to work. For example, the acceptance of high taxes and enduring compression of wage differentials as well as intergenerational solidarity over welfare distribution builds on a foundation of trust. The key to trust in this regard is not some diffuse quality of social capital accumulated mysteriously in the past. The key, as suggested by Fukuyama (2011; see above), is accountability, that elites can be held to account in politics, business, associations and communities. This is where small states may have an advantage, although even in small states accountability may fall into decay, as demonstrated by the Icelandic case. Accountability must be institutionalized to work effectively. In modern, democratic states accountability is largely achieved through free and fair elections. But that is not the end of the story. It should also be pointed out that the Nordic states have other features that contribute to accountability: a rich associational tradition and local government with substantial welfare functions and concomitant discretion. These institutions, interwoven with everyday life, provide citizens with information and civic training that enhance their capacity to critically scrutinize elites and decision makers. Quebec could be an interesting counter-example of weak accountability leading to the undoing of a unique model of provincial independence.

In any case, mechanisms of accountability should be high on the research agenda of future small states studies.

References

Abramitzky, Ran, Leah Platt Boustan and Katherine Eriksson (2012), *A Nation of Immigrants: Assimilation and Economic Outcomes in the Age of Mass Migration*, Working Paper No. 18011, Cambridge, MA: National Bureau of Economic Research.

Aðalsteinsson, Gylfi Dalmann (2006), 'Verkföll og verkfallstíðni á íslenskum vinnumarkaði 1976–2004', *Stjórnmál og stjórnsýsla*, **2** (2), 175–196.

Adler-Nissen, Rebecca (2014), 'Symbolic power in European diplomacy: the struggle between national foreign services and the EU's external action service', *Review of International Studies*, **40** (4), 657–681.

Alesina, Alberto and Roberto Perotti (1999), 'Budget deficits and budget institutions', in James M. Poterba (ed.), *Fiscal Institutions and Fiscal Performance*, Chicago: Chicago University Press, pp. 13–36.

Alesina, Alberto and Enrico Spoloare (2003), *The Size of Nations*, Cambridge, MA: MIT Press.

Almond, Gabriel and Sidney Verba (1965), *The Civic Culture: Political Attitudes and Democracy in Five Nations*, Boston, MA: Little, Brown.

Almond, Gabriel and Sidney Verba (1980), *The Civic Culture Revisited*, Boston, MA: Little, Brown.

Althingi (2010), 'Summary of the report's main conclusions', in *Report of the Special Investigation Commission to Investigate and Analyse the Processes Leading to the Collapse of the Three Main Banks in Iceland*, available at http://sic.althingi.is/pdf/RNAvefKafli2Enska.pdf (accessed 14 October 2014).

Anckar, Dag (2002), 'Why are small island states democracies?', *Round Table*, **91** (365), 375–390.

Andersen, Søren Kaj and Ove Kaj Pedersen (2010), *De nordiske landes konkurrencedygtighed – fra flexicurity til mobication*, report, Copenhagen: Nordic Council of Ministers.

Andersen, Søren Kaj, Jon Erik Dølvik and Christian L. Ibsen (2014), *De nordiske aftalemodeller i åbne markeder – udfordringer og perspektiver*, report, Oslo: Fafo.

Andersson, Jenny (2004), 'A productive social citizenship? Reflections on the concept of productive social policies in the European tradition', in Lars Magnusson and Bo Stråth (eds), *A European Social Citizenship?*

Preconditions for Future Policies from a Historical Perspective, Brussels: PIE – Peter Lang, pp. 69–88.

Andersson, Staffan, Torbjon Bergman and Svante Ersson (2014), *The European Representative Democracy Data Archive*, Release 3.

Andrews, Kieran (2014), 'Flaws found in Scottish Government 2014's flagship child care plans', *Courier*, 4 April, p. 7.

Archer, Clive (2010), 'Small states and the European security and defence policy', in Robert Steinmetz and Anders Wivel (eds), *Small States in Europe: Challenges and Opportunities*, Ashgate: Farnham, pp. 47–62.

Archer, Clive (2014), 'The Nordic states and security', in Clive Archer, Alyson J.K. Bailes and Anders Wivel (eds), *Small States and International Security: Europe and Beyond*, London: Routledge, pp. 95–112.

Archer, Clive and Neill Nugent (2002), 'Small states and the European Union', *Current Politics and Economics of Europe*, **11** (1), 1–10.

Armstrong, Harvey W. and Robert Read (1995), 'Western European micro-states and EU autonomous regions: the advantages of size and sovereignty', *World Development*, **23** (7), 1229–1245.

Armstrong, Harvey W. and Robert Read (1998), 'Trade and growth in small states: the impact of global trade liberalisation', *World Economy*, **21** (4), 563–585.

Arter, David (1999), *Scandinavian Politics Today*, Manchester: Manchester University Press.

Åslund, Anders and Mikhail Dmitriev (1999), 'Economic reform versus rent seeking', in Anders Åslund and Martha Brill Olcott (eds), *Russia after Communism*, Washington, DC: Brookings Institution Press.

Austermann, Frauke (forthcoming), 'Representing the EU in China: European bilateral diplomacy in a competitive environment', in David Spence and Jozef Bátora (eds), *The European External Action Service: European Diplomacy Post-Westphalia*, London: Palgrave.

Avdagic, Sabina, Martin Rhodes and Jelle Visser (2011), *Social Pacts in Europe: Emergence, Evolution and Institutionalization*, Oxford: Oxford University Press.

Bailer, Stefanie (2004), 'Bargaining success in the European Union: the impact of exogenous and endogenous power resources', *European Union Politics*, **5** (1), 99–123.

Bailes, Alyson J.K. (2008), *What Role for the Private Sector in 'Societal Security'?*, EPC Issue Brief No. 56, Brussels: European Policy Centre, available at http://www.epc.eu/documents/uploads/725649730_EPC%20 Issue%20Paper%2056%20What%20role%20for%20private%20sector% 20in%20societal%20security.pdf (accessed 21 January 2015).

Bailes, Alyson J.K. (2009), *Does a Small State Need a Strategy?*, Reykjavik: Centre for Small State Studies, University of Iceland, available at http://

ams.hi.is/wp-content/uploads/old/Bailes_Final%20wh.pdf (accessed 21 January 2015).

Bailes, Alyson J.K. (2014), 'Societal security and small states', in Clive Archer, Alyson J.K. Bailes and Anders Wivel (eds), *Small States and International Security: Europe and Beyond*, London: Routledge, pp. 66–79.

Bailes, Alyson J.K. and Carolina Sandö (2014), *Nordic Cooperation on Civil Security: The Haga Process 2009–14*, Reykjavik: Centre for Small State Studies, University of Iceland, available at http://ams. hi.is/wp-content/uploads/2014/04/The-Haga-Process-PDF.pdf (accessed 19 January 2015).

Bailes, Alyson J.K. and Baldur Thorhallsson (2013), 'Instrumentalizing the European Union in small state strategy', *Journal of European Integration*, **35** (2), 99–115.

Bailes, Alyson J.K., Baldur Thorhallsson and Jean-Marc Rickli (2014), 'Small states, survival and strategy', in Clive Archer, Alyson J.K. Bailes and Anders Wivel (eds), *Small States and International Security: Europe and Beyond*, London: Routledge, pp. 26–45.

Baldacchino, Godfrey (2014), 'The security concerns of designed spaces: size matters', in Clive Archer, Alyson J.K. Bailes and Anders Wivel (eds), *Small States and International Security: Europe and Beyond*, London: Routledge, pp. 241–254.

Baldersheim, Harald and Jozef Bátora (2012a), 'Prospects for two small countries in a turbulent world', in Harald Baldersheim and Jozef Bátora (eds), *The Governance of Small States in Turbulent Times: The Exemplary Cases of Norway and Slovakia*, Opladen: Barbara Budrich Publishers, pp. 262–271.

Baldersheim, Harald and Jozef Bátora (eds) (2012b), *The Governance of Small States in Turbulent Times: The Exemplary Cases of Norway and Slovakia*, Opladen: Barbara Budrich Publishers.

Bale, T., C. Green-Pedersen, A. Krouwel, K.R. Luther and N. Sitter (2010), 'If you can't beat them, join them? Explaining social democratic responses to the challenge from the populist radical right in Western Europe', *Political Studies*, **58** (3), 410–426.

Balfour, Rosa and Kristi Raik (2013), *The European External Action Service and National Diplomacies*, EPC Issue Paper No. 73, Brussels: European Policy Centre.

Bátora, Jozef (2005), 'Does the European Union transform the institution of diplomacy?', *Journal of European Public Policy*, **12** (1), 44–66.

Bátora, Jozef (2013), 'The "mitrailleuse effect": the EEAS as an interstitial organization and the dynamics of innovation in diplomacy', *Journal of Common Market Studies*, **51** (4), 598–613.

Beaudoin, Louise (1977), 'Origines et développement du rôle international du gouvernement du Québec', in Paul Painchaud (ed.), *Le Canada sur la scène internationale*, Montréal and Québec City: Centre québécois de relations internationales et Presses de l'Université du Québec.

Bélanger, Louis (1994), 'La diplomatie culturelle des provinces canadiennes', *Études internationales*, **25** (3), 421–452.

Bell, David and David Eiser (2014), *Inequality in Scotland: Trends, Drivers, and Implications for the Independence Debate*, Edinburgh: ESRC Scottish Centre on Constitutional Change.

Berge, Øyvind (2009), *De nordiske modellene etter 2000 – tiltak for å dempe finanskrisa i Norden*, report, Oslo: Fafo.

Bergh, Trond (1981), 'Norsk økonomisk politikk 1945–65', in Trond Bergh and Helge Pharo (eds), *Vekst og velstand: Norsk politisk historie 1945–65*, Oslo: Universitetsforlaget, pp. 11–97.

Berglund, Tomas and Ingrid Esser (2014), *Modell i förändring: Landrapport om Sverige*, report, Oslo: Fafo.

Bernier, Luc (1996), *De Paris à Washington: La politique internationale du Québec*, Sainte-Foy: Presses de l'Université du Québec.

Birch, Kean and Vlad Mykhnenko (2009), 'Varieties of neoliberalism? Restructuring in large industrially dependent regions across Western and Eastern Europe', *Journal of Economic Geography*, **9** (3), 355–380.

Björkdahl, Annika (2008), 'Norm advocacy: a small state strategy to influence the EU', *Journal of European Public Policy*, **15** (1), 135–154.

Blais, André (2000), *To Vote or Not to Vote? The Merits and Limits of Rational Choice Theory*, Pittsburgh, PA: University of Pittsburgh Press.

Bohle, Dorothee and Béla Greskovits (2012), *Capitalist Diversity on Europe's Periphery*, Ithaca, NY: Cornell University Press.

Bohn, Henning and Robert P. Inman (1996), 'Balanced-budget rules and public deficits: evidence from the U.S. states', *Carnegie-Rochester Conference Series on Public Policy*, **45** (1), 13–76.

Bollard, Alan, Ralph G. Lattimore and Brian Silverstone (1996), 'Introduction', in Brian Silverstone, Alan Bollard and Ralph G. Lattimore (eds), *A Study of Economic Reform: The Case of New Zealand*, Amsterdam: Elsevier, p. viii.

Bolton, Grace and Gezim Visoka (2010), 'Recognizing Kosovo's secession: remedial secession or earned sovereignty?', St Antony's Occasional Paper No. 11/2010, available at http://www.sant.ox.ac.uk/seesox/pdf/RecognizingKosovosindependence.pdf (accessed 25 January 2015).

Börzel, Tanja A. (2003), *Environmental Leaders and Laggards in Europe: Why There Is (Not) a Southern Problem*, London: Ashgate.

Börzel, Tanja A. and Thomas Risse (2000), 'When Europe hits home: Europeanization and domestic change', *European Integration On-line*

Papers, **4** (15), available at http://eiop.or.at/eiop/texte/2000-015a.htm (accessed 17 January 2015).

Boston, Jonathan (1991), 'The theoretical underpinnings of public sector restructuring in New Zealand', in Jonathan Boston, John Martin, June Pallot and Pat Walsh (eds), *Reshaping the State: New Zealand's Bureaucratic Revolution*, Auckland: Oxford University Press, pp. 1–26.

Boston, Jonathan and Chris Eichbaum (2014), 'New Zealand's neoliberal reforms: half a revolution', *Governance*, **27** (3), 373–376.

Bourdieu, Pierre (1998), 'Utopia of endless exploitation: the essence of neoliberalism', in *Le Monde diplomatique*, December, English edn, available at http://mondediplo.com/1998/12/08bourdieu (accessed 1 February 2015).

Bourque, Gilles (2000), *Le modèle québécois de développement*, Montréal: Presses de l'Université du Québec.

Bourque, Gilles and Benoît Lévesque (1999), *Le modèle québécois en question*, Cahiers du CRISES No. 9910, Montréal: Centre de recherche sur les innovations sociales.

Bourque, Gilles, Jules Duchastel and Jacques Beauchemin (1994), *La société libérale duplessiste*, Montréal: Presses de l'Université de Montréal.

Boven, Rick, Dan Bidois and Catherine Harland (2010), *A Goal Is Not a Strategy*, Discussion Paper No. 2010/1, Auckland: New Zealand Institute.

Brandal, Nikolai, Øivind Bratberg and Dag Einar Thorsen (2013), *The Nordic Model of Social Democracy*, Basingstoke: Palgrave Macmillan.

Bretherton, Charlotte and John Vogler (1999), *The European Union as a Global Actor*, London: Routledge.

Briguglio, Lino, Gordon Cordina and Eliawony J. Kisanga (2006), *Building the Economic Resilience of Fragile States*, Valletta: Formatek Publishing for the Islands and Small States Institute of the University of Malta and the Commonwealth Secretariat, London.

Brooking, Tom (2014), 'A noisy sub-imperialist: Richard Seddon and the attempt to establish a New Zealand empire in the Pacific, 1894–1901', *Journal of New Zealand and Pacific Studies*, **2** (2), 121–137.

Browning, Christopher S. (2006), 'Small, smart and salient? Rethinking identity in the small states literature', *Cambridge Review of International Affairs*, **19** (4), 669–684.

Brubaker, Roger (1996), *Nationalism Reframed: Nationhood and the National Question in the New Europe*, Cambridge: Cambridge University Press.

Brückner, Markus (2010), 'Population size and civil conflict risk: is there a causal link?', *Economic Journal*, **120** (544), 535–550.

Brunsson, Nils and Björn Rombach (1982), *Går det att spara – kommunal budgetering under stagnation*, Stockholm: Doxa.

Bunse, Simon, Paul Magnette and Kalypso Nicolaidis (2005), *Is the Commission the Small Member States' Best Friend?*, Stockholm: SIEPS.

Buzan, Barry (2007), *People, States and Fear: An Agenda for International Security Studies in the Post-Cold War Era*, 2nd edn, Colchester: ECPR Press.

Buzan, Barry, Japp de Wilde and Ole Wæver (1998), *Security: A New Framework for Analysis*, Boulder, CO: Lynne Rienner Publishers.

Cameron, David R. (2012), 'European fiscal responses to the Great Recession', in Nancy Bermeo and Jonas Pontusson (eds), *Coping with Crisis: Government Reactions to the Great Recession*, New York: Russell Sage Foundation.

Central Bank of Iceland [Seðlabanki Íslands] (2010), 'Peningastefnan eftir höft: Skýrsla Seðlabanka Íslands til efnahags- og viðskiptaráðherra', Sérrit 4, 20 December, available at http://www.sedlabanki.is/lisalib/getfile.aspx?itemid=8358 (accessed 14 October 2014).

Chapman, Jeff and Grant Duncan (2007), 'Is there now a new "New Zealand model"?', *Public Management Review*, **9** (1), 1–25.

Chayes, Abram and Antonia Handler-Chayes (1993), 'On compliance', *International Organization*, **47** (2), 175–205.

Chillaud, Matthieu (2006), *Territorial Disarmament in Northern Europe: The Epilogue of a Success Story?*, SIPRI Policy Paper No. 13, Stockholm: Stockholm International Peace Research Institute, available at http://books.sipri.org/product_info?c_product_id=329 (accessed 20 January 2015).

Cini, Michelle (2007), *European Union Politics*, Vol. 2, Oxford: Oxford University Press.

Clague, Christopher, Suzanne Gleason and Stephen Knack (2001), 'Determinants of lasting democracy in poor countries: culture, development, and institutions', *Annals of the American Academy of Political and Social Science*, **573** (1), 16–41.

Coase, Ronald (1937), 'The nature of the firm', *Economica*, **4** (16), 386–405.

Coleman, James S. (1988), 'Social capital in the creation of human capital', *American Journal of Sociology*, **94** (Supplement), 95–120.

Collier, Paul and Anke Hoeffler (2009), *Democracy's Achilles Heel or, How to Win an Election without Really Trying*, Centre for the Study of African Economies Working Paper No. 2009-08, Oxford: University of Oxford, Department of Economics.

Commonwealth Advisory Group (1997), *A Future for Small States: Overcoming Vulnerability*, London: Commonwealth Secretariat.

Compston, Hugh (2002), 'The strange persistence of policy concertation', in Stefan Berger and Hugh Compston (eds), *Policy Concertation and Social Partnership in Western Europe*, Oxford: Berghahn.

Cooper, Andrew F. and Timothy M. Shaw (2009), *The Diplomacies of Small States: Between Vulnerability and Resilience*, London: Palgrave Macmillan.

Corbett, Richard, Francis Jacobs and Michael Shackleton (2011), *The European Parliament*, London: John Harper.

Cordina, Gordon and Nadina Farrugia (2005), *Measuring Vulnerability: A Methodological Review and Refinement Based on Partner Country and Price Volatility Issues*, Occasional Papers on Islands and Small States No. 4/2005, Valletta: Islands and Small States Institute of the University of Malta.

Cottey, Andrew (2009), *Sub-regional Cooperation in Europe: An Assessment*, BRIGG Papers (College of Europe) No. 3/2009, available at http://www.cris.unu.edu/fileadmin/workingpapers/BRIGG_papers/ BRIGG_3-2009_Andrew_Cottey.pdf (accessed 25 January 2015).

Crandall, Matthew (2014), 'Soft security threats and small states: the case of Estonia', *Defence Studies*, **14** (1), 30–55.

Criekemans, David (2010), 'Regional sub-state diplomacy from a comparative perspective: Quebec, Scotland, Bavaria, Catalonia, Wallonia and Flanders', *The Hague Journal of Diplomacy*, **5** (1–2), 37–64.

Crocombe, Graham T., Michael J. Enright, Michael E. Porter, Tony Caughey and New Zealand Trade Development Board (1991), *Upgrading New Zealand's Competitive Advantage*, Auckland: Oxford University Press.

Cronberg, Tarja (2006), 'The will to defend: a Nordic divide over security and defence policy', in Alyson J.K. Bailes, Gunilla Herolf and Bengt Sundelius (eds), *The Nordic Countries and European Security and Defence Policy*, Oxford: Oxford University Press, pp. 315–322.

Crouch, Colin (2013), 'Class politics and the social investment welfare state', in Michael Keating and David McCrone (eds), *The Crisis of Social Democracy in Europe*, Edinburgh: Edinburgh University Press, pp. 156–168.

Curran, James, Sharon Coen, Toril Aalberg and Shanto Iyengar (2012), 'News content, media use and current affairs knowledge', in Toril Aalberg and James Curran (eds), *How Media Inform Democracy: A Comparative Approach*, New York: Routledge, pp. 81–97.

Curtice, John and Rachel Ormiston (2011), *Is Scotland More Left-wing than England?*, Edinburgh: Scottish Centre for Social Research.

Cyert, Richard M. and James G. March (1963), *A Behavioral Theory of the Firm*, Englewood Cliffs, NJ: Prentice Hall.

Dahl, Robert Alan (1982), *Dilemmas of Pluralist Democracy: Autonomy vs. Control*, New Haven, CT: Yale University Press.

Dahl, Robert Alan and Edward R. Tufte (1973), *Size and Democracy*, Stanford, CA: Stanford University Press.

Dellepiane, Sebastian and Niamh Hardiman (2012), 'Governing the Irish economy: a triple crisis', in Niamh Hardiman (ed.), *Irish Governance in Crisis*, Manchester: Manchester University Press, pp. 83–109.

de Mestral, Armand and Evan Fox-Decent (2008), 'Rethinking the relationship between international and domestic law', *McGill Law Journal*, **53** (4), 573–648.

Deutsch, Karl (1966), *Nationalism and Social Communication*, Cambridge, MA: MIT Press.

De Ville, Ferdi (2012), 'European Union regulatory politics in the shadow of the WTO: WTO rules as frame of reference and rhetorical device', *Journal of European Public Policy*, **19** (5), 700–718.

Dieckhoff, Alain (2000), *La Nation dans tous ses États: Les identités nationales en mouvement*, Paris: Flammarion.

DiMaggio, Paul and Walter Powell ([1983] 1991), 'The iron cage revisited: institutional isomorphism and collective rationality in organizational fields', in Walter Powell and Paul J. DiMaggio (eds), *The New Institutionalism in Organizational Analysis*, Chicago: University of Chicago Press, pp. 63–82.

Djuve, Anne Britt and Anne S. Grødem (eds) (2014), *Innvandring og arbeidsmarkedsintegrering i Norden*, report, Oslo: Fafo.

Dølvik, Jon Erik (2013), *Grunnpilarene i de nordiske modellene: Tilbakeblikk på arbeidslivs- og velferdsregimenes utvikling*, report, Oslo: Fafo.

Dølvik, Jon Erik, Tone Fløtten, Jon M. Hippe and Bård Jordfald (2014), *The Nordic Model towards 2030: A New Chapter?*, report, Oslo: Fafo.

Duncan, Grant and Jeff Chapman (2010), 'New millennium, new public management and the New Zealand model', *Australian Journal of Public Administration*, **69** (3), 301–313.

Dunn, William (2008), *Public Policy Analysis*, 3rd edn, Upper Saddle River, NJ: Pearson.

Easterly, William and Aart Kraay (2000), 'Small states, small problems? Income, growth, and volatility in small states', *World Development*, **28** (11), 2013–2027.

Economist (1997), 'Finland and Europe: in and happy', 9 October, available at http://www.economist.com/node/102291.

EEAS [European External Action Service] (2013), *EEAS Review 2013*, Brussels: EEAS, July, available at http://eeas.europa.eu/library/publications/2013/3/2013_eeas_review_en.pdf (accessed 19 January 2015).

Ehin, Piret and Mihkel Solvak (2012), 'Party voters gone astray: explaining independent candidate success in the 2009 European elections in Estonia', *Journal of Elections, Public Opinion and Parties*, **22** (3), 269–291.

Eiríksson, Stefán (2004), 'Deeply involved in the European project: membership of Schengen', in Baldur Thorhallsson (ed.), *Iceland and European Integration: On the Edge*, New York: Routledge, pp. 50–60.

Electoral Reform Society (2013), *Democracy Max: An Inquiry into the Future of Scottish Democracy – A Vision for a Good Scottish Democracy*, Edinburgh: Electoral Reform Society Scotland.

Elschner, Christina and Verner Vanborren (2009), *Corporate Effective Tax Rates in an Enlarged European Union*, Brussels: European Commission.

Elster, John (1992), 'Arguing and bargaining in the Federal Convention and the Assemblée Constituanté', in Raino Malnes and Arild Underdal (eds), *Rationality and Institutions: Essays in Honour of Knut Midgaard*, Oslo: Univeritetsforlaget, pp. 13–50.

Erk, Jan and Wouter Veenendaal (2014), 'Is small really beautiful? The microstate mistake', *Journal of Democracy*, **25** (3), 35–148.

Esping-Andersen, Gøsta (1990), *The Three Worlds of Welfare Capitalism*, Princeton, NJ: Princeton University Press.

Esping-Andersen, Gøsta (1996), *Welfare States in Transition: National Adaptations in Global Economies*, London: Sage.

European Parliament, Committee on Employment and Social Affairs (2010), *The Lisbon Strategy 2000–2010: An Analysis and Evaluation of the Methods Used and Results Achieved*, final report, Brussels: European Parliament.

European Union (2007), *Treaty of Lisbon*, available at http://europa.eu/lisbon_treaty/full_text/ (accessed 21 January 2015).

Fearon, James (1998), 'Bargaining, enforcement, and international cooperation', *International Organization*, **52** (2), 269–305.

Fearon, James and David Laitin (2003), 'Ethnicity, insurgency, and civil war', *American Political Science Review*, **97** (1), 75–90.

Ferguson, Yale H. and Richard W. Mansbach (1996), *Polities: Authority, Identities, and Change*, Columbia: University of South Carolina Press.

Fernandez-Pasarin, Ana Mar (forthcoming), 'Towards an EU consular policy', in David Spence and Jozef Bátora (eds), *The European External Action Service: European Diplomacy Post-Westphalia*, London: Palgrave.

Fløtten, Tone, Jon Kvist, Lilja Mósesdóttir and Lisbeth Pedersen (2014), *Velferdsstatsutfordringer: Ulikhet, arbeidsintegrering, tjenesteproduksjon og likestilling*, report, Oslo: Fafo.

Forsberg, Tuomas (2013), 'The rise of Nordic defence cooperation: a return to regionalism?', *International Affairs*, **89** (5), 1161–1181.

Fox, Annette Baker ([1959] 2006), 'The power of small states: diplomacy in World War II', reprinted in Christine Ingebritsen, Iver Neumann,

Sieglinde Gstöhl and Jessica Beyer (eds), *Small States in International Relations*, Seattle: University of Washington Press, pp. 39–54.

Fraser, Graham (2007), *Sorry, I Don't Speak French: Confronting the Canadian Crisis That Won't Go Away*, Toronto: McClelland & Stewart.

Freeman, Richard B. (2013), *Little Engines That Could: Can the Nordic Economies Maintain Their Renewed Success?*, report, Oslo: Fafo.

Fukuyama, Francis (2011), *The Origins of Political Order*, New York: Farrar, Straus and Giroux.

Fukuyama, Francis (2014), *Political Order and Political Decay: From the Industrial Revolution to the Globalization of Democracy*, New York: Farrar, Straus and Giroux.

Gagnon, Alain-G. and Daniel Latouche (1991), *Allaire, Bélanger, Campeau et les autres*, Montréal: Éditions Québec/Amérique.

Galbreath, David J. (2006), 'Latvian foreign policy after enlargement: continuity and change', *Cooperation and Conflict*, **41** (4), 443–462.

Galbreath, David J. and Jeremy W. Lamoreaux (2007), 'Bastion, beacon or bridge? Conceptualising the Baltic logic of the EU's neighbourhood', *Geopolitics*, **12** (1), 109–132.

Gerring, John and Dominic Zarecki (2011), *Size and Democracy Revisited*, DISC Working Papers No. 2011/17, Budapest: Center for the Study of Imperfections in Democracies.

Geys, Benny (2006), 'Explaining voter turnout: a review of aggregate-level research', *Electoral Studies*, **25** (4), 637–663.

Giddens, Anthony (1998), *The Third Way: The Renewal of Social Democracy*, Cambridge: Polity Press.

Golden, David G. and James M. Poterba (1985), 'The price of popularity: the political business cycle reexamined', *American Journal of Political Science*, **24** (4), 696–714.

Government of Denmark, Government of Greenland and Government of the Faroes (2011), *Kingdom of Denmark Strategy for the Arctic 2011–2020*, Copenhagen, Nuuk and Tórshavn: Ministry of Foreign Affairs (Denmark), Department of Foreign Affairs (Greenland) and Ministry of Foreign Affairs (Faroes).

Government of Finland (n.d.), 'Security in society', webpage, available at http://yhteiskunnanturvallisuus.fi/en (accessed 29 January 2015).

Government of Norway (2006), *The Norwegian Government's High North Strategy*, available at https://www.regjeringen.no/globalassets/upload/ud/vedlegg/strategien.pdf (accessed 25 January 2015).

Government of Sweden (2014), *International Defence Cooperation: Efficiency, Solidarity, Sovereignty*, available at http://www.icds.ee/file-admin/media/icds.ee/failid/Bertelman2014.pdf (accessed 25 January 2015).

Granovetter, Mark (1985), 'Economic action and social structure: a theory of embeddedness', *American Journal of Sociology*, **91** (3), 481–510.

Graubard, Stephen R. (ed.) (1986), *Norden: The Passion for Equality*, Oslo: Norwegian University Press.

Greif, Avner (1994), 'Cultural beliefs and the organization of society: a historical and theoretical reflection on collectivist and individualist societies', *Journal of Political Economy*, **102** (5), 912–950.

Griffiths, Richard T. (2014), 'Economic security and size', in Clive Archer, Alyson J.K. Bailes and Anders Wivel (eds), *Small States and International Security: Europe and Beyond*, London: Routledge, pp. 46–65.

Gulbrandsen, Trygve, Fredrik Engelstad, Trond Beldo Klausen, Hege Skjeie, Marit Teigen and Øyvind Østerud (2002), *Norske makteliter*, Oslo: Gyldendal Akademisk.

Gustafson, Thane (1999), *Capitalism Russian-style*, Cambridge: Cambridge University Press.

Habermas, Jürgen (1992), 'Handlungen, Sprechakte, sprachlich vermittelte Interaktion und Lebenswelt', in Jürgen Habermas (ed.), *Nachmetaphysisches Denken: Philosophische Aufsätze*, Frankfurt am Main: Suhrkamp, pp. 63–104.

Habermas, Jürgen (1995a), *Theorie des kommunikativen Handelns*, Vol. 1: *Handlungsrationalität und gesellschaftliche Rationalisierung*, Frankfurt am Main: Suhrkamp.

Habermas, Jürgen (1995b), *Theorie des kommunikativen Handelns*, Vol. 2: *Zur Kritik der funktionalistischen Vernunft*, Frankfurt am Main: Suhrkamp.

Hall, Peter A. and David Soskice (2001), 'An introduction to varieties of capitalism', in Peter A. Hall and David Soskice (eds), *Varieties of Capitalism: The Institutional Foundations of Comparative Advantage*, Oxford: Oxford University Press, pp. 1–68.

Handel, Michael (1981), *Weak States in the International System*, London: Frank Cass.

Hanf, Kenneth and Ben Soetendorp (eds) (1998), *Adapting to European Integration: Small States and the European Union*, London: Longman.

Hegre, Håvard and Nicholas Sambanis (2006), 'Sensitivity analysis of empirical results on civil war onset', *Journal of Conflict Resolution*, **50** (4), 508–535.

Hemerijck, Anton (2013), *Changing Welfare States*, Oxford: Oxford University Press.

Hendrickx, Frank (ed.) (2008), *Flexicurity and the Lisbon Agenda: A Cross-disciplinary Reflection*, Cambridge: Intersentia Publishers.

Hettne, Björn and Fredrik Söderbaum (2005), 'Civilian power or soft imperialism? The EU as a global actor and the role of interregionalism', *European Foreign Affairs Review*, **10** (4), 535–552.

Higley, John and Michael Burton (2006), *Elite Foundations of Liberal Democracy*, Oxford: Rowman & Littlefield.

Higley, John and György Lengyel (2000), 'Introduction: elite configurations after state socialism', in John Higley and György Lengyel (eds), *Elites after State Socialism: Theories and Analysis*, Oxford: Rowman & Littlefield, pp. 1–21.

Hippe, Jon M., Øyvind Berge et al. (2013), *Ombyggingens periode: Landrapport om Norge 1990–2012*, report, Oslo: Fafo.

Hix, Simon (2006), *The Political System of the European Union*, Basingstoke: Palgrave.

Hoen, Herman W. (2011), 'Crisis in Eastern Europe: the downside of a market economy revealed?', *European Review*, **19** (1), 31–41.

Hood, Christopher (1991), 'A public management for all seasons?', *Public Administration*, **69**, 3–19.

Howlett, Darryl and John Glenn (2005), 'Epilogue: Nordic strategic culture', *Cooperation and Conflict*, **40** (1), 121–140.

Hutchison, I.G.C. (2001), *Scottish Politics in the Twentieth Century*, Basingstoke: Palgrave.

IISS [International Institute for Strategic Studies] (2014), *The Military Balance 2014*, London: Routledge.

Ingebritsen, Christine (2002), 'Norm entrepreneurs: Scandinavia's role in world politics', *Cooperation and Conflict*, **27** (1), 11–23.

Ingimundarson, Valur (2011), *The Rebellious Ally: Iceland, the United States, and the Politics of Empire*, Dordrecht: Republic of Letters Publishing.

Ingólfsdóttir, Auður H. (2014), 'Environmental security and small states', in Clive Archer, Alyson J.K. Bailes and Anders Wivel (eds), *Small States and International Security: Europe and Beyond*, London: Routledge, pp. 80–92.

Ivanov, Kalin (2008), 'Legitimate conditionality? The European Union and nuclear power safety in Central and Eastern Europe', *International Politics*, **45** (2), 146–167.

James, Colin (1987), *The Quiet Revolution: Turbulence and Transition in Contemporary New Zealand*, Wellington: Allen & Unwin.

Jensen, Nathan M. (2012), 'Fiscal policy and the firm: do low corporate tax rates attract multinational corporations?', *Comparative Political Studies*, **45**, 1004–1026.

Jenson, Jane (2012), 'Redesigning citizenship regimes after neoliberalism: moving towards social investment', in Nathalie Morel, Bruno Palier and Joakim Palme (eds), *Towards a Social Investment*

Welfare State? Ideas, Policies and Challenges, Bristol: Policy Press, pp. 61–87.

Jenson, Jane and Denis Saint-Martin (2003), 'New routes to social cohesion? Citizenship and the social investment state', *Canadian Journal of Sociology*, **28** (1), 77–99.

Jimmy Reid Foundation (2013), *The Common Weal: A Model for Economic and Social Development in Scotland*, Glasgow: Jimmy Reid Foundation.

Joenniemi, Pertti (1999), 'The Barents Euro-Arctic Council', in Andrew Cottey (ed.), *Subregional Cooperation in the New Europe*, London: Macmillan, pp. 23–45.

Jones, Daniel Stedman (2012), *Masters of the Universe: Hayek, Friedman, and the Birth of Neoliberal Politics*, Princeton, NJ: Princeton University Press.

Jones, Erik (2008), *Economic Adjustment and Political Transformation in Small States*, Oxford: Oxford University Press.

Jørgensen, Henning and Per Kongshøj Madsen (2007), *Flexicurity and Beyond: Finding a New Agenda for the European Social Model*, report, Copenhagen: DJØF.

Kahnemann, Daniel (2011), *Thinking, Fast and Slow*, New York: Farrar, Straus and Giroux.

Kangas, Olli and Antti Saloniemi (2013), *Historical Making, Present and Future Challenges for the Nordic Welfare State Model in Finland*, report, Oslo: Fafo.

Karl, Terry L. (1997), *The Paradox of Plenty: Oil Booms and Petro States*, Berkeley: California University Press.

Karsh, Efraim (1989), *Neutrality and Small States*, London: Routledge.

Kattel, Rainer and Ringa Raudla (2013), 'The Baltic republics and the crisis of 2008–2011', *Europe–Asia Studies*, **65** (3), 426–449.

Kattel, Rainer, Tarmo Kalvet and Tiina Randma-Liiv (2010), 'Small states and innovation', in Robert Steinmetz and Anders Wivel (eds), *Small States in Europe: Challenges and Opportunities*, Farnham: Ashgate, pp. 65–85.

Katzenstein, Peter J. (1984), *Corporatism and Change: Austria, Switzerland, and the Politics of Industry*, Ithaca, NY: Cornell University Press.

Katzenstein, Peter J. (1985), *Small States in World Markets: Industrial Policy in Europe*, Ithaca, NY: Cornell University Press.

Katzenstein, Peter J. (1997), 'The smaller European states, Germany and Europe', in Peter J. Katzenstein (ed.), *Tamed Power: Germany in Europe*, London: Cornell University Press, pp. 251–304.

Katzenstein, Peter J. (2003), '"Small states" and small states revisited', *New Political Economy*, **8** (1), 9–30.

Keating, Michael (1997), *Les défis du nationalisme moderne: Québec, Catalogne, Écosse*, Montréal: Presses de l'Université de Montréal.

Keating, Michael (2008), 'Culture and social science', in Donatella della Porta and Michael Keating (eds), *Approaches and Methodologies in the Social Sciences: A Pluralist Perspective*, Cambridge: Cambridge University Press, pp. 99–117.

Keating, Michael and Malcolm Harvey (2014), *Small Nations in a Big World: What Scotland Can Learn*, Edinburgh: Luath Press.

Keating, Michael, John Loughlin and Kris Deschouwer (2003), *Culture, Institutions and Economic Development*, Cheltenham, UK and Northampton, MA, USA: Edward Elgar.

Keller, Suzanne (1991), *Beyond the Ruling Class: Strategic Elites in Modern Society*, Piscataway, NJ: Transaction Publishers.

Kelsey, Jane (1995), *The New Zealand Experiment: A World Model for Structural Adjustment?*, Auckland: Auckland University Press with Bridget Williams Books.

Kelsey, Jane (2002), *At the Crossroads: Three Essays*, Wellington: Bridget Williams Books.

Keohane, Robert O. (1969), 'Lilliputians' dilemmas: small states in international politics', *International Organization*, **23** (2), 291–310.

Keukeleire, Stephan (2000), *The European Union as a Diplomatic Actor*, DSP Discussion Papers No. 71, Leicester: Centre for the Study of Diplomacy.

Keukeleire, Stephan (2003), 'The European Union as a diplomatic actor: internal, traditional and structural diplomacy', *Diplomacy and Statecraft*, **14** (3), 31–56.

Kickert, Walter, Erik Hans Klijn and Joop Koppenjan (1997), *Managing Complex Networks: Strategies for the Public Sector*, London: Sage.

Kirton, Mark (2013), *Caribbean Regional Disaster Response and Management Mechanisms: Prospects and Challenges*, Washington, DC: Brookings Institution, available at http://www.brookings.edu/~/media/research/files/reports/2013/07/caribbean%20regional%20organizations%20disasters/caribbean%20regional%20disaster%20response.pdf (accessed 20 January 2015).

Klitgaard, Michael G. (2007), 'Why are they doing it? Social democracy and market-oriented welfare reforms', *West European Politics*, **30** (1), 172–194.

Klus, Adam (2014), 'The Nordic dimension of the Ukrainian crisis', *New Eastern Europe*, 12 June, available at http://www.neweasterneurope.eu/interviews/1242-the-nordic-dimension-of-the-ukrainian-crisis (accessed 8 January 2015).

Knight, Daniel M. (2013), 'The Greek economic crisis as trope', *Focaal: Journal of Global and Historical Anthropology*, **65**, 147–159.

Knill, Christoph (2001), *The Transformation of National Administrations in Europe: Patterns of Change and Persistence*, Cambridge: Cambridge University Press.

Koenig, Thomas (2008), 'Analysing the process of EU legislative decision-making to make a long story short', *European Union Politics*, **9** (1), 145–165.

Laffan, Brigid (1998), 'Ireland: the rewards of pragmatism', in Kenneth Hanf and Ben Soetendorp (eds), *Adapting to European Integration: Small States and the European Union*, London: Longman, pp. 69–83.

Laffan, Brigid (2006), 'Managing Europe from home in Dublin, Athens and Helsinki: a comparative analysis', *West European Politics*, **29** (4), 687–708.

Lamoreaux, Jeremy W. and David J. Galbreath (2008), 'The Baltic states as "small states": negotiating the "East" by engaging the "West"', *Journal of Baltic Studies*, **39** (1), 1–14.

Lehmbruch, Gerhard (1984), 'Concentration and the structure of corporatist networks', in John H. Goldthorpe (ed.), *Order and Conflict inContemporary Capitalism*, Oxford: Oxford University Press, pp. 60–80.

Lehti, Marko (2006), 'Eastern or Western, new or false: classifying the Balts in the post-Cold War era', in Fabrizio Tassinari, Pertti Joenniemi and Uffe Jakobsen (eds), *Wider Europe: Nordic and Baltic Lessons to Post-enlargement Europe*, Copenhagen: Danish Institute of International Studies, pp. 69–88.

Le Mière, Christian and Jeffrey Mazo (2013), *Arctic Opening: Insecurity and Opportunity*, IISS Adelphi Series, Abingdon: Routledge.

Lemieux, Thomas (1999), 'Disparités des revenus et croissance de l'emploi: y a-t-il un trade-off?', in Suzanne Lévesque (ed.), *L'Après-déficit zéro: des choix de société*, Montréal: Association des économistes québécois.

Leslie, John and Annmarie Elijah (2012), 'Does n = 2? Trans-Tasman economic integration as a comparator for the single European market', *JCMS: Journal of Common Market Studies*, **50** (6), 975–993.

Lewis, Jeffrey (2005), 'The Janus face of Brussels: socialization and everyday decision-making in the European Union', *International Organization*, **59** (4), 937–971.

Lieven, Anatol (1994), *The Baltic Revolution: Estonia, Latvia, Lithuania and the Path to Independence*, New Haven, CT: Yale University Press.

Lijphart, Arend (1984), *Democracies*, New Haven, CT: Yale University Press.

Lijphart, Arend and Markus L. Crepaz (1991), 'Corporatism and consensus democracy in eighteen countries: conceptual and empirical linkages', *British Journal of Political Science*, **21** (2), 235–246.

Lindvall, Johannes (2012), 'Politics and policies in two economic crises: the Nordic countries', in Nancy Bermeo and Jonas Pontusson (eds), *Coping with Crisis: Government Reactions to the Great Recession*, New York: Russell Sage Foundation, pp. 233–260.

Listhaug, Ola (2007), 'Oil wealth dissatisfaction and political trust in Norway: a resource curse?', in Øyvind Østerud (ed.), *Norway in Transition: Transforming a Stable Democracy*, London: Routledge, pp. 130–147.

Local, The [Swedish news website] (2015), 'Sweden's Opposition votes in woman leader', 10 January, available at http://www.thelocal.se/20150110/swedens-opposition-vote-in-new-woman-leader (accessed 10 January 2015).

Lunde Saxi, Håkon (2006), 'Norwegian and Danish defence policy in the post-Cold War period: a comparative study', MA thesis, University of Oslo, available at https://www.duo.uio.no/bitstream/handle/10852/23764/1/Saxi_MA_Thesis.pdf (accessed 21 January 2015).

Lundvall, Bengt-Åke and Edward Lorenz (2012), 'Social investment in the globalising learning economy: a European perspective', in Nathalie Morel, Bruno Palier and Joakim Palme (eds), *Towards a Social Investment Welfare State? Ideas, Policies and Challenges*, Bristol: Policy Press, pp. 235–257.

MacRae, Duncan C. (1975), 'A political model of the business cycle', *Journal of Political Economy*, **85** (2), 239–263.

Made, Vahur (2010), 'Successes and failures in representing small state interests in European Union decision-making: the case of Estonia', *Acta Societatis Martensis*, **4** (1), 109–138.

Maes, Ivo and Amy Verdun (2005), 'Small states and the creation of EMU: Belgium and the Netherlands, pace-setters and gate-keepers', *Journal of Common Market Studies*, **43** (2), 327–348.

Magnette, Paul and Kalypso Nicolaidis (2005), 'Coping with the Lilliput syndrome: large vs. small states in the European Convention', *European Public Law*, **11** (1), 83–102.

Männik, Erik (2004), 'Small states: invited to NATO – able to contribute?', *Defense and Security Analysis*, **20** (1), 21–37.

Mapp, Wayne (2014), *The New Zealand Paradox: Adjusting to the Change in Balance of Power in the Asia Pacific over the Next 20 Years*, Washington, DC and Lanham, MD: Center for Strategic and International Studies and Rowman & Littlefield.

March, James G. (1999), 'A learning perspective on the network dynamics of institutional integration', in Morten Egeberg and Per Laegreid (eds),

Organizing Political Institutions: Essays for Johan P. Olsen, Bergen: Universitetsforlaget, pp. 129–155.

Marien, Sofie (2011), 'Measuring political trust across time and space', in Sonja Zmerli and Marc Hooghe (eds), *Political Trust: Why Context Matters*, Colchester: ECPR Press, pp. 13–46.

Marshall, T.H. (1950), *Citizenship and Social Class: And Other Essays*, Cambridge: Cambridge University Press.

Martin, Pierre (1995), 'When nationalism meets continentalism: the politics of free trade in Quebec', *Regional and Federal Studies*, **5** (1), 1–27.

Matláry, Janne H. and Øyvind Østerud (eds) (2007), *Denationalization of Defence: Convergence and Diversity*, Aldershot: Ashgate.

McCann, Philip (2009), 'Economic geography, globalisation and New Zealand's productivity paradox', *New Zealand Economic Papers*, **43** (3), 279–314.

McElroy, G. (2006), 'Committee representation in the European Parliament', *European Union Politics*, **7** (1), 5–29.

McLean, Ian (1978), *The Future for New Zealand Agriculture: Economic Strategies for the 1980s*, Wellington: Fourth Estate Books for the New Zealand Planning Council.

McRoberts, Kenneth and Dale Posgate (1983), *Développement et modernisation au Québec*, Montréal: Boréal Express.

Menon, Anand (2008), *Europe: The State of the Union*, London: Atlantic Books.

Mérand, Frederic (2008), *European Defence Policy: Beyond the Nation State*, Oxford: Oxford University Press.

Mesli, Samy (2014), *La coopération franco-québécoise dans le domaine de l'éducation: De 1965 à nos jours*, Montréal: Septentrion.

Michaud, Nelson and Isabelle Ramet (2004), 'Québec et politique étrangère: contradiction ou réalité?', *International Journal*, **59** (2), 303–324.

Michelmann, Hans J. and Panayotis Soldatos (1990), *Federalism and International Relations: The Role of Subnational Units*, Oxford: Clarendon Press.

Milward, Alan (1992), *The European Rescue of the Nation State*, Berkeley: University of California Press.

Misiunas, Romuald J. and Rein Taagepera (1993), *The Baltic States: Years of Dependence 1940–1990*, London: Hurst & Company.

Moene, Karl Olav (2005), 'Social democracy as a development strategy', in Pranab Bardhan, Samuel Bowles and Michael Wallerstein (eds), *Globalization and Egalitarian Redistribution*, London: Sage, pp. 148–168.

Moene, Karl Olav and Michael Wallerstein (2006), 'The Scandinavian model and economic development', *Development Outreach* (World Bank Institute), February.

Moravcsik, Andrew (1999), *The Choice for Europe: Social Purpose and State Power from Messina to Maastricht*, London: Routledge.

Morel, Nathalie, Bruno Palier and Joakim Palme (2012), 'Beyond the welfare state as we knew it?', in Nathalie Morel, Bruno Palier and Joakim Palme (eds), *Towards a Social Investment Welfare State? Ideas, Policies and Challenges*, Bristol: Policy Press, pp. 1–30.

Morin, Claude (1987), *L'art de l'impossible: La diplomatie québécoise depuis 1960*, Montréal: Boréal.

National Dairy Council [Ireland] (2013), *Strategy 2013–2015*, Dublin: National Dairy Council.

NATO (2010), 'Strategic Concept', available at http://www.nato.int/lisbon2010/strategic-concept-2010-eng.pdf (accessed 21 January 2015).

Nissinen, M. (1999), *Latvia's Transition to a Market Economy: Political Determinants of Economic Policy Reform*, London: Macmillan and the School of Slavonic and East European Studies.

Nixon, Chris and John Yeabsley (2002), *New Zealand's Trade Policy Odyssey*, Wellington: New Zealand Institute of Economic Research.

Nordic Ministers (2011), 'Declaration on solidarity', available at http://www.utanrikisraduneyti.is/media/nordurlandaskrifstofa/Norraen-samstoduyfirlysing-ENG.pdf (accessed 25 January 2015).

NOU (2015), *Finanspolitikk i en oljeøkonomi*, 2015: 9, Oslo: Ministry of Finance.

NZIER (2012), 'Grow for it: how population policies can promote economic growth', NZIER Working Paper No. 2012/1, Wellington: New Zealand Institute of Economic Research.

Oddsson, Davið (2002), 'Prime Minister of Iceland's NewYear's speech', 31 December, available at http:// www.forsaetisraduneyti.is/radherra/raedur-og-greinar/nr/378 (accessed 2 February 2004).

OECD (2002), 'Best practices for budget transparency', *OECD Journal on Budgeting*, **1** (3), 7–14.

OECD (2003), *Economic Surveys: New Zealand*, Paris: OECD Publishing.

OECD (2004), 'The legal framework for budget systems: an international comparison', *OECD Journal on Budgeting*, **4** (3).

OECD (2012), *Promoting Growth in All Regions*, Paris: OECD Publishing.

Ohmae, Kenichi (1995), *The End of the Nation State: The Rise of Regional Economies*, New York: Free Press.

Ojanen, Hanne (2014), *Nordic Defence Cooperation – Inspiration for the EU or a Lesson in Matching Expectations?*, TEPSA Policy Paper, available at http://www.tepsa.eu/tepsa-policy-paper-by-hanna-ojanen-nordic-defence-cooperation-inspiration-for-the-eu-or-a-lesson-in-matching-expectations/ (accessed 20 January 2015).

Ólafsson, Thorvardur Tjörvi and Thórarinn G. Pétursson (2010),

Weathering the Financial Storm: The Importance of Fundamentals and Flexibility, Economics Working Paper No. 2010-17, September, available at http://www.econ.au.dk/fileadmin/site_files/filer_oekonomi/ Working_Papers/Economics/2010/wp10_17.pdf (accessed 17 October 2014).

Oldberg, Ingmar (2014), *The Role of Russia in Regional Councils*, Reykjavik: Centre for Arctic Policy Studies, available at http://ams.hi.is/ wp-content/uploads/2014/08/The-role-of-Russia_Online.pdf (accessed 1 February 2015).

Olsen, Øystein (2015), 'Årstale: Økonomiske perspektiver', 12 February, available at http://www.norges-bank.no/Publisert/Foredrag-og-taler/ 2015/12_02_2015_Olsen_arstalen/ (accessed 28 February 2015).

Olstad, Finn (2010), *Frihetens århundre*, Oslo: Pax.

OSCE (2003), *OSCE Strategy to Address Threats to Security and Stability in the Twenty-first Century*, Vienna: Organization for Security and Co-operation in Europe, available at http://www.osce.org/mc/17504 (accessed 29 January 2015).

Ostry, Jonathan D., Andrew Berg and Charalambos G. Tsangarides (2014), *Redistribution, Inequality, and Growth*, IMF Staff Discussion Note 14/02, Washington, DC: International Monetary Fund.

Ott, D. (2000), *Small Is Democratic: An Examination of State Size and Democratic Development*, New York: Garland Publishing.

Oxford Analytica (2010), 'Europe: small states prefer partial EU integration', *Oxford Analytica*, Oxford: Global Strategic Analysis.

Panke, Diana (2006), 'The differential impact of communicated ideas: bridging the gap between rationalism and constructivism', *Hamburg Review of Social Sciences*, **1** (3), 312–342.

Panke, Diana (2008), *Argumentieren und Verhandeln in der Europäischen Union: Theoretische Überlegungen zum variierenden Einfluss der Europäischen Kommission*, Hamburg: Diplomica Verlag.

Panke, Diana (2010a), 'Developing good instructions in no time – an impossibility? Comparing domestic coordination practises for EU policies of 19 small and medium-sized states', *West European Politics*, **33** (4), 769–789.

Panke, Diana (2010b), *Small States in the European Union: Coping with Structural Disadvantages*, Farnham: Ashgate.

Panke, Diana (2010c), 'Why discourse matters only sometimes: effective arguing beyond the nation-state', *Review of International Studies*, **36** (1), 145–168.

Panke, Diana (2011a), 'Microstates in negotiations beyond the nation-state: Malta, Cyprus and Luxembourg as active and successful policy shapers?', *International Negotiation*, **16** (2), 297–317.

Panke, Diana (2011b), 'Small states in EU negotiations: political dwarfs or power-brokers?', *Cooperation and Conflict*, **46** (2), 123–143.

Panke, Diana (2012a), 'Being small in a big union: punching above their weights? How small states prevailed in the vodka and the pesticides cases', *Cambridge Review of International Affairs*, **25** (3), 329–344.

Panke, Diana (2012b), 'Dwarfs in international negotiations: how small states make their voices heard', *Cambridge Review of International Affairs*, **25** (3), 313–328.

Panke, Diana (2012c), 'Explaining differences in the shaping effectiveness: why some states are more effective in making their voices heard in international negotiations', *Comparative European Politics*, **10** (1), 111–132.

Panke, Diana (2012d), 'Lobbying institutional key players: how states seek to influence the European Commission, the Council presidency, and the European Parliament', *Journal of Common Market Studies*, **50** (1), 129–150.

Panke, Diana (2012e), 'Small states in multilateral negotiations: what have we learned?', *Cambridge Review of International Affairs*, **25** (3), 387–398.

Panke, Diana (2013), *Unequal Actors in Equalising Institutions: Negotiations in the United Nations General Assembly*, Houndmills: Palgrave.

Paquin, Stéphane (2004), *Paradiplomatie et relations internationales: Théorie des stratégies internationales des régions face à la mondialisation*, Brussels: PIE – Peter Lang.

Paquin, Stéphane (2013), 'Federalism and the governance of international trade negotiations in Canada: comparing CUSFTA with CETA', *International Journal*, **28** (4), 545–552.

Patry, André (1980), *Le Québec dans le monde*, Montréal: Leméac.

Pedersen, Lisbeth and Søren Kaj Andersen (2014), *Reformernes tid: Regulering af arbejdsmarked og velfærd siden 1990*, report, Oslo: Fafo.

Pelletier, Réjean (1992), 'La Révolution tranquille', in Gérard Daigle (ed.), *Le Québec en jeu: Comprendre les grands défis*, Montréal: Presses de l'Université de Montréal, pp. 609–623.

Pettifer, James (2012), *The Making of the Greek Crisis*, London: Penguin Specials.

Pétursdóttir, Solveig (1999), 'Speech at the Althingi', 7 December, available at http://www.althingi.is/altext/125/12/r07222821.sgml (accessed 3 May 2003).

Pierson, Paul (2000), 'Increasing returns, path dependence, and the study of politics', *American Political Science Review*, **94** (2), 251–267.

Plumb, John Harold (1967), *The Growth of Political Stability in England, 1675–1725*, London: Macmillan.

Porter, Michael (1990), *The Competitive Advantage of Nations*, Basingstoke: Macmillan.

Portes, Alejandro (2001), 'Social capital: its origins and applications in modern sociology', *Annual Review of Sociology*, **24**, 1–24.

Powell, Walter W. (1990), 'Neither market nor hierarchy: network forms of organization', *Research in Organizational Behavior*, **12**, 295–336.

Prime Minister of Iceland's Office (2010), 'The response of the public administration to the report of the special investigation commission to investigate and analyse the processes leading to the collapse of the three main banks in Iceland: a working group's report by the Prime Minister's Office', available at http://www.forsaetisraduneyti.is/media/Skyrslur/Skyrsla-starfshops-6-mai2010.pdf (accessed 26 October 2014).

Pryce, Vicky (2012), *Greekonomics: The Euro Crisis and Why Politicians Don't Get It*, London: Biteback Publishing.

Pryser, Tore (1988), *Arbeiderbevegelsens historie*, Vol. III, Oslo: Tiden norsk forlag.

Putnam, Robert D. (1973), *The Beliefs of Politicians: Ideology, Conflict, and Democracy in Britain and Italy*, New Haven, CT: Yale University Press.

Putnam, Robert (1993), *Making Democracy Work: Civic Traditions in Modern Italy*, Princeton, NJ: Princeton University Press.

Qvigstad, Jan F. (2012), 'Om å forvalte rikdom', *Nytt Norsk Tidsskrift*, **29**, 78–87.

Raik, Kristi (2002), 'Bureaucratization or strengthening of the political? Estonian institutions and integration into the European Union', *Cooperation and Conflict*, **37** (2), 137–156.

Raunio, Tapio and Matti Wiberg (2001), 'Parliamentarizing foreign policy decision-making: Finland in the European Union', *Cooperation and Conflict*, **36** (1), 61–86.

Rhodes, Martin (2001), 'The political economy of social pacts: "competitive corporatism" and European welfare reform', in Paul Pierson (ed.), *The New Politics of the Welfare State*, Oxford: Oxford University Press, pp. 165–194.

Rhodes, Martin (2013), 'Labour markets, welfare states and the dilemmas of European social democracy', in Michael Keating and David McCrone (eds), *The Crisis of Social Democracy in Europe*, Edinburgh: Edinburgh University Press, pp. 140–155.

Richardson, Ruth (2008), 'The fortunes and fates of reformers', in Margaret Clark (ed.), *The Bolger Years, 1990–1997*, Wellington: Dunmore Publishing, pp. 142–152.

Rickli, Jean-Marc (2008), 'European small states' military policies after the Cold War: from territorial to niche strategies', *Cambridge Review of International Affairs*, **21** (3), 307–325.

Rigaud, Benoît, Luc Bernier, Louis Côté, Joseph Facal and Benoît Lévesque

(2008), *La politique économique québécoise entre libéralisme et coordination*, Québec City: ÉNAP – Observatoire de l'Administration publique.

Rigaud, Benoît, Louis Côté, Benoît Lévesque, Joseph Facal and Luc Bernier (2010), 'Les complémentarités institutionnelles du modèle québécois de développement', *Recherches sociographiques*, **51** (1), 13–43.

Rodrik, Dani (1998), 'Why do more open economies have bigger governments?', *Journal of Political Economy*, **106** (5), 997–1032.

Rokkan, Stein (1999), *State Formation, Nation-building and Mass Politics in Europe: The Theory of Stein Rokkan*, in Peter Flora, Stein Kuhnle and Derek Urwin (ed.), Oxford: Oxford University Press.

Rokkan, Stein and Derek W. Urwin (1983), *Economy, Territory, Identity: Politics of West European Peripheries*, London: Sage.

Rommetvedt, Hilmar (2011), *Politikkens allmenngjøring og den nypluralistiske parlamentarismen*, 2nd edn, Bergen: Fagbokforlaget.

Rothstein, Robert L. (1968), *Alliances and Small Powers*, New York: Columbia University Press.

Royal Commission on Social Policy and Ivor Richardson (1988), *The April Report: Report of the Royal Commission on Social Policy*, Wellington: Royal Commission on Social Policy.

Ryggvik, Helge (2014), 'Norsk oljehistorie', *Store norske leksikon*, available at https://snl.no/Norsk_oljehistorie.

Sabatier, Paul A. and Hank C. Jenkins-Smith (1999), 'The advocacy coalition framework: an assessment', in Paul A. Sabatier (ed.), *Theories of the Policy Process*, Boulder, CO: Westview Press, pp. 117–166.

Sabel, Charles F. (1993), 'Studied trust: building new forms of cooperation in a volatile economy', *Human Relations*, **46** (9), 1133–1170.

Salmond, Patrick and Anthony J.G. Insall (2012), 'Preface to *The Nordic Countries: From War to Cold War, 1944–1951*', reprinted in *Scandinavian Journal of History*, **3** (2), 136–155.

Scheuerman, William E. (2009), *Hans Morgenthau: Realism and Beyond*, Cambridge: Polity Press.

Schick, Allen (1996), *The Spirit of Reform: Managing the New Zealand State Sector in a Time of Change*, Wellington: State Services Commission.

Schmitter, Philippe (1974), 'Still the century of corporatism?', *Review of Politics*, **36** (1), 85–131.

Scott, Graham (2001), *Public Sector Management in New Zealand: Lessons and Challenges*, Canberra: Australian National University.

Scott, Graham, Peter Bushnell and Nikitin Sallee (1990), 'Reform of the core public sector: New Zealand experience', *Governance*, **3** (2), 138–167.

Scottish Attitudes Survey (2012), *Scottish Attitudes Survey 2011 Core Module: Attitudes to Government, the Economy and Public Services in Scotland*, Edinburgh: Scottish Government.

Scottish Government (2013), *Scotland's Future: Your Guide to an Independent Scotland*, Edinburgh: Scottish Government.

Scruton, Roger (2007), *The Palgrave Macmillan Dictionary of Political Thought*, 3rd edn, Basingstoke: Palgrave Macmillan.

Sepos, Angelos (2005), *Differentiated Integration in the EU: The Position of Small Member States*, EUI Working Paper RSCAS No. 2005/17, San Domenico di Fiesole: Robert Schuman Centre for Advanced Studies.

Shaw, Timothy M. (2014), 'What Caribbean post-2015: developmental and/or fragile? Old versus new security?', in Clive Archer, Alyson J.K. Bailes and Anders Wivel (eds), *Small States and International Security: Europe and Beyond*, London: Routledge, pp. 223–240.

Sikk, Allan (2009a), 'Force mineure? The effects of the EU on party politics in a small country: the case of Estonia', *Journal of Communist Studies and Transition Politics*, **25** (4), 468–490.

Sikk, Allan (2009b), *The 2009 European Elections in Estonia*, European Parliament Election Briefing No. 41, Brighton: European Parliament and Referendums Network (EPERN).

Skilling, David (2012a), *In Uncertain Seas: Positioning Small Countries to Succeed in a Changing World*, Singapore: Landfall Strategy Group.

Skilling, David (2012b), *There Is No Such Thing as Domestic Policy*, Singapore: Landfall Strategy Group.

Skogstad, Grace (2012), 'International trade policy and Canadian federalism: a constructive tension', in Herman Bakvis and Grace Skogstad (eds), *Canadian Federalism: Performance, Effectiveness and Legitimacy*, 3rd edn, Toronto: Oxford University Press, pp. 157–177.

Smith, Eivind (2012), 'Den smale sti – Noen kommentarer om å forvalte rikdom', *Nytt Norsk Tidsskrift*, **29**, 92–97.

Smith, Michael E. (2004), *Europe's Foreign and Security Policy: The Institutionalization of Cooperation*, Cambridge: Cambridge University Press.

Spence, David (2002), 'The evolving role of foreign ministries in the conduct of European Union affairs', in Brian Hocking and David Spence (eds), *Foreign Ministries in the European Union: Integrating Diplomats*, London: Palgrave Macmillan, pp. 18–36.

Spence, David (2009), 'Taking stock: 50 years of European diplomacy', *The Hague Journal of Diplomacy*, **4** (2), 235–259.

Spence, David and Jozef Bátora (eds) (forthcoming), *The European External Action Service: European Diplomacy Post-Westphalia*, London: Palgrave.

Spruyt, Hendrik (1994), *The Sovereign State and Its Competitors: An Analysis of Systems Change*, Princeton, NJ: Princeton University Press.

Srebrnik, Henry F. (2004), 'Small island nations and democratic values', *World Development*, **32** (2), 329–341.

Statistics Iceland [Hagstofa Íslands] (2011), 'Gross domestic product 2010: revision', *Statistical Series: National Accounts*, **96** (46), 8 September, available at http://www.statice.is/lisalib/getfile.aspx?ItemID=12647 (accessed 30 October 2014).

Steen, Anton (1997), *Between Past and Future: Elites, Democracy and the State in Post-communist Countries: A Comparison of Estonia, Latvia and Lithuania*, Aldershot: Ashgate.

Steen, Anton (2007), 'Do elite beliefs matter? Elites and economic reforms in the Baltic states and Russia', *Comparative Social Research*, **23**, 79–102.

Steen, Anton (2010), 'National elites and the Russian minority issue: does EU–NATO integration matter?', *Journal of European Integration*, **32** (2), 193–212.

Steen, Anton and Øyvind Østerud (2007), 'Eliter og nyliberal stat – postsosialdemokratiske og postkommunistiske eliter', in Per Kristen Mydske, Dag Harald Claes and Amund Lie (eds), *Nyliberalisme – ideer og politisk virkelighet*, Oslo: Universitetsforlaget, pp. 185–206.

Steinmetz, Robert and Anders Wivel (eds) (2010), *Small States in Europe: Challenges and Opportunities*, Farnham: Ashgate.

Stiglitz, Joseph (2012), *The Price of Inequality*, London: Penguin.

St John, Susan and M. Claire Dale (2012), 'Evidence-based evaluation: working for families', *Policy Quarterly*, **8** (1), 39–51.

St. meld. nr. 25 (1974), *Petroleumsvirksomhetens plass i det norske samfunn*, Oslo: Ministry of Industry.

St. meld. nr. 29 (2000–2001), *Retningslinjer for den økonomiske politikken*, Oslo: Ministry of Finance.

St. meld. nr. 2 (2013–2014), *Revidert nasjonalbudsjett 2014*, Oslo: Ministry of Finance.

Stråth, Bo and Øystein Sørensen (eds) (1997), *The Cultural Construction of Norden*, Oslo: Universitetsforlaget.

Strauss-Kahn, Dominique (2009), 'Letter from IMF managing director to open civil meetings', 12 November, available at http://www.imf.org/external/np/vc/2009/111209.htm (accessed 26 October 2014).

Strömvik, Maria (2006), 'Starting to "think big": the Nordic countries and EU peace-building', in Alyson J.K. Bailes, Gunilla Herolf and Bengt Sundelius (eds), *The Nordic Countries and European Security and Defence Policy*, Oxford: Oxford University Press, pp. 199–214.

Sutch, William B. (1966), *The Quest for Security in New Zealand, 1840 to 1966*, Wellington: Oxford University Press.

Taagepera, Rein (2007), *Predicting Party Sizes: The Logic of Simple Electoral Systems*, Oxford: Oxford University Press.

Taagepera, Rein (2008), *Making Social Sciences More Scientific: The Need for Predictive Models*, Oxford: Oxford University Press.

Taagepera, Rein and Madeleine O. Hosli (2006), 'National representation in international organizations: the seat allocation model implicit in the European Union Council and Parliament', *Political Studies*, **54** (2), 370–398.

Taagepera, Rein and Stephen Recchia (2002), 'The size of second chambers and European assemblies', *European Journal of Political Research*, **41** (2), 165–185.

Taagepera, Rein and Matthew Soberg Shugart (1989), *Seats and Votes: The Effects and Determinants of Electoral Systems*, New Haven, CT: Yale University Press.

Thickett, Glen (2002), 'The influence of macro trends on the frequency of industrial disputes', *Labour, Employment and Work in New Zealand 2002*, pp. 249–256.

Thomson, Robert and Madeleine O. Hosli (2006), 'Explaining legislative decision-making in the European Union', in Robert Thomson, N. Stokman, Christopher H. Achen and Thomas Koenig (eds), *The European Union Decides*, Cambridge: Cambridge University Press, pp. 1–24.

Thorhallsson, Baldur (2004), *Iceland and European Integration: On the Edge*, London: Routledge.

Thorhallsson, Baldur (2005), 'What features determine international activities of small states? The international approaches of Iceland until the mid-1990s', *Stjórnmál og stjórnsýsla*, **1** (1), 107–140.

Thorhallsson, Baldur (2006), 'The size of states in the European Union: theoretical and conceptual perspectives', *Journal of European Integration*, **28** (1), 7–31.

Thorhallsson, Baldur (2008), 'Evrópustefna íslenskra stjórnvalda: Stefnumótun, átök og afleiðingar', in Valur Ingimundarson (ed.), *Uppbrot hugmyndakerfis: Endumótun íslenskrar utanríkisstefnu 1991–2007*, Reykjavík: Hið íslenska bókmenntafélag, pp. 67–96.

Thorhallsson, Baldur (2010), 'The corporatist model and its value in understanding small European states in the neo-liberal world of the twenty-first century: the case of Iceland', *European Political Science*, **9** (3), 375–386.

Thorhallsson, Baldur (2011), 'Domestic buffer versus external shelter: viability of small states in the new globalized economy', *European Political Science*, **10** (3), 324–336.

Thorhallsson, Baldur (2012), 'Small states in the UN Security Council: means of influence?', *The Hague Journal of Diplomacy*, **7** (2), 135–160.

Thorhallsson, Baldur (2013), *Iceland's Contested European Policy: The*

Footprint of the Past – A Small and Insular Society, Jean Monnet Occasional Paper Series No. 02/2013, Valletta: Institute for European Studies, University of Malta.

Thorhallsson, Baldur (2014), *Iceland Prefers Partial Engagement in European Integration*, Small State Brief, Reykjavik: Institute for International Affairs, available at http://ams.hi.is/wp-content/uploads/2014/04/WhitePaper1.pdf.

Thorhallsson, Baldur and Rainer Kattel (2013), 'Neo-liberal small states and economic crisis: lessons for democratic corporatism', *Journal of Baltic Studies*, **44** (1), 83–103.

Thorhallsson, Baldur and Peadar Kirby (2012), 'Financial crises in Iceland and Ireland: does European Union and Euro membership matter?', *Journal of Common Market Studies*, **50** (5), 801–818.

Thorhallsson, Baldur and Anders Wivel (2006), 'Small states in the European Union: what do we know and what would we like to know?', *Cambridge Review of International Affairs*, **19** (4), 651–668.

Thucydides (1972), *History of the Peloponnesian War*, trans. Rex Warner, London: Penguin.

Tiilikainen, Teija (2006), 'Finland – an EU member with a small state identity', *European Integration*, **28** (1), 73–87.

Tilly, Charles (1975), *The Formation of National States in Western Europe*, Princeton, NJ: Princeton University Press.

Tilly, Charles (1990), *Coercion, Capital and European States, AD 990–1990*, Oxford: Blackwell.

Tilly, Charles (1994), 'Entanglements of European cities and states', in Charles Tilly and Wim P. Blockmans (eds), *Cities and the Rise of States in Europe, AD 1000 to 1800*, Boulder, CO: Westview Press.

Torvik, Ragnar (2009), 'Why do some resource-abundant countries succeed while others do not?', *Oxford Review of Economic Policy*, **25** (2), 241–256.

Trapans, Jan Arveds (1998), 'The Baltic states: defence and geopolitics', *European Security*, **7** (3), 92–100.

Traxler, Franz (2004), 'The metamorphoses of corporatism: from classical to lean patterns', *European Journal of Political Research*, **43** (4), 571–598.

Treasury [New Zealand] (1984), *Economic Management*, Wellington: Treasury.

Treasury [New Zealand] (1990), *Briefing to Incoming Government 1990*, Wellington: Treasury.

Tulmets, Elsa (2014), *East Central European Foreign Policy Identity in Perspective: Back to Europe and the EU's Neighbourhood*, Basingstoke: Palgrave Macmillan.

UNDP [United Nations Development Programme] (1994), *Human Development Report*, available at http://hdr.undp.org/sites/default/files/reports/255/hdr_1994_en_complete_nostats.pdf (accessed 19 January 2015).

US Government Accountability Office (2011), *Federal Reserve System: Opportunities Exist to Strengthen Policies and Processes for Managing Emergency Assistance*, GAO-11-696, July, Washington, DC: US Government Accountability Office.

Vaillancourt, François and Luc Vaillancourt (2005), *La propriété des employeurs au Québec en 2003 selon leur groupe d'appartenance linguistique*, Québec: Conseil supérieur de la langue française.

Vandenbroucke, Frank and Koen Vleminckx (2011), 'Disappointing poverty trends: is the social investment state to blame?', *Journal of European Social Policy*, **21** (5), 450–471.

Vartiainen, Juhana (2014), *To Create and Share: The Remarkable Success and Contested Future of the Social-democratic Nordic Models*, report, Oslo: Fafo.

Vilpišauskas, Ramūnas (2014), 'Lithuania's double transition after the re-establishment of independence in 1990: coping with uncertainty domestically and externally', *Oxford Review of Economic Policy*, **30** (2), 223–236.

Vital, David (1967), *The Inequality of States: A Study of the Small Power in International Relations*, Oxford: Clarendon Press.

Walt, Stephen M. (1987), *The Origins of Alliances*, Ithaca, NY: Cornell University Press.

Weber, Max (1970), *Essays in Sociology*, Oxford: Oxford University Press.

Weldon, Steven (2006), 'Downsize my polity? The impact of size on party membership and member activism', *Party Politics*, **12** (4), 467–481.

Wildavsky, Aaron (1975), *Budgeting: A Comparative Theory of Budgetary Processes*, Boston, MA: Little, Brown.

Wildavsky, Aaron (1987), 'Choosing preferences by constructing institutions: a cultural theory of preference formation', *American Political Science Review*, **81** (1), 3–22.

Wilkinson, Richard and Kate Pickett (2010), *The Spirit Level: Why Equality Is Better for Everyone*, Harmondsworth: Penguin.

Williamson, Oliver (1975), *Markets and Hierarchies: Analysis and Antitrust Implications*, New York: Free Press.

Wivel, Anders, Alyson J.K. Bailes and Clive Archer (2014), 'Setting the scene: small states and international security', in Clive Archer, Alyson J.K. Bailes and Anders Wivel (eds), *Small States and International Security: Europe and Beyond*, London: Routledge, pp. 3–25.

Wunderlich, Jens-Uwe (2012), 'The EU an actor *sui generis*? A comparison of EU and ASEAN actorness', *Journal of Common Market Studies*, **50** (4), 653–669.

Young, Audrey and Claire Trevett (2014), 'NZ wins seat on Security Council: "victory for the small states"', *New Zealand Herald*, 17 October, available at http://www.nzherald.co.nz/nz/news/article.cfm?c_id=1&objectid=11343853 (accessed 16 December 2014).

Zake, Ieva (2002), 'The People's Party in Latvia: neo-liberalism and the new politics of independence', *Journal of Communist Studies and Transition Politics*, **18** (3), 109–131.

Zeniewski, Peter (2011), 'Neoliberalism, exogenous elites and the transformation of solidarity', *Europe–Asia Studies*, **63** (6), 977–994.

Index